A TALENT
FOR
ADVENTURE

A TALENT
FOR
ADVENTURE

The Remarkable Life of
Lieutenant Colonel Pat Spooner MBE (MIL)

by

Pat Spooner

Pen & Sword
MILITARY

First published in Great Britain in 2012 by
Pen & Sword Military
an imprint of
Pen & Sword Books Ltd
47 Church Street
Barnsley
South Yorkshire
S70 2AS

ISBN 978 1 84884 810 8

A CIP catalogue record for this book is
available from the British Library

Typeset in Sabon by
Phoenix Typesetting, Auldgirth, Dumfriesshire

Printed and bound in England by
CPI Group (UK) Ltd, Croydon, CR0 4YY

Pen & Sword Books Ltd includes the Imprints of Pen & Sword Aviation, Pen
& Sword Family History, Pen & Sword Maritime, Pen & Sword Military,
Wharncliffe Local History, Pen & Sword Select, Pen & Sword Military Classics,
Leo Cooper, The Praetorian Press, Remember When, Seaforth Publishing and
Frontline Publishing.

For a complete list of Pen & Sword titles please contact
PEN & SWORD BOOKS LIMITED
47 Church Street, Barnsley, South Yorkshire, S70 2AS, England
E-mail: enquiries@pen-and-sword.co.uk
Website: www.pen-and-sword.co.uk

Contents

List of Maps

DEDICATED TO

My dear friend, Jimmie,
The late Lieutenant Colonel J. Y. Ferguson MBE MC
Royal Scots

AND TO

All those brave Italians, from all walks of life,
Especially the courageous *Contandini*,
Who risked their lives to help us on our way to freedom.

'He goes seeking liberty, which is so dear,
As he knows who for it renounces life'.
Divine Comedy – Inferno
Dante Alighieri (1265–1321)

Foreword

by

Field Marshal Sir John Chapple GCB CBE DL

Like many of his generation, Pat Spooner packed in a lot during the Second World War. Very few, however, will have experienced such an adventurous and diverse set of different military exploits.

He started as a young officer, fresh out of Sandhurst, among the last Regular Army entrants to the Indian Army. He joined the 8th Gurkha Rifles in 1940 and started his service with them in the peaceful hills of Shilong, Assam. Then he moved to North West India and went with the 2nd Battalion, 8th Gurkha Rifles to Iraq. In this he was fortunate because his battalion had been under orders to move to Singapore. They were diverted to Iraq to help head off the German interest in the oilfields. He was on active service there until April 1942 after which Pat Spooner went, in a new role, to North Africa. Here, in June 1942, he was captured near Tobruk and was sent to a prisoner-of-war camp in Italy.

After fifteen months in various camps, the Italian armistice was announced in September 1943 and Pat managed to get away and head for the Allies' front line in the South. This was yet another adventurous time. He acknowledges the great help given to him by the friendly and very brave Italian *contandini*.

In the course of their escape he and his close companion, Jimmie Ferguson, were assigned by British Intelligence to help two British Generals, Sir Philip Neame VC and Sir Richard O'Connor, and Air Vice Marshal Boyd, also trying to reach the British lines. Pat describes in detail their harrowing adventures. It took until Christmas 1943 before they all got back to safety.

After a brief break back in England Pat was re-assigned to yet another role in India, operating behind the enemy lines in the Arakan, and then engaged in landing and hiding stores on remote, and Japanese-occupied, islands in the Indian Ocean. These were intended to help RAF aircrews who might not be able to make it back to their bases in India or Ceylon. This work is hardly mentioned in official histories; nor does it appear in other wartime memoirs.

Then, after the Japanese capitulation in late 1945, Pat found himself involved for nearly two years in investigating and bringing to justice Japanese who had committed horrific war crimes in South-east Asia. Again, these accounts throw light on little recorded events. This role took him to Malaya, Java, Burma and Singapore. It was challenging work and there did not appear to be too much support.

Just before Indian Independence, Pat Spooner left his parent regiment and the Indian Army. He had had over seven exciting years. Although still in his twenties he had reached the rank of Lieutenant Colonel. It had been an Adventurous time for which he had shown much Talent.

Field Marshal Sir John Chapple GCB CBE DL

Acknowledgements

This book started life as an account of my wartime experiences which I hoped might be of interest to my family and friends. My mother had kept all my letters and diaries, and it is thanks to her diligence that I was able to record my experiences with reasonable accuracy.

The gestation period was prolonged, and only recently I happened to mention an episode at the end of the war to a fellow-worshipper at my church, St Martha-on-the-Hill, near our home in Guildford, Duncan Simpson OBE, a former test pilot, who contributes articles to *The Aeroplane* magazine. He introduced me to the Deputy Editor, Nick Stroud, who commissioned me to write an article on my exploits in the Andaman Islands (reproduced as Chapter 6 in this book – 'Clandestine Catalinas'). It was Nick who badgered me to make my wartime experiences available to a wider audience. This, therefore, became the genesis of my autobiography and I am truly grateful for all his help and encouragement.

I acknowledge with gratitude the part played by Anne Hereward and Jane Demery who each spent many hours typing and re-typing chapters from my draft. I am indebted to my brother, John, a retired English teacher at a college in Vancouver, Canada, for his critical comments on the initial draft manuscript; also to Angela Blaydon, Director, AB Publishing Ltd, for her help in the final editing of the manuscript. Maggie Nelson produced the maps for the book and a special word of thanks is due to her for her endeavours and the excellent end product.

Likewise, my daughter-in-law, Andrea Spooner, offered invaluable advice on the preparation of the manuscript for submission to publishers, in her capacity as Senior Executive Editor at Little, Brown Books for Young Readers in New York.

Last, but by no means least, I am most grateful to my wife, Frances, whose patience, understanding and constant encouragement was a great source of inspiration without which this book would never have seen the light of day.

Chapter One

Starting with Sandhurst

The taxi drew level with the imposing wrought-iron gates at the entrance to the Royal Military College, Sandhurst. Heart pounding with a mixture of anticipation and excitement, I asked the driver to proceed slowly up the driveway lined with pines and birches leading to the College where I was to spend the next eighteen months as a 'Gentleman Cadet' training to be a fully fledged army officer.

Passing the Lower Lake I saw, through the trees, and beyond a further stretch of water, the impressive buildings of the Old College. Immediately in front was a large parade ground with which I was to become painfully familiar. I had heard of new cadets failing the testing first six weeks of 'square bashing', the purpose of which was to weed out the weakest cadets. Guards' sergeants, I soon learned, were instructed to put the fear of God in their charges, and this they did with relish. One false step and the sergeant would emit a high-pitched screech - 'You miserable little worm! Yes, you - Sir! What the bleeding hell do you think you're doing - Sir?!' However grievous the crime, Gentlemen Cadets must, at all costs, be treated with due respect, even by ferocious drill staff.

Early in 1937, aged sixteen, I was destined to attend the University of Heidelberg on leaving college. Instead I applied for and was awarded a Kitchener Memorial Scholarship for entry to the Royal Military College, Sandhurst. The threat of war loomed over Europe in 1937, and it was clear that any venture into the academic world would have been short-lived.

I joined Sandhurst in September 1938 and was assigned to No. 5 Company in the Old Buildings. Our eighteen-month course, however, was severely curtailed by the declaration of war with

1

Germany in September 1939, by which time the top brass of the War Office had decamped from Whitehall to the RMC, displacing 5 Company which was moved into cramped quarters in the New Buildings.

In the months preceding the outbreak of war, the cadets were put to work digging slit trenches in the college grounds. Normal military studies were suspended. I was by then in the Intermediate division and had been promoted to the lofty rank of corporal. Orders were issued to stop cadets from saluting red-tabbed, gold-braided staff officers at every corner. 'Square-bashing' was cut to the barest minimum, much to our relief.

On return from leave in September 1939, we learned that Intermediate Term cadets were to leave the college forthwith, having first been enlisted into the Queen's Royal Regiment (West Surrey) of the Territorial Army. Sadly, we were to be deprived of the traditional Passing-Out Parade, ending with marching up the steps of the Grand Entrance, with the Adjutant taking up the rear on his grey charger, to the strains of *Auld Lang Syne*.

Having been awarded a King's India Cadetship, I was in the fortunate position of being able to apply for an Indian regiment, regardless of my academic or military record at the RMC. Normally, only those who had done well would be accepted into the Indian Army. This applied even more so to the Gurkha Regiments who tended to take the cream of the crop.

Commissioned as a Second Lieutenant on 22 October 1939, I joined some twenty other ex-cadets (all appointed to the Unofficial List of the Indian Army) on a voyage to India, which I recorded daily in diary form. Entitled *An Account of my Journey to India – October 1939* the following is an extract:

We had crossed the English Channel on a dark and stormy night, the sea so rough that I had vowed never again to go by boat to France. Lying immobilized on a bunk, wishing for a speedy end to the nightmare, my prayers were answered by a loud bang and the sound of rushing waters. Convinced we had hit a mine I lurched to my feet only to discover that some idiot, stumbling down the stairwell, had dislodged a large fire extinguisher from its bracket on the wall. Foam gushed in every direction, creating instant panic, followed by hysterical laughter amongst the other occupants of the cabin. Somehow, my own sense of humour had deserted me.

A train transported us through France to Marseilles where we embarked on a troopship crammed with troops destined for the Middle East and beyond. There was nothing for us to do except eat, drink, read, play card games and sleep. The food was excellent, drinks were cheap and all we lacked was female company. The sole members of the fair sex on board were the wife and two teenage daughters of General Wavell, C-in-C Middle East, who were joining him in Cairo. None of our group, however, was bold or brash enough to court their company. A few high-spirited members found it amusing, after dinner, to seat themselves in the lounge within hearing distance of the Wavell ladies and tell risqué stories. For a while, the unfortunate Lady Wavell, acutely embarrassed, would endure this childish behaviour, a pained expression on her patrician features, before bustling her blushing offspring away to the safety of their cabins.

Although we were part of a small convoy, escorted by a destroyer, there were no 'alarums or excursions' during our passage through the Mediterranean. It was three months before the Italians entered the war, and the German navy and air force were not yet active in that area. Indeed, I recall no blackout of the ship itself or at any of the ports where we stopped.

We stopped briefly in Malta and arrived a few days later at Alexandria, where we were given shore leave. Another ULIA officer and I made our way to the well-known Cecil Hotel for a drink before lunch. Standing self-consciously in the lobby, I saw General Wavell enter the hotel with his family in tow. His well-starched khaki bush-shirt, bedecked with rows of ribbons, the scarlet tabs on his lapels, and the gold oak-leaf embroidery around the peak of his cap, combined to make his appearance awesomely intimidating to a very junior sub-altern. To my consternation the General marched straight up to us, leaned ominously forward, and demanded to know who we were and where we were bound. For an awful moment I thought he was about to confront us with the insulting behaviour suffered by his wife and daughters on board ship. I stammered something about being on our way to India. Wavell smiled broadly, shook our hands warmly, wished us good luck and promptly whisked his family off to the dining room. My relief was such that I almost saluted the General bareheaded and cap less – a heinous military crime.

I was often to recall this encounter during my army career. General Wavell was a brilliant and much-loved commander who was held in the highest esteem, not least by Winston Churchill himself. Later, as Field Marshal the Earl Wavell, he became Commander-in-Chief, India. His anthology of poetry, *Other Men's Flowers*, comprising all the poems he could repeat from memory, was a constant companion and comfort during the latter stages of my army career.

Arriving in Bombay, we were immediately shunted off by train to the Officers' Training School, Belgaum, some 200 miles south of Bombay, beyond Poona, and not far from the neutral Portuguese colony of Goa, then crawling with Germans. There we were introduced to the Indian climate, language (Urdu) and way of life in a military cantonment very different from Sandhurst. Tough-talking British sergeants, seconded from line regiments, soon had us drilling their way instead of the foot stamping taught us by Guards non-commissioned officers at the RMC. Amongst the first batch of trainees was a group of hard-drinking tea planters from Ceylon and Darjeeling who took malicious delight in persuading us nineteen-year olds to quaff gins and tonics at lunchtime, often with dire results. One of them took me big game hunting in the jungles south of Belgaum, with a hired *shikari* (Indian hunter). This proved to be a nerve-racking experience, especially on the day we encountered a *barra bagh* (large tiger) face to face on a jungle track in broad daylight. Fortunately for us the beast seemed singularly dis-interested in our presence, and loped off into the undergrowth. We spent a sleepless night perched on a *machan* (platform) up a tree to which had been tethered an understandably petrified goat. Climbing down at dawn was daunting, but thankfully uneventful.

Meanwhile, I had applied to the 7th and the 8th Gurkha Rifles, with both of which Regiments I had close family connections. On 4 April 1940 I received word that I had been accepted by 8th Gurkha Rifles and was posted to their Headquarters in Shillong, Assam. En route, I stayed a few memorable days with the English

Commanding Officer of the Bhopal State Rifles, an old friend of the family, where I fell instantly and madly in love with the young Prince's English governess.

On arrival in Shillong I was welcomed by Nick McKenzie, the Adjutant, who wheeled me before the CO, Lieutenant Colonel Gordon, and introduced me to Major Chris Yates, second in command, and the few other officers there. The battalion had just returned from an extended tour of active service on the North West Frontier, and were enjoying much deserved rest and relaxation. Of the twelve or so British officers, several were on leave or on courses, so the mess was fairly empty.

I well remember the mess tucked away amongst the pine trees on the hill, known as The Peak, overlooking Shillong. There was hardly any training, and Thursdays were Race Days, when we adjourned to the race course where the Gurkha band played stirring marches, a wonderfully civilized and relaxed atmosphere. In the early days, much of the time was taken up in distributing calling cards around town. As a result invitations poured in – to lunches, cocktail parties and dinners. Often one had several engagements from which to choose, an idyllic situation, which, however, led to a feeling of guilt. Thousands of miles away a world war raged in which many of my former Sandhurst colleagues were actively engaged, in stark contrast to the tranquillity and scenic beauty of Shillong.

This was at a time when wives and children left the intense heat of Calcutta and made for the coolness of the hill stations, such as Shillong and Darjeeling, in the foothills of the Himalayas on the border of Nepal and Tibet. With the advent of young, unattached daughters, single officers were much in demand.

Lunches, cocktail parties, dinners, and dances at the Officers' Club proliferated. Picnics at Cherrapungi, a beauty spot an easy drive from Shillong, were frequent. Reputedly this was the wettest place on the planet, but it never rained once when I was there.

All this fun and games came to an abrupt halt when I was sent on a Vickers Machine Gun course at Saugor, a thousand or more miles away in the Punjab. Whilst there, the battalion moved to Quetta, Baluchistan, where I rejoined them after the course ended. There we were to mobilize for active service. We were billeted in wooden huts a mile or so out of the town. The contrast with

Shillong was dramatic. Heat, dust, sandstorms and mosquitoes brought us down to earth with a bump. Intensive training at platoon, company and finally battalion levels quickly produced the results required to make the battalion battle-worthy. Long marches by day and night, sometimes for days on end found us trudging in the bleak, rugged landscape on the edge of the mountains of Afghanistan.

I was given command of the Machine Gun Platoon, with a *Jemadar* (Second Lieutenant) as my second in command, a *Havildar* (Sergeant), and a dozen Gurkha soldiers, armed with Vickers machine guns, tripod-mounted on 15cwt trucks. Relics of the Great War these weapons, with their water-cooled barrels and cumbersome mechanism, were apt to jam at awkward moments. Nevertheless, they served a useful purpose and could be extremely effective. I was the only officer who knew anything about the tactical handling of the machine-gun platoon, so I enjoyed an independence which suited me very well.

Carriers arrived on the scene at about the same time. These were small, open-top, light vehicles with tracks, armed with Bren light machine guns. I desperately wanted to command the Carrier Platoon but obviously this proved impossible. The junior officer appointed to this role was seriously wounded in North Africa and died of his injuries. Carriers were no match for the German equivalent and proved almost useless in desert warfare.

We were half-way through our allotted training and mechanization period when orders came for us to prepare for active service in Malaya. With two other Indian Army battalions our Brigade, 20 Indian Infantry Brigade, entrained for the port of Karachi where we boarded a troopship. Anchored offshore, sealed orders were received (we learned later) diverting us to Iraq.

Equipped (if by no means fully trained) for jungle warfare, we were now facing a possible campaign in desert conditions. As it turned out, fate was on our side: had we proceeded to Singapore, we would very likely have ended up in the debacle which followed the Japanese invasion of Malaya.

We were told little about the situation in Iraq, only that a nasty character called Rashid Ali, the Iraqi leader, had been wooing the Nazis, encouraging them to take over the country and its valuable oilfields. Indeed, it transpired that the Luftwaffe had taken control of the main airfields near Baghdad and Basra. The threat was such that immediate countermeasures had to be taken. So it was that our Brigade became, overnight, the spearhead of an Expeditionary Force sent to prevent the Germans, already hovering on the Turkish border, from taking over the country.

As we steamed up the Persian Gulf, escorted by a couple of destroyers, we learned that we might have to face bombardment from an Iraqi coastal defence gun at Faro at the entrance to the Shat-el-Arab. I was detailed to place my machine guns on deck, packed down with sandbags, to provide covering fire in the event of such an attack. As it was, we sailed silently past Faro in the dead of night without incident. As the channel narrowed we became more vulnerable to rifle or machine-gun fire from the western shore. On the other side was the coast of Persia, which posed no threat.

Our arrival at night in the port of Basra was, in fact, an anti-climax. There was no opposition, no sign of any soldiers. We duly disembarked and made camp in the dockyard area. There we stayed for a few days before moving off to Shu'aiba to set up defensive positions around the airfield. The RAF had bombed the airfield continuously and scattered around were damaged German fighters.

Orders came for our Brigade to move north and take Baghdad. It soon became apparent that our worst enemy was not the Iraqi army who were conspicuous by their absence, but the intense heat. Temperatures at midday reached 40 to 45 degrees C, which made movement of any kind almost unbearable. Water was strictly rationed. Our Gurkhas were hill men brought up in a temperate climate to whom this extreme heat was totally alien. Being sturdy and always cheerful, whatever the conditions, they carried on without complaint.

Our mechanized column drove up the road to Baghdad which ran alongside the Tigris River. We passed Ur of the Chaldees of Biblical fame, founded in 2006 BC, and then the centre of civilization, in what had been a 'land of milk and honey'. All that remains now, in a vast area of arid desert, is a small mound in a sandy landscape.

Further on, we skirted Kut-al-Amara where my father had been an Anglican padre in a garrison besieged by the Turks in the First World War. By an amazing coincidence I was following in his footsteps, both having been members of an expeditionary force sent from India to protect the oil supplies in the Persian Gulf. However, in his case, the end result was disastrous. In December 1915, the Division he joined attacked Baghdad unsuccessfully and was forced to retreat to Kut where they were besieged by a much larger Turkish force for 134 days (until then, the longest in British military history).

Kut had an Arab population of 6,000 to which were added some 10,000 British and Indian fighting men, 3,500 Indian non-combatants and 2,000 sick and wounded. Many died of starvation and the death toll from shellfire and snipers' bullets mounted daily. Most of the garrison's horses and mules had been eaten and the bread ration reduced to four ounces a day. Starving men consumed meat from dogs, cats, hedgehogs, sparrows, starlings – anything remotely edible. During the siege, 1,746 of the Garrison had been killed or died of disease.

In a book about my father, *God on Our Side*, the author, Michael Moynihan, quotes from his voluminous diary: '. . . General Townsend was forced to surrender, and some 12,000 emaciated British and Indian troops were rounded up for a 1,200-mile forced march across the scorching desert towards a brutal captivity only the toughest were to survive'. My father, as a priest, was offered repatriation, but he refused, insisting on staying with his men. The strain of the five months' siege, followed by the march through the deserts of Iraq and Turkey, left an indelible mark on many of the officers and men. In captivity, some 1,700 British and 1,300 Indian other ranks were to die. My father's health had been further undermined by very serious maltreatment on the part of a Turkish dentist in the PoW camp at Kastamoni.

After the war, my father returned to India to continue his work as an Army chaplain. He refused to admit that he was a sick man, suffering from insomnia, depression and severe mood swings. In 1926, six years after I was born in Simla, and the year my brother, John, was born in England, he had a serious nervous breakdown and was invalided home to England for good. He spent the next sixteen years in a Nottingham nursing home specializing in mental casualties of the war. He was in state of limbo, a Rip van Winkle, unable even to recognize my Mother when she visited him. Thankfully, he was one of the first to receive electric shock treatment (then in an experimental stage) which miraculously cured him completely. In Moynihan's book, I am quoted as saying:

> I knew very little at that time about my father's experiences during the siege. . . . . I found Kut a hell-hole of a place, a drab stinking little town which must have been the hottest place on earth. He asked if there was anything to show that once a besieged British garrison had held out there for five months. All I had seen had been the crumbling remains of some trenches around the town. No sign of a cemetery: no indication of where the hospital had been.

Our Brigade halted a short distance south of Baghdad. An artillery field battery fired warning shots in the general direction of the city, presumably to let it be known that we had serious intentions and would meet any resistance with force. Nothing happened. We proceeded cautiously into the suburbs. Still no sign of the 'enemy'. And so we entered Baghdad and set up a tented camp in the open ground in the centre of the city, and where I was ignominiously bitten by a scorpion (see Chapter 10). There we stayed for a few days before moving out to the airfield where we established our temporary headquarters. Later, we were relieved by another Brigade and advanced north to Mosul on the border of Turkey. Having endured the vicious heat of the height of the summer in southern Iraq, we now had to face a winter under canvas in the bitter cold of the Northern provinces where temperatures dropped to minus 20 degrees C. My orderly brought me hot shaving water at 6 am. Unless I used it at once, it would freeze over.

There was little or no contact with the Iraqi army. They kept well out of our way, wisely perhaps, and left it to the Assyrian Guards, trained by the British Army, to put up at least a modicum of resistance. The odd assault on the main railway line and attempted ambushes and acts of sabotage were the most we had to deal with. Our Brigade's main tasks were to defend the airfields and protect main roads. Later, the troops were put to work digging deep tank trenches from east to west to stop German armour penetrating the southern oilfields. It was a back-breaking task for our little Gurkhas in the searing heat. Amongst the best fighting men in the world (if not the best), they kept their kukris (curved knives) keenly sharpened, ready for use. Digging trenches was viewed with deep distaste.

There was little for my machine-gun platoon to do, apart from rushing round the desert in our trucks on tactical exercises against an imaginary enemy. The Brigade Major asked our Colonel if he could spare an officer to be seconded to Brigade HQ as the Chemical Warfare Officer. Colonel Clark offered my services and I was duly appointed. I was the obvious choice, of course, from the army's standpoint. I had absolutely no knowledge of chemicals; indeed at school I had failed miserably at the subject, which I loathed, mainly due to the chemistry master's inability to teach it with any degree of enthusiasm.

My allotted task was to experiment with the use of crude oil, of which there was an abundance, for defence purposes. I visited an oil refinery on the Iraq/Persia border. The man in charge gave me a tour of the refinery, explaining its functions and purpose. He suggested filling a deep trench with crude oil and igniting it as a deterrent to advancing enemy troops. I thought this was a brilliant idea and determined to test it on return to Baghdad. Before leaving I asked him: 'How do you put up with the foul, acrid smell of burning oil?' 'What smell?' he replied.

My efforts to harness oil for military purposes culminated in an ambitious demonstration laid on in the desert outside Baghdad for the benefit of Divisional staff officers. With reckless abandon my small staff and I exploded oil barrels filled with sharp stones and topped up with oil, dug into a bank on the corner of the road. This was to be used to ambush enemy transport and cause casualties and confusion as a result of the ensuing fireball and deadly rain of stony shrapnel.

Encouraged by the audience's positive reaction, we proceeded to shower a simulated tank with Molotov cocktails which evinced even greater plaudits. These crude weapons had been used to great effect by the Russians in their defence of Stalingrad. In those early days, these were glass bottles filled with petrol. An oil-soaked rag was placed in the neck of the bottle. The rag was then lit and the bottle thrown at the objective. Several variations were developed. One was to place the rag on the side of the bottle and keep it in place with a rubber band, making sure the bottle was capped. Later on, the mixture was modified to half petrol and half motor oil, or tar, which sticks well to surfaces and burns very hotly indeed.

It so happened that I had been introduced to an elderly Iraqi, a former chemical engineer, who claimed he had worked for Lawrence of Arabia in the First World War. Adapting the Russian model, he filled a wine bottle with crude oil and fitted to the neck an ingenious 'fuse' consisting of a cork through which were passed dual pipettes, one containing concentrated sulphuric acid and the other glycerol. On impact with the tank's metal exterior the bottle would break, the two chemicals would ignite instantaneously and burning oil would cascade through the tank's turret, to the obvious discomfort of the occupants. At least that was the theory. Large numbers of these bottles would be distributed to the units in the field.

My *pièce de résistance* and grand finale was to be the 'Ignition of the Oil Trench'. In the experimental stages, I had successfully set fire to a trench of oil by firing into it a shell from a Very pistol, normally used to illuminate battlefields at night. I vaguely knew that crude oil takes a lot to set it alight, but was confident that I had solved the problem. The magnesium in the shell had done the trick before and would do so again. Pointing the pistol at a corner of the trench I pulled the trigger and the shell shot into the black, oily liquid. It disappeared for a few seconds and could then be seen wriggling along just beneath the surface. It promptly fizzled out. There were audible sounds of mirth from the distinguished audience. Much to my chagrin and embarrassment the same thing happened when I fired two more rounds into the trench. I had to admit defeat. Apart from those slight hiccups, the consensus was that the demonstration had been a success. At least it had provided an interlude of harmless entertainment for the Division's top brass.

Next I was given yet another task for which, again, I had no qualifications. It was to test captured enemy weapons. I don't remember when or where they were captured, but they were probably issued to Iraqi soldiers from German or Italian ordnance supplies.

I used a firing range outside Baghdad to try out German rifles and machine pistols, Italian hand grenades and a 2-inch mortar of unknown origin. The latter caused me some anxiety and trepidation, wondering whether the barrel would explode when the shell was dropped down the barrel, this being the primitive but accepted method of arming and firing a mortar. Holding my breath and uttering a silent prayer I released the shell, whereupon it duly shot skywards. In that instant, I spotted a little old Arab woman, obviously terrified, scurrying across the open ground just where I estimated the shell would fall. To my great relief the shell failed to explode on impact and no harm was done.

Breakdowns in wireless communication were frequent, so I found myself offered yet another role, that of Brigade Liaison Officer, a sort of glorified messenger boy. I was given a powerful motorbike which enabled me to transport important confidential signals from one unit HQ to another. This I enjoyed, at least until I encountered my first real sandstorm. Whipped up by a gale-force wind, the sand blew horizontally such that visibility was reduced almost to zero. It stung the face and any uncovered part of the body, and particles got into every crevice of one's clothing. Given the effect of almost complete disorientation, one loses all sense of direction and can easily end up going round in circles.

The battalion's official interpreter, an intelligent, well-educated Iraqi, rode with me in my 15cwt truck whenever we moved from one place to another. I had picked up a few words of Arabic and, being interested in languages, I decided to study it enough to take the elementary Arabic exam, albeit with an ulterior motive. I put in to the Adjutant a formal request to go to Baghdad to take the exam. I was summoned to his tented office where I found the interpreter standing behind the Adjutant, who told the Iraqi to test my knowledge by asking me a few questions. The fact that I appeared to be quite fluent astonished the Adjutant. Little did he know that the interpreter and I had rehearsed the Q and A session until I was word perfect. And so off I went to the fleshpots of the city, staying at the Semiramis Hotel on the banks of the Tigris River, sleeping in a bed on the roof to escape the nocturnal heat. The fact that I failed (only just) the exam was of no great importance. At least I had enjoyed a few days of civilized luxury.

I have every reason to be grateful for the opportunities given to me to exercise what turned out to be an innate ability to function independently. I learned to use simple common-sense to offset a serious lack of knowledge and experience in whatever I was charged to do. I revelled in my independence to such an extent that much later, when the decision came whether or not to stay in the Regular Army, I opted out, in the belief that I would never make a

good Regular Army officer, hidebound by boring rules and regulations. It also led me to seize chances that came my way in civilian
life to take on jobs, again for which I had no qualifications but
which offered me an 'independent command', away from the Head
Office. This included becoming, inter alia, the Midwest Manager
at The British Travel Association's office in Chicago; General
Manager of The British-American Chamber of Commerce in New
York; Director of the multi-million pound Appeals for St Paul's and
Canterbury Cathedrals, and for the Royal Opera House, Covent
Garden.

And so it was that all the varied if unspectacular jobs I had done
in Iraq had apparently so impressed the Brigade Major that he
recommended me for the Intelligence Course in Cairo. There was
a vacancy for the job of Brigade Intelligence Officer and, for whatever reason, he thought I would be a suitable candidate. The
Brigadier agreed and early one morning, in April 1942, I left Iraq,
never to return.

Chapter Two

'For you the war is over!'

At the tender age of twenty-one my war was brought to an abrupt, inglorious standstill. During the night of Wednesday 17 June 1942, in the Western Desert of North Africa, near Tobruk, I was rudely deprived of my liberty by crack German Panzer troops.

The fact of being taken prisoner is so overwhelming a disaster that for days one fails to grasp its significance, let alone its reality. Losing one's freedom is degrading, a devastating deprivation, akin, one imagines, to the loss of virginity through rape. Lurking in the subconscious of the combatant lies a tacit acceptance of the prospect of being killed or wounded on the field of battle. Yet the thought of being put 'in the bag' scarcely enters one's head, the possibility too remote even to contemplate.

I had survived ten months of uneventful active service with the 2nd Battalion of the 8th Gurkha Rifles in Iraq. Much to my surprise, in April 1942 I was sent on the much-prized course at the Middle East Intelligence School, at Helwan, outside Cairo.

I left Baghdad on 10 April in a rickety civilian motor coach, its springs much the worse for wear, which followed the rough, bumpy road that ran alongside the oil pipeline all the way to Syria. The 600-mile trek through the Syrian Desert took three long, wearisome days. We stopped at night to allow the driver to sleep, starting again at dawn as the sun's first rays peeked over the far horizon, with frequent breaks in the heat of the day to give the steaming radiator a chance to simmer down.

On the third day we skirted the southern end of the Sea of Galilee. Descending slowly into the fertile valley of the Jordan we approached the land of milk and honey. Starved of greenery for so many months, it was heart-lifting suddenly to see green grass, orchards of fruit trees, sparkling streams, birds (other than

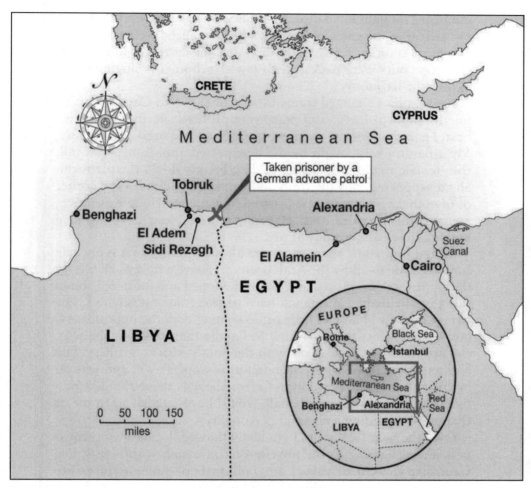

Map 1 – Western Desert

vultures) and wild wayside flowers. One realized then how Moses must have felt as he led the Israelites out of their Egyptian bondage across the desert into the Promised Land.

The bus rattled through Nazareth, scattering groups of children in a cloud of dust, and reached Haifa in time for me to catch the night train to Ismailia, 300 miles south on the Suez Canal. Exhausted from the long, tiring journey, I quickly fell into a deep sleep. Suddenly I was awakened by a wondrous sound. For a moment I thought I had died, that this was a celestial choir greeting my arrival at the gates of heaven. Then I realized we had stopped at a large station (Tel Aviv, in fact) and the carriages in the train alongside ours were packed with Jewish schoolgirls singing softly in melodic harmony.

At Ismailia I changed trains for the final run to Cairo. Waiting for the train to leave, and perspiring profusely in the oppressive heat, I gazed out of the window, feeling badly in need of company. My attention was caught by the unexpected appearance of a tall, trim female figure in uniform striding briskly down the platform. She disappeared into the train and I relaxed back into the corner of my otherwise empty first-class compartment. There was movement in the corridor and, glancing round, I saw a young face looking down enquiringly at me.

'May I join you?' she said, and without waiting for a reply, she stepped aside to allow the Arab porter to heave a bulky valise onto the empty rack opposite me. I was tongue-tied and muttered something unintelligible, struggling hard to overcome my shyness. For twelve months I had had little or no contact with the opposite sex, and was at a loss to know how to handle the situation. She was, she informed me, a sergeant with the South African artillery. She had served in a coastal defence unit near Cape Town, and was on her way to join another unit in Cairo. She was slender and attractive (but then almost any female would have seemed so to me at that point), exuding a cheerful personality.

Over the next two hours I gradually thawed, losing my nervousness and delighting in the novelty of conversing with a real, live Caucasian girl. On arrival in Cairo I plucked up courage to invite her to dine with me, promising to call her when I knew where I was staying. She responded graciously and said she would look forward to hearing from me. Sadly, I lost her address, and never saw her again.

The course started on 20 April so I was able to take several days' welcome leave sampling the fleshpots of Cairo. It was marvellous to be in a metropolitan city after more than a year in the arid deserts of Iraq. Rooms were scarce, but I was lucky to find one at the Grand Hotel (a gross misnomer) in the heart of Cairo. I found myself sharing with a young South African Officer in the Corps of Engineers. He was friendly and easy-going, if rather shy, and a delightful companion. He had been on active service in Eritrea and

Abyssinia, and was enjoying a week's leave before rejoining his unit in the Western Desert. Modest and frugal in his ways, he even did his own laundry, washing his 'smalls' in the basin and hanging them out of the window to dry. We spent a memorable evening together getting pleasantly plastered at a popular night club boasting the finest belly dancers in the Middle East.

The day after he left, someone came to the door asking for 'Captain Jan Smuts'. Astonished, I enquired, 'Any relation to the Field Marshal?' 'Yes,' came the reply; 'His eldest son.'

Helwan stands on the Nile, twenty miles south of Cairo, and from the Intelligence School the Pyramids were plainly visible. It was almost unbearably hot and humid, not at all conducive to the application of the intelligent thought processes demanded of the students. The course, condensed from three months to three weeks to cater for the urgent needs of the military, was intensive, mentally exhausting and even physically demanding. The 'cloak and dagger' aspect, however, appealed to the innately secretive side of my nature.

From 7 am to late at night we were pushed to our limits. Harassed instructors crammed our heads with every conceivable facet of intelligence work: how to identify German and Italian military, naval and air force units; the coding and decoding of clandestine messages; enemy orders of battle; the collection, collation and dissemination of information about enemy dispositions; acceptable methods of interrogating captured enemy personnel; and much more besides.

During the last few days we were subjected to rigorous tests and frantic exercises to determine our suitability to become fully fledged intelligence officers. One over-zealous instructor, in an attempt to emulate battle conditions, suddenly flung wide the windows to expose the papers and maps neatly laid out on our desks to a near-hurricane force gust of wind. This had the desired catastrophic effect, severely testing our ability to remain cool, calm and collected under adverse conditions such as one might encounter in the heat of battle.

The course finished on 16 May and I was posted to my old brigade (20 Indian Infantry) as Brigade Intelligence Officer. Meanwhile (and unknown to me), my battalion, the 2nd Battalion 8th Gurkha Rifles, had been transferred from 20 to 21 Indian

Infantry Brigade, both under the command of the 10th Indian Division, Iraq.

The Staff Captain I saw at the General Headquarters, Cairo, was strangely reticent as to the location of the Brigade to which I had been assigned. Not wishing to embarrass him, or to show off my newly acquired intelligence acuity, I refrained from mentioning that the previous day I had spotted a column of army transport, emblazoned with the 10th Indian Divisional signs, driving slap through the centre of Cairo in broad daylight. So much, I reflected morosely, for military security in a city well known to be teeming with enemy agents and others vociferously longing for the German displacement of the British.

I was told to report back to GHQ in ten days' time, when he hoped to have more precise information. 'And in the meantime, old boy, how about going on another course?'

As an embryonic intelligence officer, keen to impress, I readily agreed. And so, the following day I found myself seated next to an attractive WAAF (Women's Auxiliary Air Force) officer, and peering myopically through a magnifying glass at enlarged aerial photographs. The object of the course was to teach Army and RAF officers how to interpret photographs of enemy positions taken from the air. Photos, shot in pairs at slightly different angles, when placed side by side and looked at with one eye through a magnifying glass mounted on metal legs, become miraculously stereoscopic, the combined images giving the impression of three-dimensional depth and solidity.

A stack of 10 x 8-inch prints in black-and-white landed on our desks first thing each morning. We were invited to record what we could detect, from the shape and pattern of shadows cast onto the ground, as being potential enemy gun emplacements, tanks, parked aircraft and so on, however ingeniously concealed by camouflage. To the initiated it was, we were assured, perfectly possible to assess the precise depth, to the nearest inch, of a slit trench photographed from 5,000 feet or more above ground.

By the end of the first day I was cross-eyed and confused, my pile of photographs only marginally reduced. Vainly, I struggled to find anything remotely suspect, from time to time glancing furtively at the adjacent WAAF's desk for helpful clues. She and her two fellow WAAFs, however, made short work of their respective piles and departed, looking faintly smug, well before the afternoon tea break. Discreet enquiries revealed that these paragons were there on a 'refresher' course. They were, in fact, ace operators from the War Office in London, where their PIU (Photo Interpretation Unit) had successfully identified such sophisticated and vital strategic targets as German submarine pens in Baltic ports.

*   *   *

Ten days and several hundreds of photographs later I reported back to GHQ, this time to be told to make my way to Alexandria, the main Egyptian port on the Mediterranean. There I would receive my marching orders for joining the Brigade to which I had been posted, and which, it now transpired, was firmly entrenched 'somewhere in the Libyan desert'.

Early next morning, after a final night 'on the town', I took the train to Alexandria where I booked into the Cecil Hotel on the sea front. Entering the lobby brought back memories of my previous visit. In March 1940, I had been one of forty keen young officers, fresh from Sandhurst, who stopped off in Alex en route to India. A dozen of us were to join Gurkha battalions; the others had been assigned to Indian cavalry and infantry units. On the previous occasion I had encountered General Wavell who came to meet his wife and two daughters off our troopship.

Considerable confusion reigned in the Western Desert during May and June 1942 when Rommel renewed his offensive, with Egypt as his goal. Once again, I experienced difficulty in determining the precise whereabouts of my elusive Brigade. A sympathetic staff officer at the headquarters in Alexandria suggested politely that I 'proceed forthwith' (a popular phrase in army jargon) in the direction of Tobruk, and 'there to ask again'.

I arranged to hitch a ride with an Indian captain, a field cashier, whose 15cwt truck was loaded with steel boxes stuffed with cash with which to pay the troops in Tobruk. Moreover, he seemed better informed than the staff officer, confiding that my Brigade was very likely in the vicinity of Sidi Rezegh, not far south of Tobruk itself, and offered to deliver me there safely.

Next day, we set off early and followed the coast road, reaching Sidi Barrani, some 200 miles away, in the late afternoon. We stayed overnight in a transit camp, the truck parked safely in front of the guard room. Next morning we drove for a further 150 miles, still

on the coast road, passing through the derelict towns of Sollum and
Bardia, until we reached the road that ran due south to Sidi Rezegh.
Here we were confronted by a military policeman who warned us
that a tank battle was in progress several miles down the road near
Sidi Rezegh. Under the circumstances, and having no desire to
become prematurely embroiled in a battle, we headed at some
speed for the dubious safety of Tobruk.

On 26 May 1942, Rommel launched his major offensive aimed
at destroying our armoured forces in the desert and capturing
Tobruk. His initial efforts failed miserably, and he suffered severe
losses in men and material.

During the first week of June he renewed his attacks on positions
southwest of Tobruk, including those of the Free French Brigade at
Bir Hacheim, and succeeded in regaining the initiative. German
88s, equally effective as anti-aircraft and anti-tank guns, wrought
widespread havoc. By the end of the second week of June, our
armour, outgunned and outmanoeuvred by the German Mark III
and IV tanks in the fierce battles for possession of the area known
as the 'Cauldron' (between El Adem and 'Knightsbridge'), was
forced to withdraw towards Tobruk.

The brigade I was to join was holding the Sidi Rezegh 'box',
twenty-five miles southeast of Tobruk. The two other brigades of
the 10th Indian Division occupied similar 'boxes' fifteen miles
further west, at Belhamed and Gambut.

There was a perceptible air of despondency in Tobruk. The
general opinion was that the fortress could not endure yet another
siege. For one thing there were food supplies for only ninety days.
Secondly, as I quickly discovered, it was subjected daily to devastating air attacks by the Luftwaffe from airfields in Sicily, taking
full advantage of their air superiority. Hundreds of Stukas would
descend on Tobruk in long screaming dives, scattering their deadly
bombs far and wide, inflicting severe damage on ordnance workshops, engineer parks, ammunition dumps, NAAFI stores and
other vital targets.

The garrison's air defences were insufficient to prevent such
determined attacks. Anti-aircraft guns put up intensive 'box
barrages'; every available machine gun was brought to bear on the
diving planes and rifles were fired from slit trenches, all to little
effect.

Water was so scarce a desalination plant struggled to process sea water for drinking purposes. But it was scarcely drinkable. Filling a glass one-third with gin (if you were lucky), one-third with lime juice, topping it up with water, you could still taste the chlorine.

At last, news came that the road to Sidi Rezegh was clear. The German attempt to capture the airfield had been beaten off; the Sidi Rezegh 'Box', one of several defensive positions running south from the coast, had been vacated by 21 Indian Infantry Brigade (of which my battalion, the 2nd Battalion 8th Gurkha Rifles, was now part) and was occupied by 20 Brigade, my old brigade from Iraq.

I reported for duty in a cramped underground bunker which served as the Brigade Headquarters. The Brigadier, eyes red-rimmed from lack of sleep, welcomed me back and wished me well. The Brigade Major (his senior staff officer) briefly outlined the situation which he calmly, but not reassuringly, described as 'rather critical, if not exactly desperate'.

My first impression was of a dogged determination to hang on to the 'Box' at all costs. The second, in contrast, was of a sense of vague confusion: no one seemed to have much idea of the enemy's dispositions, nor what they were likely to do next. 'It's what's known, Pat, as the fog of war,' the Brigade Major explained grimly. This was caused, no doubt, by the fluidity of the battles that had raged in the area for several days, including the one that had precluded my earlier arrival.

My immediate task was to determine the composition and whereabouts of any German forces lurking in our vicinity. Trying hard not to duck every time a shell burst nearby, I busied myself studying signals and situation reports, quizzing staff officers and anyone coming within earshot, making contact by radio and field telephone with divisional and battalion intelligence officers, and marking up my meagre findings in coloured crayons on my pristine Perspex-covered brigade situation map.

One of our reconnaissance patrols identified a concentration of German tanks on an escarpment a mile or so southwest of our 'Box'. Immediately, I called up the RAF base at El Adem, a few miles to our rear, giving them the map reference of the reported tank assembly. Within minutes, I had the vicarious thrill of hearing a squadron of our fighter-bombers thunder overhead and, moments later, the distant crump of bombs exploding, hopefully on target. This afforded a strange, satisfying sense of power which, sadly, was to prove ephemeral.

Following recently-learned textbook procedures, I interrogated a German soldier, caught the night before on patrol near our wire perimeter fence. The youth, however, was singularly unforthcoming. Apart from giving the minimum statutory information – name, rank and number – no amount of persuasion, subtle or otherwise, would extract anything that might help to identify German units or their intentions. On the contrary, he was cockily confident that his spell in captivity would be short-lived. I was left with the uneasy suspicion that he knew something I didn't.

Within a week of my arrival our Brigade was suddenly, and without warning, ordered to withdraw, under cover of darkness, to the coast road. (Incidentally, one's own side carries out a 'tactical withdrawal': only the enemy 'retreats'.) There, the 30cwt trucks already on their way from a rear staging area, would turn about, pick up the three battalions of infantry, plus 'odds and sods', and transport them back to Mersa Matruh, where the Brigade was to reform.

Together with another staff officer I rode in a station wagon driven by a swarthy Sikh soldier. Bumping along the rough track that led northwards through the barbed-wire perimeter defences, we came across an ambulance that, moments before had strayed off the track and detonated a mine, blowing the front end into a tangled wreck. Fortunately, the driver and wounded occupants had escaped injury and were safely transferred to another vehicle.

An hour or so later we reached the coast road and turned sharp right towards the Egyptian frontier. After a few miles, I spotted our Brigadier on the roadside, bending over an abandoned 15cwt lorry, calmly extracting the battery. 'Can't afford to let this fall into Jerry's hands,' he declared righteously. He must have spent twenty vital minutes performing this inane salvage operation. Then, ordering us to give him a five-minute head start, he drove off into the dusty darkness.

We covered a short distance, when, perched precariously on the roof of the station wagon and peering ahead in the pitch dark, I saw what I took to be empty oil drums on either side of the road. Suddenly these objects leapt to life as a dozen German soldiers surrounded the car, brandishing sub-machine guns, and shouting

'*Raus*! *Raus*!' ('Get out! Get out!'). These troops, it later transpired, were the advance guard of a Panzer Brigade assigned to sweep round from the south in a broad arc and cut off 10th Indian Division's line of withdrawal. In fact, they must have reached the road just seconds before, as I later learned that the Brigadier had got through safely. Had he not been so hell-bent on the salvation of one miserable car battery, we would have escaped the ambush and been spared the miseries of many months' captivity. Such, as they say, are the fortunes of war.

Guarded by a youthful, blond-haired Panzergrenadier we were forced to squat on the sand, in the bitterly cold night air, while the German infantry prepared to ambush the rest of our Brigade. Impotently we watched the quiet, ruthless efficiency with which they set the trap. Soon, the faint squeals of tank and carrier tracks and the drone of engines were heard as the motorized column, with dog-tired men asleep in the backs of the lorries, came rumbling slowly towards us.

Next, we heard the whispered 'stand by' orders to the German gunners, followed a moment later by the barked '*Feuer*', whereupon all hell broke loose. Star shells illuminated the exposed column. Withering streams of tracer bullets and mortar shells rained on the hapless troops as they leapt, stunned and bleary-eyed, from their lorries and ran for cover to escape the cold-blooded slaughter.

Somehow, a group of gallant Gurkhas succeeded in mounting a brief but abortive counter-attack. Their rifle and machine-gun fire forced us to flatten ourselves in the sand, while our boyish guard, with commendable courage, remained upright, unflinching. The thought of being on the receiving end of slashing kukris did little to improve my morale, already at its lowest ebb.

When dawn broke, the scene was one of utter devastation. As far as the eye could see the desert was littered with burning lorries, dead and wounded everywhere. German stretcher parties attended the scattered casualties. Pathetic groups of British, Gurkha and Indian prisoners were slowly herded into an ever expanding laager beside the road.

Later that day, we saw a column of German transport rapidly approaching us from the east. It was customary for both sides in this fluid so-called 'gentlemen's' desert warfare to abandon prisoners whenever circumstances demanded a withdrawal. However, our hopes were soon dashed by the appearance, in an open staff car, of the legendary Rommel himself. To our astonishment, the Field Marshal (as he had just been appointed by Hitler) personally disentangled a traffic jam right in front of us, his barked orders accompanied by much springing to attention and sharp saluting. The German officer in charge of us said, with undisguised relish, that Rommel was returning personally to oversee the capture of Tobruk before launching his final assault on Egypt.

In this theatre of war, if not in others, German troops, on Rommel's explicit orders and also perhaps from a sense of mutual respect, were punctilious in their treatment of Allied prisoners. 'For you the war is over,' declared the interrogating officer, with a hint of envy. PoWs were not, however, the responsibility of front-line troops, and the next day we were handed over to the Italians, whom the Germans openly despised as 'the jackals of Rommel's desert army: useless, scented, degenerate creatures, utterly unwarlike'. Conversely, and with equal fervour, the Italians loathed and feared the Germans.

An officious *capitano* of the *Ariete* Division took charge of our small, disconsolate band of British officers. A Gilbert and Sullivan character, he was resplendent in waisted uniform, polished riding boots and sun helmet adorned with crimson plumes. He reeked, moreover, of cheap scent and brilliantine. After endless delays, this preening pretty boy and his minions herded us onto large, open Lancia diesel trucks into which we were crammed like cattle, and forced to stand, without food or water, in the fierce midday sun.

The long line of transport waited at the road-side for the order to move off. After two hours, driven desperate by thirst, I risked life and limb by jumping over the tailgate and crawling beneath the truck behind. Feverishly, I opened the radiator drain tap and swallowed the filthy fluid, warm, brackish, oily, as it dripped slowly into my gaping mouth. Hearing the barked orders for the convoy to move off, I clambered back on board, mercifully unscathed but my thirst unquenched.

Skirting Tobruk, we passed German 88s (heavy artillery guns) lined up in a wide arc, almost wheel-to-wheel, pouring a continuous barrage of murderous fire into the hapless beleaguered garrison. It was a dispiriting sight.

*   *   *

Two days later, after a harrowing journey of some 300 miles along the Cyrenaica coast, and twice machine gunned by the RAF, we reached the port of Benghazi. En route, we stopped overnight in a filthy, fly-infested prison at Derna, sleeping on rush mats on the concrete floor. After a gap of sixty-nine years memory plays strange tricks. But never shall I forget that particular night. With the bright moonlight streaming through the barred cell windows, a dozen officers from the South Wales Borderers sang in soft, sweet harmony the haunting melodies of traditional Welsh songs. I can still hear, too, their poignant renderings of *Abide with me* and *Land of My Fathers*.

Once a day we were fed Italian hard rations, consisting usually of a four-inch square, yellowish dog biscuit, a half-pound tin of *carne bollito* (probably horse meat), and small lumps of stale bread. Very soon most of us developed 'gippy-tummy', a moderate form of dysentery which saps one's strength and lowers one's resistance to more virulent infections. Survival is the chief preoccupation: any thoughts of escape diminish rapidly as the body weakens and the spirit succumbs to a sense of resignation and despondency.

Our brief sojourn in Benghazi, where we were incarcerated in a disused warehouse, was punctuated by RAF bombing raids on a nearby airfield. These attacks, heart-warming though they were, nevertheless caused us no small unease, the bombs too often falling perilously close to our makeshift camp, the RAF pilots blissfully unaware of our existence. But our discomfort was as nothing compared to the fearful alarm and confusion created amongst our Italian guards, who disappeared like rabbits into their warren, to reappear only when the aircraft had long gone.

From there we were flown in an ancient Savoia transport plane to the town of Lecce on the heel of Italy, and then taken to a deserted tobacco factory, commandeered by the Red Cross as a temporary transit camp for officer prisoners. A few days later we were moved by train to a much larger transit camp on the outskirts of the port of Bari, on the Adriatic coast.

At Bari we joined several hundred officer PoWs, all recently captured in the Western Desert. Many had been caught in Tobruk, and from them we learned the dismal story of its capitulation on 20 June. The garrison had consisted of the 2nd South African

Division plus a Guards Brigade and 11 Brigade of the 4th Indian Division (comprising 2/7th Gurkha Rifles, 5th Mahrattas and the Cameron Highlanders), a total of 33,000 men, one-third of whom were non-combatants, such as service corps personnel.

The German offensive had opened on 13 June. The 15th and 21st Panzer Division and the 90th Light Infantry Division attacked the Gazala Line with ferocity, and the Luftwaffe intensified their raids, bombing ammunition and storage dumps by night, a departure from their former daylight raids.

Official records relate that Churchill, concerned about the grave situation in North Africa, ordered General Auchinleck, Commander-in-Chief, Middle East, to leave Cairo and take over personal command of the desert battle from General Ritchie. But by then it was too late.

On 14 June, Churchill telegraphed the Auk (as General Auchinleck was known): 'Presume there is no question . . . of giving up Tobruk. As long as Tobruk is held no serious enemy advance into Egypt is possible . . . ' Next day, the Auk replied:

' . . . I have no intention whatever of giving up Tobruk . . . ' He went on to assure Churchill that General Ritchie considered the Tobruk garrison adequate to hold it 'even if it should become temporarily isolated by the enemy'.

On the night of 16/17 June (the night I was captured) the coast road was cut, leaving Tobruk once again in a stage of siege. Rommel was hot in pursuit of our forces, retreating in some disarray towards El Alamein, 700 miles to the east.

Even though the fortress was surrounded by a thirty-six-mile perimeter of minefields, anti-tank ditches and barbed wire, its defences had been badly neglected over the past six months and were in very poor shape.

The commander of the garrison was General Klopper, an Afrikaaner and a controversial character. Later on, discussing the fall of Tobruk with non-Afrikaaners in our camp, the whole conduct of the defence of Tobruk was severely questioned. What caused, for example, the failure of Klopper's counter-attack? Moreover, when Klopper surrendered, why was no *sauve qui peut* order given? Tacit suspicions of treachery were rife, extending even to accusations of fifth-column activity amongst the Boer element. Certainly a good deal of tension existed between the British and the

South Africans in the PoW camp. The Springboks, for their part, vehemently resented any odious comparisons with the Australians who, in 1941, had held out for eight months and never surrendered Tobruk.

After the war, General Klopper faced a Court of Enquiry and was duly exonerated of any blame. There were, indeed, extenuating circumstances, quite apart from his heritage of the seriously decayed defences. At that time of the year the hours of darkness, when troops can be moved and defences improved, are short. There had been a breakdown in communications with General Ritchie's HQ. There was a limited area of movement within the perimeter, coupled with a serious shortage of transport. But above all, there were almost continuous and devastating air attacks during daylight hours.

Not surprisingly, morale in the Bari camp was poor. The prospect of languishing behind barbed-wire for the rest of the war was not one to relish. By the time we arrived reaction had set in and an air of gloom permeated the camp. Tempers became frayed and discipline suffered. Contrary to King's Regulations, some of the more unruly inmates had grown beards, until ordered by the Senior British Officer to remove them forthwith. Some semblance of order, even under these strained circumstances, has to be maintained.

Led to believe that our stay in Bari would be short – no more than a few days – we remained there, in squalid surroundings, for two depressing months. In these sordid surroundings we settled down as best we could to a dreary routine of roll-calls and restless nights on hard wooden bunks in crowded huts. We queued for sparse rations, armed with a kidney-shaped Italian dixie into which was doled out, from a huge metal tureen, a concoction of watery soup with a faint tinge of onion, to which, almost as an afterthought, a few grains of rice had been added. A lump of bread, half the size of a tennis ball, completed our meagre daily diet.

Soon after we arrived, there was an incident calculated to depress our morale even further. Four officers escaped but were recaptured and brought back to the camp. They were ordered to demonstrate how and where they had escaped. While doing so, crawling through the barbed-wire surrounding the camp, they were shot in cold blood 'in the act of escaping'. On another occasion, a young officer, stricken with dysentery, wandered out in the night to the latrines. Challenged by the sentry, he called out several times 'Latrina', only to be brutally shot through the stomach.

From this wretched place I and a number of others were moved by train up the Adriatic coast to the port of Pescara, thence inland some ten miles to Chieti, a small town perched on a hill. Alighting at the station (Chieti Scala) at the foot of the hill, and carrying our blankets and meagre possessions, we were marched the few hundred yards to Campo PG 21, our 'home' for many months to come.

Chapter Three

Captive in Chieti

PG 21 was a new camp, the largest of its kind in Italy. Later, it contained 1,200 officers, mostly British, but also many South Africans captured in Tobruk, as well as a number of Canadians, Australians and Americans. It lay in a wide coastal valley, to the west of which were the Abruzzi mountains, dominated by the spectacular snow-capped Gran Sasso mountain (8,800 ft). High on the hillside behind the camp, the town was reached by a funicular railway from which the locals would often wave to us. Rumour had it that the previous occupants, an Italian cavalry regiment, had been drafted to the dreaded Russian front where they were duly decimated, thus releasing their barracks for more mundane purposes.

Surrounding the camp was a fifteen-foot wall, guarded by sentries armed with machine guns, and searchlights on platforms at each of the four corners and halfway along each side. Escape was further discouraged by rolls of barbed-wire at the foot of the wall, both inside and outside, and by a single strand of trip-wire beyond which one ventured at the risk of being shot.

Here, to my surprise and delight, I found two fellow-officers from 2nd Battalion 8th Gurkha Rifles, Major Rick Wall and Captain Eddie Edwards. They had both been with my battalion throughout the Iraq campaign, and were captured in June in the fighting around Mersa Matruh. Sadly, we were billeted in separate huts so I did not see them as much as I would have wished. There were several officers, too, from 2/7th Gurkha Rifles, who had been part of the ill-fated Tobruk garrison.

As usual, the living quarters were cramped. Each single-storey building housed some 120 officers in rooms jam-packed with double-tier bunks. The bottom of the bunk consisted of movable slats, placed crossways, those surplus to requirements becoming

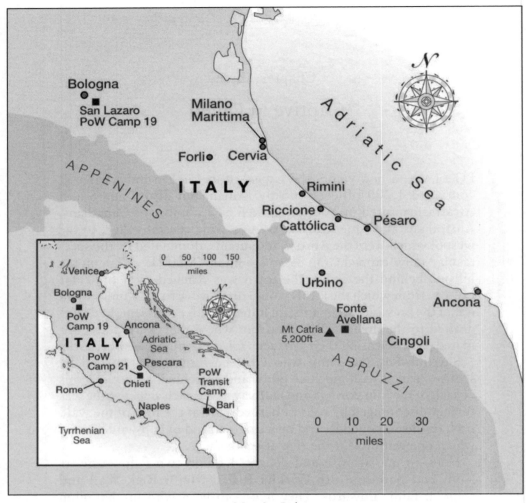

Map 2 – Italy

useful sources of fuel. Each block boasted communal ablutions, with washbasins and showers, and toilets graced with mahogany swing doors. Unfortunately, these masterpieces of Italian plumbing rarely saw the luxury of water! This scarce commodity was procured from a well, sited between each block. Into this we lowered an empty can on a string and then shuffled off to wash our bodies or our eating utensils, or to flush the toilets.

Except for a metal Italian-army dixie, no eating or cooking utensils were ever issued. We had to use our ingenuity to make cups out
of cans, plates and rudimentary stoves from biscuit tins, and knives
and forks from whatever came to hand.

The Italians, as captors, were neither cruel nor kind. Any
maltreatment was mainly due to sheer neglect, inefficiency and
almost total disinterest in our well-being. Unlike the Germans, the
Italians supplied no clothing. Most of us possessed only the thin
desert uniform in which we were captured – cotton shirts and
stockings, 'bush' shorts or trousers, and suede desert boots,
commonly known as 'brothel creepers'. Within weeks these
summer uniforms became tattered and threadbare, and when
winter came we resorted to cutting a hole in one or both of the two
scratchy army blankets issued to us, wearing them like prairie
Indians. It was to be many months before we received clothing
parcels from home.

For the first six months, before the spasmodic issue of Red Cross
parcels, thoughts of food preoccupied our minds. The daily ration
varied little, except that, in the summer, there was fruit to supple-
ment our diet. Monotonously, the 'Eyeties' dished out bitter ersatz
coffee and 200 grammes of bread for breakfast; for supper, we were
rationed to a third of a dixie of thin, soupy stew, to which was
added a modicum of rice, macaroni or beans. Hunger rapidly
moderates squeamishness. Weevils in the soup, for example,
became nutritious and edible for their protein content.

In the early days, lack of food made climbing up onto a top bunk
a major operation. Many prisoners lay listlessly on their palliasses
(straw mattresses) fantasizing about past or future gastronomic
delights. Red Cross parcels were a sensitive subject. We were
entitled, in theory, to one each per month. In practice, we were
lucky to share an occasional parcel between four. Only once (at
Christmas) do I recall enjoying a whole parcel to myself. Many
were mysteriously 'lost' en route to the camp, or pilfered by the
guards who prized in particular the chocolate, condensed milk and
butter, as well as other unobtainable luxuries. Canadian parcels
were the best, containing such delicacies as powdered eggs,
porridge oats, biscuits and dried fruit.

Later on, the Italians allowed us to open a canteen where we
could buy boiled sweets, biscuits, jam, onions, fish paste, fig bars,

Italian cigarettes and tobacco, and essential toiletries, such as soap and toothpaste. We paid for these in paper currency called '*buone*', issued on the basis of rank – second lieutenant, 750 lire per month; lieutenant, 950 lire; captain, 1,100 lire (valued then at 72 lire to the pound).

When personal (i.e., non-Red Cross) food, clothing, tobacco parcels began to arrive, morale (of the recipients, at least) soared. The names of the lucky ones were posted on the notice-board daily. Bartering became rife. Everything had a market value, which fluctuated according to supply and demand.

It was sad to see the heavy smokers prowling the campus, heads down, searching the ground for discarded stub ends. They would go to excessive lengths, even swap their precious food rations, to satisfy their craving for nicotine. Some even smoked dried-out used tea-leaves, but were forbidden to do so inside their hut, the smell being so thoroughly obnoxious.

Apart from physical discomforts there was the mental problem of coping with excruciating boredom. For months we had no books, other than the few cherished, dog-eared copies, circulated within each block, and possessively guarded by their owners.

Gradually, various activities were organized which did much to alleviate the soul-destroying monotony. Academic graduates, of whom there were many, covering diverse subjects, began to surface and offer their specialized knowledge to any who were eager to learn. There were courses on subjects such as engineering, science, philosophy, literature, languages, art and even military studies. Societies proliferated, catering to special interests such as sketching, angling, motoring and poetry. Yet, after a while, attendance gradually dwindled: the debilitating diet made concentration difficult and weakened the will to learn, however absorbing the subject.

News of the outside world, vital for morale, was provided by the Camp newspaper with a weekly analysis of the progress of the war. Information was culled from Italian newspapers, newly arrived PoWs, bribed guards, and, rather more accurately, from the BBC on an ingeniously hidden secret radio.

Thanks to their innate love of music, the Italians encouraged music-making in many of its forms. Instruments were supplied through the Red Cross or lent by the Italians. Our maestro, Tony

Baines, created a superb symphony orchestra, and their concerts were amongst the camp's most popular events. Tony wrote and conducted his first symphony in Chieti. There was music to satisfy all tastes, from string quartets to the Big Band led by jazz trumpeter, Tommy Sampson, whose brilliant rendering of *In the Mood* still rings in my ears.

Plays produced in the camp theatre were professional, with consistently high standards of performance. Often on Saturday nights there was a slickly-produced variety show. One came to accept, without demur, young men made up as gorgeous girls playing passionate love scenes, evoking never a titter from the audience. A particularly handsome, blond South African youth became notorious for his credible and utterly convincing portrayal of slinky, sexy females.

On one notable occasion the theatre was ingeniously converted into a glamorous night club. Volunteers were invited to appear as dancing partners. A dozen from our block transformed themselves into ravishing maidens, heavily made up and dressed to kill. The effect was startling, so much so that several of us spread the rumour that the Commandante had finally relented and allowed a bevy of local lasses into the camp for the evening. Not surprisingly, tickets rapidly sold out, and when the doors opened there was a stampede of spruced-up officers falling over each other for the favours of a 'comely wench'. A special brew of camp vino helped to make the evening go with a swing. It was indeed a riotous occasion. And even when the cruel deception was revealed, there were no hard feelings. A good time, as they say, was had by all.

In summer, life was easier. We could lie in the sun, chatting, dozing or reading. In the cool of the late afternoon, as the burning sun sank slowly over the Abruzzi, there were games to watch – football, baseball (introduced by the American contingent), basketball, or even cricket, played by those with the energy to do so on the open space in the centre of the camp. In the evening, there was a daily issue of rough, vinegary vino which, if consumed too liberally, offered temporary oblivion but invariably produced an horrendous hangover.

At morning and evening roll-calls we would parade in front of our building to be counted by an Italian officer. Those too sick or weak to stand were counted on their bunks, and those in the camp hospital were checked separately. Interminable delays were caused by any discrepancy, so the Senior British Officer sensibly insisted on our tacit co-operation. Spot roll-calls and building searches were frequent.

A squad of *Carabinieri* (military police), fondly known as 'Snow White and the Seven Dwarfs', armed with hammers and chisels, would appear without warning and solemnly troop in single file into each block in turn. Sometimes their progress through the camp was accompanied by a whistled or hummed chant of 'dum-de-dum, dum-de-dum, dum-de-diddle-de-dumdedum . . . ' Systematically, they tapped the floors, examined the tiles in the washrooms with scrupulous care, and peered down the toilet bowls, their every fibre finely tuned to the uncovering of tunnels. They were a source of constant merriment to the PoWs, and the cause of no little anxiety to anyone engaged in seriously nefarious activities.

There was, of course, the inevitable Escape Committee. Their tasks were to monitor and co-ordinate escape plans, to weed out the more bizarre conceptions, to recommend those that had some hope of success to the Senior British Officer for his final approval, and to provide the lucky ones with whatever material help they could offer.

As an Intelligence officer with particular interest in maps, I was put in charge of their reproduction, using the silk versions, smuggled into the camp by RAF Officers, as 'masters'. Drawn with meticulous care on handkerchiefs, these were hidden all over the camp in hollowed-out bedposts, Red Cross tins ingeniously fitted with false bottoms, spines of books, etc.

One day, to check progress, I gathered all the maps together and was inspecting them when the bell rang for a surprise roll-call. Concealing them in a Red Cross box covered with a blanket, I jumped out of the window into the courtyard, as did others from my hut. Something must have aroused the suspicion of the sentry on the wall, because the next thing I knew a guard appeared from nowhere, calmly picked up the box and marched off triumphantly towards the administration building, leaving me stunned and mortified. Undoubtedly, it was one of the worst moments of my captivity.

Tunnels abounded. Started and discovered with monotonous regularity, at one time there were at least five on the go. Once, while

Italian 'ferrets' busily filled in a detected tunnel, several picks and shovels carelessly left unattended were quietly expropriated for future excavations.

On another occasion, a hammer, borrowed from the Italians, somehow managed to 'fall down one of the wells'. Convinced that it had been hidden, the Commandante called in the Chieti Fire Brigade to pump the well dry. While they were thus engaged, several of us sat at intervals along the hose which we proceeded to slice with our home-made knives! Not content with these acts of blatant sabotage, we then turned our attention to the fire engine's tyres, which we succeeded in puncturing, much to the frustrated fury of the official in charge. Sadly, these childish pranks backfired. In retribution, the entire camp's pay was summarily docked for a month.

Then there was the incident of 'The General Salute'. At a morning roll-call the Commandante announced that we must learn the bugle call for the Italian General Salute, to prepare us for the day when an Italian general honoured the camp with a visit. Thereupon, a diminutive bugler mounted the platform and sounded the call. To the Commandante's obvious delight and surprise (if not amazement), the entire parade dutifully stood smartly to attention, and then stood at ease when a single note was blown.

Intoxicated with his new-found power, Il Colonnello repeated the performance several times. At last the absurdity of the situation overcame military discipline, our collective patience by then exhausted. In mutinous silence the entire camp, taking their cue from the Senior British Officer, promptly sat on the ground. The Commandante fretted and fumed; the Italian Adjutant, a bearded Mephistophelian character, who sported a monocle, looked suitably aghast; and the guards, in a feeble attempt to appear menacing, proceeded to unsling their rifles. Reinforcements were hurriedly summoned from the local barracks. As they attempted to force their way through our serried ranks, one of them 'accidentally' tripped up and, in the ensuing melee, was temporarily relieved of his rifle.

Beside himself with impotent rage, the Commandante stamped his jack-booted feet and yelled imprecations all to no avail. This farce continued well into the afternoon, until, at last, a compromise was reached. The Senior British Officer would call us all to attention simultaneously with the sound of the bugle – likewise for the 'stand at ease'. Thus honour was satisfied.

Amongst many interesting personalities incarcerated at PG 21 were 'Pip' Gardner, London's first VC of the war; Freddie Brown, the England Test captain and manager; Bill Bowes, the Yorkshire and England fast bowler; and Tony Roncoroni, the much-capped English Rugby international. John Dugdale, the London theatre critic, wrote and reviewed plays. Eric Newby, the well-known travel-writer, author of *Love and War in the Apennines* and many fascinating travel sagas, was a valued camp colleague. He had been captured in a Commando raid on the Sicilian coast and shared my burning desire for freedom.

We followed, with growing excitement, the seemingly sluggish progress of the Allied forces. Over our illicit radio came news of the First Army's landing in North Africa, the surrender of Tunisia and the capture of Sicily. The Italians, fearful that the Allies would invade their country half-way or further still up the peninsula, ordered the gradual evacuation of PoW camps in our area to others farther north. So it was that, in early August, I was amongst 200 or so packed off to PG 19, a new camp on the outskirts of Bologna.

Rumours, rife at all times, grew daily that an Armistice was imminent. On 26 July 1943, at the King of Italy's invitation, Marshal Badoglio replaced Mussolini as head of the Italian government. Although the landing of the Allies on the mainland was hundreds of miles to the south, it seemed entirely possible that the Italian guards might desert, leaving the way clear for a mass walk-out.

Six weeks later, on 7 September, came Badoglio's dramatic announcement, blazoned across the front page of the *Corriere della Sera*. Headed in four-inch black lettering: 'ARMISTIZIO', it read: 'I, as head of the Government, recognizing the impossibility of continuing the war against the vast preponderance of enemy forces, have asked the Allied Governments for an Armistice.' The satisfaction of reading of our enemy's unconditional surrender in one of their own newspapers, was a heart-warming experience. But no one had any illusions that the Germans would sit back and watch thousands of Allied PoWs calmly walk free.

The Times reported on 9 September that 'an armistice was signed on 8 September by a representative of General Dwight D. Eisenhower, Commander-in-Chief of the Allied Forces in the Mediterranean, and the representative of Marshal Badoglio . . . . Hostilities between the armed forces of the United Nations and those of Italy terminate at once'. The article went on to ask: 'What next in Italy? In the northern regions strongly garrisoned by German divisions there can be no sharp cut between past and present for some time'. Badoglio even hinted in a radio message that the Italian people, so far as they could, should turn to fight against the Germans.

All that day we prepared, with mounting excitement, for a mass exodus. In the afternoon, to calm our strained nerves, Tony Baines conducted a memorable performance of Beethoven's Fifth Symphony in the canteen. The cooks somehow managed to dish out double rations to fortify us for the demands anticipated on our physical resources.

That night we lay on our bunks fully clothed, armed with a supply of hard rations and ready for a prearranged signal. This came in the early hours of the morning. Sure enough, the guards had vanished; the gates were wide open; our hour of deliverance had come. I made swiftly for the door in the wall behind the cook-house. No sooner had I gone outside the walls a few yards when there was a frantic cry of 'Look out! Germans!' We had been betrayed. Armed with sub-machine guns, German paratroopers had surrounded the camp and were herding the PoWs back inside. I crawled under the nearest thick bush, praying that somehow I would escape notice in the darkness. Unhappily, dawn broke and I was spotted by a German soldier who pointed his gun at me and said what sounded like: 'Go back into ze garten!' I had no choice but to obey.

We were marshalled into groups on the parade ground, surrounded by rolls of barbed-wire and machine guns mounted on tripods, and kept there, without food or water, for the rest of that day and overnight. It was clear the Germans meant business. One officer had been killed and several others wounded, attempting escape. On the other hand, it quickly became evident that these were front-line troops unaccustomed to handling PoWs and, therefore, not up to our wily ways.

Next morning we were allowed to return to our huts, but warned that we were to be transferred to Germany within the next couple of days. I had already reconnoitred the camp for likely hiding-places and settled on the loft of my hut. I found that a handful of other officers had the same idea. So, together, we prepared our refuge, laying in stores of food and water in the small space between the rafters and the ceiling of the hut. The washroom trapdoor, which provided access to the loft, was cunningly fixed so that it could be secured from above, after the last person had been heaved through the opening by an accomplice below.

On learning that the move to Germany was imminent, we clambered up into our hideaway. It was pitch dark in the loft and great care had to be taken not to put one's foot between the joists onto the flimsy ceiling. The pitch of the roof being low, there was room neither to stand nor sit upright; all movements had to be slow and deliberate, and we conversed in monosyllabic whispers.

Early next day, 10 September, we heard the sound of transport rumbling into the central courtyard. For several hours we overheard our colleagues below us packing such belongings as they could carry and moving out of the building. Eventually there was silence.

Thinking the coast was clear, we were about to prepare for our candle-lit evening meal when there were muffled voices and sounds of activity beneath us. Just in time, we realized that those Germans left behind were going through and pillaging abandoned belongings. Next came the sound of a record being played on a gramophone, followed shortly by raucous laughter. Then, later, the sound of heavy boots tramping through the building gradually became fainter – until, once more, there was silence.

We were all set to resume our cold collation when someone sneezed, right below us, someone engrossed, perhaps, in an English book or magazine left on one of the bunks? Again we waited for what seemed an age, scarcely daring to breathe, until the sound of receding footsteps told us that the last scavenger had left the building.

For two days and nights we stayed in our cramped quarters, afraid to move. On the second night, a volunteer bravely went down to recce the situation. On his return, he reported that the lights had been switched off on the walls, the sentry boxes were empty, and that the only sign of life came from the guardroom near the main gates, at the far end of the camp.

We drew lots to decide the order of departure from our hiding place. I was paired with Captain Jimmie Ferguson, Royal Signals. When our turn came, Jimmie and I lowered ourselves to the wash-room floor, climbed out of the window, and crept stealthily over to the wall. I gave Jimmie a leg-up onto the wall and he, in turn, pulled me up beside him. Together, we scrambled through the barbed-wire and dropped gently down to the ground, fifteen feet below.

Swiftly and silently, we made our way to the shelter of a nearby olive grove. It was 3 am on the 11 September. Jimmie and I had never met before, so we had no pre-arranged escape plan. Like other escaped PoWs, we thought it would be only a matter of weeks, perhaps days, before our troops arrived. It was simply a question of lying low, up in the hills, and waiting patiently . . .

How wrong we were! Little did we realize it would be three frustrating and hazardous months before we reached the Allied lines – and final freedom.

Chapter Four

Flight to Freedom

Scrambling headlong through the trees and undergrowth we came to a stream, and followed it until we reached a bridge across a main road. There we decided to risk walking on the road itself, expecting little (if any) traffic at such an early hour. Our first concern was to cover as much ground as possible before dawn.

Suddenly Jimmie froze. Pointing across the fields to our right he whispered, 'See those lights? They're floodlights on our camp walls, for God's sake!' He was right; somehow we had come full circle and were heading back towards our prison camp, now only a few hundred yards away.

Then we saw, looming out of the pre-dawn mist, a squad of German soldiers marching briskly along the road towards us. Attempting to emulate a farm lad, I spat coarsely as they approached. Too late, I realized the idiocy of such reckless provocation. Happily, the Germans ignored what might have been construed as an act of impertinence by an insolent Italian peasant, and marched straight past us.

Dawn was imminent. We needed urgently to find somewhere to hide. Turning sharp left, down a rough track, we hurriedly crossed open fields that led to a thick copse. Here we remained hidden in dense undergrowth for the rest of the day, utterly exhausted and emotionally drained by the dramatic events of the past few days. We slept fitfully and ate some of our 'escape' rations.

Waiting for darkness to fall, we discussed our situation and considered the alternatives. We could either make for the Swiss border, some 150 miles to the north, or go southeast to the coast and beg, borrow or steal a boat in which to cross the Adriatic to Yugoslavia. On the other hand, we could head due south in the hope of crossing the front lines, then some 400 miles away. I favoured the latter course, since this gave us an important further option: should penetration of the lines prove difficult or impossible, we could lie low, up in the mountains, and wait patiently for the Allied forces to arrive. Jimmie had reached more or less the same conclusions.

Our immediate objective, therefore, was to find the nearest wayside station and board a southbound train. The plan was to make our way as far south as fast as possible, taking advantage of the turmoil created by the recent Italian capitulation.

That evening, uncertain of the reception we could expect, we cautiously approached an isolated farmhouse. Declining the offer of shelter for the night, preferring to press on under cover of darkness, we thankfully accepted a meal of pasta and bitter ersatz coffee. The farmer told us where, a few miles away, we could board a train without attracting attention. To our surprise and delight he unearthed some old civilian clothes which we exchanged for our inadequately disguised battle-dress jackets and tunics.

As darkness fell we set off again, this time avoiding the main road and, following the farmer's directions, skirted the nearby hamlet of Idice. After a mile, we encountered the railway line and followed this until we reached the wayside station of Mirandola, no more than eight miles from Bologna, still much too close for comfort.

Our luck was in. Soon after daybreak a southbound train stopped to pick up a handful of locals. We clambered aboard. Too late, we found it crammed with German troops. They took no notice of us, however, as we pushed our way down the narrow corridor. Squeezing ourselves into a compartment occupied by German soldiers and Italian labourers, we flopped into the only two empty seats and pretended to doze off. Hardly daring to breathe, we prayed that no one, especially the Italians, would speak to us. The Italian I learned in camp might well deceive a German, but certainly not an Italian.

The train chugged slowly south, stopping at every station, taking its time and adhering to no apparent timetable. At noon it reached the town of Rimini on the Adriatic coast, some hundred miles from Bologna. As we hoped, it then continued south, hugging the coast, and still stopping briefly at each station. This gave us frequent opportunities to leave the train whenever the need arose. We dared not risk getting too close to the front lines where civilians would

be conspicuous and likely to attract unwelcome attention. Our plan
was to leave the train somewhere near the Adriatic port of Pesaro,
and head up into the mountains. There we would lie up until the
Allied forces reached us.

In the late afternoon, I gave Jimmie the prearranged signal
(clenching the right fist) that we should leave the train at the next
station, at the same time raising my eyebrows questioningly.
Jimmie signified agreement by repeating the coded gestures. As the
train slowed we got to our feet and made our way into the corridor.
The train drew into the wayside station of Gradara. Jimmie swung
open the carriage door and leapt onto the platform, closely
followed by me. To our relief, we found the platform deserted: no
sign of a ticket collector.

We strolled casually out into the main street beside the station.
Feeling vulnerable and conspicuous, we hurried away from the
village, heading for the hills and the mountains, beyond which the
sun was fast sinking. It was early autumn and the nights were
becoming cooler. Both of us wore old army raincoats which helped
to keep out the chill. Mine, swapped in the camp for cigarettes, had
pockets sewn into the inside, large enough to take flat tins of emergency rations. These contained solid slabs made up of precious
chocolate melted down and mixed with condensed milk and egg
powder, all saved, with considerable will-power, from our rarely
issued Red Cross parcels.

For the next five days we plodded due south, farther and farther
up into the hills. We slept rough in the open or in cow barns,
devouring succulent grapes fresh from the vine, raw eggs taken
from chicken coops, and hunks of doughy, home-made bread
offered by kindly farmers. '*Molto grazie per la vostra ospitalita*' I
would say haltingly but with genuine feeling, as we took our leave.

On 16 September (the day before my twenty-third birthday), I
wrote a letter to my mother 'from somewhere in Italy' and left it
with a farmer who had fed and sheltered us to pass on to our troops,
'in case we should get recaptured'. In fact, it was to be eighteen
months before the Allies reached the Pesaro area, so I preceded the
letter's arrival in England by more than a year. In it I said:

We had our first sleep for four days last night, so are feeling
much fitter now. All the houses we have visited have received

us with open arms and given us all the assistance within their power – they really have been wonderful. I just *can't* describe what it feels like to be free (even if it is only temporary). We have already come over 150 miles, and have about another 200 to go . . . '

I gave Jimmie's mother's address in Fife, Scotland, asking my mother to contact her as soon as possible; and ended 'Be seeing you soon (I hope)'.

The nights by now, at the higher altitude, were distinctly chilly, fine for walking but not for sleeping rough outside, exposed to the biting wind and occasional rainstorms that swept up the valleys. Foot-slogging in the dark was becoming increasingly perilous as the hills became steeper and more dangerously precipitous and the roads more scarce.

One evening, in the pouring rain, we approached a sturdy young lad tending a flock of sheep on a rock-strewn plateau and asked for shelter for the night. He led us to his farm where we were welcomed warmly, served hot soup and invited to dry ourselves by the kitchen hearth. The boy's father, apologizing for not being able to accommodate us, then brought us to the house of the local priest who greeted us cordially and offered us a bed for the night, which we gratefully accepted. During supper, our host, a sly-faced gentleman with a robust, well-fed physique, suddenly begged to be excused and left the room. We heard the front door close and his footsteps clattering on the cobbled street outside. He sounded in a hurry – too much hurry for our liking. Jimmie and I looked at each other, instinctively guessing the sinister purpose of our host's hasty departure. By now we could almost read each other's thoughts: words were superfluous.

Leaving hurriedly by the back door which opened onto a small enclosed yard, we clambered over a stone wall and dashed into the open fields beyond. Shouts came from the front of the house and the sound of running feet. Shots rang out, fired wildly in our direction, accompanied by yells of '*Alto!*' ('Stop!'). Ignoring these, we stumbled on in the darkness until we were well beyond reach. We found shelter that night in a derelict barn where we reflected on our narrow escape, the first of many. It was, too, a lesson well-learned – henceforth to be more cautious in accepting hospitality, even from a Catholic cleric.

My gym shoes, received from home a few days before our escape, were by now wearing thin. I had chosen them only to facilitate climbing over the camp walls, oblivious to the obvious defects of such flimsy footwear for cross-country trekking. After only a week the soles began to wear thin, and then to disintegrate, forcing me to walk barefooted and bleeding on stony paths and rough, rocky ground, much to Jimmie's consternation and concern. Clearly, I could not continue in this way for much longer. Somehow, somewhere, I had to find shoes.

Then, quite by chance, we heard that some English people were being hidden up in the mountains, at a monastery called Fonte Avellana, and decided to investigate. At least we could rest and recuperate for a day or two, giving us a chance to find our bearings and decide what to do.

The next ten miles were tough going. We followed a steep, winding road up a long, narrow valley. In the distance was a snow-capped peak which we identified on our make-shift map as Monte Catria (5,200ft), in the lee of which lay our immediate goal. Rounding a corner, there before us at the road's end, stood the monastery, its tiled roofs and white walls gleaming in the autumn sunset. Cautiously, we approached a modest dwelling near the entrance to the monastery, and Jimmie knocked on the door. '*Siamo inglesi* . . . ' I began, as the door slowly opened. 'Well, hi there! Come on in!' exclaimed a female voice with a broad American accent, almost as if she was expecting us. Overcome with relief, we stumbled, slightly dazed, into the dimly-lit parlour and found ourselves amongst an astonishing group of people: they consisted of a small band of refugees from a civilian internment camp near the port of Ancona, on the nearby Adriatic coast.

Cold, wet and famished as we so obviously were, the farmer and his wife immediately sat us down by a roaring log fire. Steaming bowls of soup and pasta were brought, which we devoured ravenously. The wife then placed on the stone floor a wooden tub of hot water in which to bathe my bleeding feet. Next, she produced, miraculously, a pair of brown shoes which, with the help of thick rough socks, fitted me remarkably well, thus solving my most pressing problem.

As we were to discover over the next few weeks, these impover-ished peasant farmers, who had suffered so much privation during the war years, not only provided us (total strangers and erstwhile enemies) with food and shelter, but invariably insisted on opening a bottle of their best home-made wine to celebrate our safe arrival.

The lady who had greeted us at the door introduced us to her husband, a portly, middle-aged American named Fred Foster. The others were an attractive Anglo-Indian girl, who had been a minor film star in Cinecitta, Rome's Hollywood; Derek Oldham, a well-known English baritone; and a young Canadian lady and her eight-year-old daughter. Understandably, they were all in an acute state of jitters. Somehow, back in the internment camp, Mr Foster had managed to acquire a sizeable sum of Italian money, in hard cash. With this he had bribed a local merchant to provide a van in which he had himself driven his party of fugitives to the monastery. Now he was busy trying to organize their repatriation through 'a high-level contact in Rome'.

After supper, Jimmie and I were taken into the monastery to meet Padre Lorenzo and Padre Leone, both of whom spoke fluent English. They greeted us warmly and showed us (apologizing profusely as they did so) to the bare cell where we were to sleep on straw mattresses on the stone floor. The monastery, built in the sixth century, was occupied by Brothers of the strict Benedictine Order whose way of life differed little from those of its original occupants. They suffered the same austerity – bare cells, a basic diet of bread and water, no creature comforts whatsoever, and spent the same long hours in prayers and meditation. No members of the opposite sex were ever permitted to enter the monastery. Dante, the great thirteenth-century poet and philosopher, had taken refuge there. The cell he had occupied, and where he had written his masterpiece, *Divine Comedy*, was preserved as a place of historic interest.

Surrounded by a low brick wall, an inner courtyard contained an orchard of lime and cherry trees. Beyond were clusters of yews and hazel bushes, which gave their name to the monastery, and a well-cultivated fruit and vegetable garden, the produce of which supplemented the monks' modest diet.

Hiding in the monastery, too, were several Italian officers. Like many others, they had deserted in the days following the Armistice and taken refuge in the mountains to avoid being deported to a labour camp in Germany or, even worse, to the Russian Front. None of them was ever aware of our presence, not even the one in the cell next to ours.

Early on the third day, we were roused by a monk who rushed into our cell to warn us of the imminent arrival of a German patrol. Breathlessly, he exclaimed/explained that an army lorry and two motorcycles, spotted in the distance winding their way up the valley road, would very soon reach the main gate. While we dressed hastily, the monk produced a length of rope which he proceeded to dangle out of the cell window. In turn, we slid down the rope to the inner courtyard twenty feet below (see photo), and sprinted out of the monastery by the rear gate which led to the safety of the wooded hill behind. There we stayed hidden all day, working our way slowly round, through the bushes and trees, to a vantage point on the hillside from where we could observe the buildings clustered below us.

As darkness fell we observed a German guard standing silhouetted against the open door of the farmhouse, his fixed bayonet reflecting the light from the front parlour. An hour or so later the guard turned, slammed the door shut and disappeared from view. We heard the sounds of the lorry's engine and motorcycles starting up and moving away down the valley. After a while Jimmie crept gingerly down to recce the situation. I could see the light stream out from the farmhouse as he cautiously opened the door. Then he turned and signalled the all-clear and I hurriedly joined him.

The scene in the parlour was a piteous sight. The women and young girl were in a state of near hysteria, weeping copiously, the men standing to one side, grim faced, all of them speechless with shock. Mrs Foster, the first to regain her composure, described the day's traumatic events. The German officer had questioned each of them closely, demanding to know where they had come from, how long they had been there, where were the British officers whom they had been 'reliably informed' were being hidden in the monastery, and so on. Repeatedly issuing dire threats to the farmer and his wife if they were caught hiding '*der Englander*', they left, taking the unfortunate Mr Foster with them 'for further questioning'. His distraught wife, in no way comforted by the officer's curt assurance that her husband would be returned safely within a day or so, nevertheless put on a remarkably brave face. We never learned of Mr Foster's fate, but guessed the worst.

Later, Padre Leone told us that the Germans had scoured the monastery thoroughly, searching, they had said, for the British officers. Courageously, the two Brothers and their fellow monks had stoutly denied all knowledge of their existence. Nor were they questioned about the Italian officers, all of whom had evaded the German search party. And so the Germans left empty-handed (apart from the hapless Foster), if unconvinced.

Early next morning, we told Padre Leone that we had decided to leave at once, fearing our presence was jeopardizing the lives and safety of the monks, as well as the Marini family who had already put themselves at considerable risk by harbouring civilian refugees. The Padre, however, urged us to wait another day. He explained that he was expecting two important visitors the following morning, and he was very anxious for us to meet them.

Sure enough, next day, while Jimmie and I were strolling through the monastery gardens, quietly contemplating our future, one of the monks came to take us to Padre Lorenzo. With the padre were two men to whom we were introduced. One was an Italian Jew called Rogero Cagnazzo. The other was an unnamed Frenchman who, it transpired, had come from occupied France, where he was a leader of the Maquis (the French Resistance organization), to advise on ways and means of establishing a guerrilla group in the nearby mountains. Cagnazzo, leader of the local partisan group, had learned of our presence in the area and wanted to discuss with us the possibility of obtaining help from the Allied forces in the south.

Since the Armistice, he told us, large numbers of soldiers had deserted the Italian Army, many still armed, and were either making their way home or roaming the countryside at will. A few escaped PoWs were also on the loose, as were thousands of male civilians who had left the cities and towns of northern and central Italy, taking refuge in the country to avoid deportation to Germany. Many of these fugitives, he said, were known to be camping out in the nearby woods and foothills of the Apennines. Now was the time, he felt, to organize the Italian deserters into guerrilla bands, which, if properly armed and trained, could effectively harass the Germans in the surrounding region. There would be no problem, he thought, in rallying support from the local farmers and '*Contandini* ' (peasants), most of whom were known to be sympathetic to their cause.

On the political front, the Germans had restored Mussolini as the head of a new radical Fascist regime, based in northern Italy on the shores of Lake Garda, known as the Republic of Salo, the King having escaped to southern Italy. Cagnazzo explained that the fluid situation caused by the internal upheaval had created an ideal opportunity for anti-Fascist elements, some of whose leaders had money, organizational ability and fighting experience. The Communist Party, until then relatively small and ineffective, was growing rapidly and had formed so-called 'Garibaldi Brigades', seizing the chance to foment revolution, particularly in industrial cities like Milan and Turin where they encouraged strikes. Aware of the Allies' efforts to crush the Communist partisans in Greece, they realized that little or no support would be forthcoming from that quarter. At the same time, as a result of the sudden collapse of civil order, there were spontaneous uprisings against the hated Fascist authorities and the German occupation.

There was little doubt, from what the French resistance leader told us, that partisans, properly organized, could pose a considerable threat to the Germans and contribute much to the Allied cause. They would help to tie down German forces (there were no less than twenty-six divisions in Italy), deprive the Germans of manpower, disrupt their war production and harass their troop movements.

Cagnazzo and his French colleague outlined their plans to organize guerrilla operations in the Apennines based on Fossombrone, ten miles north of the Monastery. They would mount surprise attacks on military convoys, sabotage ammunition dumps, blow up bridges and seize weapons and equipment. That they were in deadly earnest there was little doubt. Their ability to carry out such bloodthirsty operations seemed to us, however, more debatable. It was obvious that, in their present state – poorly prepared and ill-equipped – they would be no match for the Germans or even the Italian Militia.

Nevertheless, the partisans, particularly in central Italy, became a thorough scourge to the German High Command over the ensuing months; so much so, in fact, that the Germans were forced to deploy large numbers of troops to counter their activities. In retaliation, the Germans often took extreme measures, even going so far as to burn down villages and shoot the inhabitants.

We learned much later that, from the autumn of 1943 to the end of the German occupation, some 40,000 partisans and 10,000 civilians were believed to have been killed in central and northern Italy: but the veracity of these figures has to be questioned.

Aged about thirty-five, Cagnazzo was small of stature and slimly built. By profession he was a civil engineer – a very successful one, we were told. With his dark hair and intelligent eyes he was distinctively Jewish in appearance, a dangerous feature at a time when vicious anti-Semitism amongst Italian Fascists was rife. He possessed many of the Jews' finer traits – he was sensitive, resourceful, imaginative and very determined. He was also exceptionally brave and seemed to revel in adventure. In many ways, apart from his Jewishness, he made a model secret agent.

Before the war there were no more than 45,000 native-born Italian Jews, plus another 10,000 or so born abroad, mostly refugees from the Nazis. There had been an attempt, in 1939, to deport foreign Jews. And the Government had gone so far as to forbid Italian Jews from marrying Aryans, to hold public office or to run businesses of one hundred or more employees.

Since the war began, the Fascist anti-Jew movement had grown in strength. Jews were excluded from the army due to their supposed 'lack of martial spirit', and from the civil service. The Germans themselves stepped up their anti-Semitic campaign on taking control of northern Italy at the time Jimmie and I were 'on the run'. During the winter of 1943/44 more than 7,500 Jews were deported to German concentration camps. Most of them died in the gas chambers. It was all the more remarkable, therefore, that Cagnazzo undertook such huge and deliberate risks at that crucial time.

Cagnazzo astonished us still further by volunteering to accompany one of us to the Allied lines as an advocate for the guerrillas' cause. He seemed singularly undeterred by the perils of such a mission. Moreover, he was confident that he would have little difficulty in procuring a boat for the journey south. First, however, he would arrange for Jimmie and me to be sheltered by a group of

partisans in the Pesaro area. There we would await further word
from him once he had made all the necessary arrangements.

And so, on the evening of 27 September 1943, Jimmie and I left
the monastery in an elderly Fiat saloon car, driven by Cagnazzo at
hair-raising speed down the winding, precipitous road to the
coastal plain. Before setting off, he warned us that if he encountered a German or Italian checkpoint, he did not intend to stop. To
do so would mean our instant return to a PoW camp (if we were
lucky) and almost certainly a firing squad for him. With so much
at stake he was prepared to crash through or round any barriers
that blocked his way.

To our profound relief we reached our destination, a small farm
in the village of Pozzo Alto, a few miles outside Pesaro, without
incident and were warmly welcomed by the farmer, Signore
Terenzi, aged seventy-three, and his wife, Rosa. Like many others
of their kind, they had bravely volunteered to help British prisoners
on the run, knowing the awful retribution meted out by the
Germans to those caught doing so. Leaflets, scattered far and wide,
threatened to shoot anyone harbouring escaped prisoners. As
already mentioned, the Germans were indeed ruthless; we had
heard of whole families being taken outside and shot. The extent
of the Germans' 'anti-terrorist' action is borne out by the following
edict issued by the German High Command:

**Edict from the Commander-in-Chief of the German Armed
Forces:**

Until now the German Armed Forces have done correctly and
with the greatest respect for the population everything they
were compelled to do by the exigencies of war. This amicable
conduct requires unfailingly amicable conduct on the part of
the population. If the attempted murders and attacks by the
bandits, which have so far been isolated, individual cases,
were to escalate, the High Command of the German Armed
Forces would immediately have to alter its own conduct and
the population in question would be responsible for the consequences of such a decision.

To guarantee security of communications in the army's rear

zone and of its logistical services, I give the order that from this moment:

1) anyone in possession of weapons or explosives who does not report them to the nearest German command post WILL BE SHOT;

2) anyone who gives shelter to bandits, protects them or gives them clothing, food or weapons, WILL BE SHOT;

3) if it is found that someone knows about a group of rebels or even about one individual rebel, without having informed the nearest command post, WILL BE SHOT;

4) anyone who gives information to the enemy or the bandits about the location of German command posts or military depots, WILL BE SHOT;

5) every village where it can be proved that there are bandits or that attempts have been made on the lives of German or Italian soldiers, or acts of sabotage aimed at damaging or destroying war material, WILL BE COMPLETELY BURNT DOWN. In addition, the male inhabitants of the village of or over the age of 18 years WILL ALL BE SHOT. The women and children will be interned in labour camps.

Italians!

The welfare of your country and the fate of your families now lie in your hands. The German Armed Forces, as specified in this edict, will act justly but without mercy in pursuing each case with the utmost rigour.

The Commander-in-Chief of the German Armed Forces

The farmers who sheltered us were mostly peasants eking out a paltry living from smallholdings, mostly owned by the Church, to whom they paid an annual tithe, leaving the barest minimum for them to live on. Since the war began, any sons in their teens or older had been called up for compulsory military or 'industrial' service; many had been deported to German internment camps and used as cheap labour, never to be heard from again. Some ended their young lives on the Russian front. And so it was on their women-folk that nearly all of the heavy manual labour devolved.

These courageous and devout people were simple country folk. They loathed the Fascist regime and scarcely concealed their deep hatred of the German occupiers. The latter, in turn, treated Italians generally with the utmost contempt. Time and again these splendid '*Contandini*' risked their lives for Allied escapees, without a moment's hesitation and with no thought of financial or any other gain.

Over the next two weeks, to minimize the chance of discovery, Jimmie and I were moved every two or three days from one 'safe house' to another. We travelled either on foot or by bicycle, invari-ably accompanied by a young Italian guide, twenty-six-year-old Anacleto Gabani, a local plumber and shoemaker, always making sure to arrive at our destination before the curfew started at 9.30 pm.

There being little else to do, Jimmie and I spent much of our time talking and exchanging views on many diverse subjects – our school days, our likes and dislikes, food (a recurrent theme), our views on women in general and girls in particular, army life, our wartime experiences, PoW camps, and, of course, our present dilemma. Seven years my senior, Jimmie was more worldly-wise, due perhaps to a less inhibited upbringing. Born and raised in Burntisland, Fife, on the banks of the Forth opposite Edinburgh, Jimmie had gradu-ated from university and spent several years before war broke out in the textile trade. I enjoyed listening to graphic accounts of his earlier years, travelling around Scotland, first as a trainee manager with an Edinburgh firm called Patrick Thompson, and later with Dickson & Benson of Middlesbrough, achieving the distinction of becoming the youngest buyer in the textile trade in Britain.

On the subject of the opposite sex – a popular topic – Jimmie was far more experienced. I had no sisters and had spent my adoles-cence in isolation from female company of my own age. There was, however, no lack of interest on my part: I was nothing if not keen to learn. I had been smitten by the charms of a young lady in Shillong, Assam, an idyllic hill station where, early in 1940, I had joined 8th Gurkha Rifles as a junior subaltern. Together we had enjoyed Sunday picnics at Cherrapunji, a local beauty spot twenty miles south of Shillong. Renowned for being the wettest place on earth, it offered a staggering view of the distant Syhlet Plains, some 1,500 feet below, from the edge of a steep escarpment, itself the cause of the exceptionally heavy rainfall. I escorted her, too, to formal dances at the Shillong Officers' Club, and occasionally to the races on Thursday afternoons. But the moment things began to get interesting I was posted to the Machine Gun Course at Saugor, several hundred miles away in central India.

In those days, young subalterns were firmly discouraged from becoming entangled with the fair sex. It was the Colonel's duty to protect them from such dangerous pursuits, and to keep their minds on strictly military matters. Any hint of physical intimacy and one was immediately sent on a course to some remote part of the country; as indeed I was, quite unjustly, as it happened. Nor could a young officer marry without the Colonel's permission. Had he been brazen enough to do so, the young officer would have run the risk of being posted out of the regiment to the Indian Pioneer Corps, or, even worse, banished to Movement Control.

Later, on active service with my battalion in Iraq, I had met an attractive young Anglo-Syrian girl, who lived under the ever-watchful eyes of her wealthy parents, at the Semiramis Hotel on the banks of the Tigris, in the heart of Baghdad. On the rare occasions when visits to the 'big city' were permissible (as, for example, when I sat for an Arabic exam), we frolicked together at the Swimming Club, and danced, perspiring profusely, to an atrocious 'Palm Court' trio in the hotel's dingy dining room. Once, we even managed an unchaperoned picnic by moonlight on a small sand-bank island in the middle of the murky river, catching and cooking fish on an open wood fire. Again, this pseudo-romantic, strictly platonic relationship was rudely interrupted by my unexpected, but not unwelcome posting to the Intelligence Course in Cairo, never again to return to the fleshpots of Baghdad.

Jimmie and I debated, too, the respective merits and demerits of civilian versus service life. Like me, he had foreseen the advent of war, obtaining a peacetime commission in the Territorial Army. On the outbreak of war he was posted to the Royal Corps of Signals. Jimmie was scathing about the red tape, square-bashing, 'traditional' side of army life, and said he could not wait for the war to end to return to civilian life. In the event, it was ironical that, after the war, Jimmie stayed on and enjoyed an outstanding military career, ending up as a Colonel in the Royal Scots. I resigned my commission, my Gurkha regiment having been 'Indianized' after the partition of India, spending the rest of my working life in 'civvy street'.

A man of keen intelligence and very decided views, Jimmie was typical, in many ways, of 'wartime' officers who, by this time, formed the majority of those serving their country in the armed forces. They had brought a breath of fresh air into a system still dominated by old-fashioned, stereotyped traditions. Impatient with dogma, and what seemed to them out-dated, petty rules and regulations, they were apt to be more pragmatic, logical and straightforward in their thinking than the average 'regular' officer. Emergency Commissioned Officers (known as ECOs) were signed up only 'for the duration', so had little to lose by expressing what the older and more staid professionals tended to regard as a 'confoundedly bolshie attitude'.

I myself came from Army stock. My grandfather and great grandfather, on my mother's side, were both generals, and my father had been Chaplain General to the Forces in India, where I was born. My first six years were spent within sight of army barracks; and I had fond memories of church parades on the dusty parade grounds of British Army cantonments in northern India.

Even so, I never aspired to make the Army my career. I disliked the Officers' Training Corps at my public school so much that I joined the Corps' band to avoid some of the dreary parades and infantry training (based on outmoded First World War tactics) that were otherwise compulsory. Having won a Lord Kitchener's Memorial Scholarship, in the summer of 1938 I was all set to go to the University of Heidelberg, to read languages and economics.

Then, in September, came what Churchill described as 'the tragedy of Munich', followed by the Nazi rape of Czechoslovakia. It seemed certain that Britain was heading for another war with Germany. I decided it would be prudent to join up well before the war started. So, having ascertained that the scholarship was acceptable to the Royal Military College, I applied for and was granted a place there. I wanted to join the Indian Army, preferably the

Gurkhas, so was fortunate not only in gaining entry to Sandhurst but also to be awarded a King's India Cadetship. This meant that I was guaranteed a commission in an Indian regiment; regardless of how badly (short of failure) I did in the final exams.

As a graduate of Sandhurst I felt obliged to defend the Army against Jimmie's well-meant criticisms. Yet I was secretly unconvinced that military life and my recently acquired taste for independence were compatible. As a Liaison Officer with the headquarters of 20 Indian Infantry Brigade in Iraq, where my battalion, 2nd Battalion 8th Gurkha Rifles, had been sent in 1940 to help quell Rashid Ali's Nazi-inspired rebellion, I had tasted and enjoyed the benefits of a 'roving commission'. After the Iraqis had been soundly defeated, we became bogged down for months on end in a static situation, digging endless defensive positions against possible German invasion from the north, through Turkey. Occasional sorties into Syria and Persia, and a spell under canvas in Mosul, northern Iraq (in bitter Arctic conditions) alleviated the depressing boredom to some extent.

But the freedom of careering about in the desert, first as a Liaison Officer, and later as the Brigade Chemical Warfare Officer (for which I had not the remotest qualifications) was much more to my liking. It was hardly surprising, therefore, that I jumped at the chance to attend the Intelligence School in Cairo. My sole regret was leaving the Gurkhas of whom I had become inordinately fond, as are all British officers who have the privilege to serve with them.

To our astonishment, Jimmie and I found that we had served in Quetta, India at the same time, had both been in the Indian Infantry Brigade sent to Iraq in April 1941, had moved to the Western Desert and been captured within a couple of weeks of each other, and had even been in the same PoW camps in Italy, before landing up together in a PoW camp in Bologna. And yet, after nearly two years' service in the same places, we met for the very first time in the loft of our hut at the Bologna camp, where we had each of us chosen to hide before making our escape!

It was fortunate that Jimmie and I got on so well together. Our characters and personalities were markedly different, yet we respected and trusted each other. He was more outgoing and extroverted. I was inclined to be rather reserved, more of a good listener. Living cheek by jowl with someone you don't know, under exceptionally trying conditions, one's nerves often stretched to breaking point, is in itself a severe test. I tended to defer to Jimmie as my senior in age, though not in rank. But he always listened patiently and politely, and invariably asked my opinion on what action we should take, never did we blame each other if anything went wrong. And, most importantly, we shared a sense of humour, which stood us in good stead whenever things looked bleak. Above all, we were both aware that our best hope of reaching the Allied lines safely lay in our ability to work together amicably as a team.

During this interim period in limbo, while waiting to hear from Cagnazzo, we came to appreciate and admire the sterling qualities of our 'host' families, above all their astonishing hospitality. They went out of their way to make life bearable for us. What meagre food they had they ungrudgingly shared with us, even if it meant depriving themselves. Most farms owned a few modest grape vines from which they made wine for their own use. The best vintages they kept for special occasions, such as when we arrived on their doorstep. They were well aware of the dreadful risks they took in harbouring escaped PoWs; the danger of our being discovered, and of their betrayal, was omnipresent. Outwardly, however, they never appeared to be fearful or apprehensive. On the contrary they were consistently cheerful and unconcerned about their own safety, a trait which Jimmie and I found quite remarkable.

One morning we were sitting in the parlour while the farmer's wife was busy preparing the midday meal. There came a knock on the front door. There was no time for us to hide, no alternative but to stay put. It had been agreed that should someone arrive unexpectedly, we would be passed off as Yugoslav immigrant workers who spoke no Italian. The visitor was the wife of a neighbouring farmer, a dumpy lady with sharp eyes and a ruddy complexion. For a moment she looked quizzically at us, and then turned to our 'hostess' and the two of them gabbled away in the local patois, of which neither Jimmie nor I understood a word. (It was surprising how even the poorest uneducated 'Contandina' could speak good, standard Italian as well as their own regional dialect, almost as if they were bilingual). Meanwhile, Jimmie and I exchanged a few mock-Yugoslav words, before lurching to our feet and disappearing upstairs.

Sometimes local German units would despatch small foraging

parties into the countryside, to collect eggs, chickens, vegetables, fruit or anything else they fancied. Fortunately for us, one such party was sighted by the farmer's two young children who were playing outside the farm in which we were hidden. They rushed in to warn their mother, who hurriedly ushered us out of the back door, telling us to hide on top of a haystack behind the cowshed until she gave us the all-clear.

There were, of course, no spare beds in these modest farm dwellings. Invariably we slept on straw in a barn, usually with the cows, but on one memorable occasion with a family of pungent, snorting pigs. By now we were accustomed to such primitive arrangements. The nocturnal rustling of rats in the straw, however, did take more getting used to. Once I woke to find a particularly voracious specimen gnawing at my fly buttons. Rarely now do I hear farmyard sounds without recalling the rustic hospitality we experienced in the autumn of 1943, in the depths of the Italian countryside.

Late one evening Jimmie and I were making our way through the back streets of Pesaro, for once unaccompanied, en route to our next sanctuary, the Convent of San Giovanni. Approaching the heavy wooden front door set into the high wall surrounding the convent, we noticed, some 300 yards away down the narrow street, a small group of German soldiers lurching drunkenly towards us. Vigorously, I pulled the iron ring by the side of the door and heard a bell clang somewhere inside the convent. We waited apprehensively, hearts pounding, but there was no response. Again we tried – and again, to no avail. We faced two simple alternatives: stay put and hope for the best, or walk away in the opposite direction. To run could well court disaster. By now the Germans were less than a hundred yards away. I was sure they would accost if not assault us; we were easy prey for a gang of inebriated soldiery on the loose in the dimly-lit streets. 'Let's go,' Jimmie whispered. As we turned to move away, the door swung open and we were swept inside. Moments later the Germans staggered past, shouting raucously.

Several days later, we were moved to the house of Signore Canastrari, a timber merchant in Borgo Santa Maria, a mile away on the main road to Urbino, and thence to Luigi Delpiccolos' farm. We had been there for three days when Cagnazzo arrived to take Jimmie (who had 'won the toss' – a dubious victory – as to which of us would accompany Cagnazzo on his trip south) to the home of Signora Elisa Cognetti-Fratini at No.2 Viale della Republica, situated in an affluent section of Pesaro, where they spent the night. A charming, cultured lady in her mid-forties, Elisa was a Professor of English at the local Commercial College. Living with her were Maria, her sister, and Luisa, her faithful retainer.

The following evening, 6 October, a taxi arrived to take Jimmie and Cagnazzo to Cattolica, a fishing village ten miles up the coast. There they boarded a motor fishing boat, hired by Signore Ezio Galluzzi, a friend of Cagnazzo, and skippered by a gallant local fisherman called Signore Gueriono.

All fishing was subject to rigorous control by the Germans and the Fascist police who guarded the ports all along the coast. Boats had to be registered; they had to return to port before nightfall; they were liable to be searched before departure and on their return, and so on. Often aircraft would be sent to search for overdue fishing vessels; and if found at sea they could be machine-gunned without warning. Both the owner and skipper were, therefore, taking an immense calculated risk. Discovery would have meant a heavy fine (at the very least), imprisonment or worse.

Leaving at dawn, they passed, unheeded, the German control post at the harbour entrance and sailed out into the Adriatic Sea. Early next morning they safely reached the port of Termoli, 200 miles to the south and a few miles below the Allied lines.

Meanwhile, I was moved yet again, this time to the farm of Signore Berzigotti at Chiusa di Ginestrelo, five miles south of Santa Maria. One day a local barber came to cut my hair. He was told that I was Berzigotti's brother who had just arrived from France where he had lived all his life, and for this reason could not speak Italian. The barber, a friendly soul, swallowed this fabrication without question, and proceeded to do things to my hair it had never before experienced.

I shared a large, lumpy bed with the eldest son, Enzio, a gormless, unwashed youth whose sonorous snores seriously disturbed my efforts to sleep. The bedroom overlooked the main road and on Sundays I enjoyed watching the local farmers and their families, dolled up in their best clothes, passing by on their way to church, a colourful and heart-warming sight.

Cooped up in a small farmhouse with little to occupy the mind, my humdrum existence was all-too rarely enlightened by a young lady called Nazarena Guidi, the daughter of a close friend of Cagnazzo. This attractive and vivacious girl, who lived with her family in what sounded like a grand villa in Pesaro, rode out to the farm on an expensive-looking bicycle. She brought me food, cigarettes, fruit, even money, which she carried in a saddlebag, in so doing running grave risks on my behalf. Born in France of a French mother and Italian father, Nazarena spoke in fluent, rapid French which I could mostly understand if not respond to with equal fluency.

On one occasion she came with information about German fortifications being built in the Pesaro area. She told me the Germans were rounding up Italian youths to use as forced labour. All this, and other military intelligence, was gleaned either from her own observation or, more remarkably, through the indiscretion of German officers billeted in her father's villa. On another visit she proudly produced an automatic pistol which I politely, but firmly, declined for reasons less obvious to her than to me.

Always smartly dressed, with her hair immaculate, Nazarena exuded bonhomie and high spirits. Well educated and intelligent, she was romantically inclined and a trifle quixotic: thus her eagerness, I surmised, to indulge in a conspiratorial venture by tending to the material needs of an escaped British officer. I looked forward eagerly to her visits which brought welcome interludes of friendly companionship to alleviate an otherwise monotonous existence.

I was, however, worried that Nazarena's exuberant rashness might attract unwanted attention, thus inviting trouble. Also, I felt that too many people knew of my existence, that sooner or later I would be betrayed. Nevertheless, I was totally in the hands of the local partisan group, so there was little I could do about this. One day, as if to reinforce my anxiety, Signore Berzigotti's padrone (the owner of his farm) told him he had heard that there were some escaped British prisoners in the neighbourhood. He cautioned my host to keep a sharp look out, and to let him know if he heard anything so that he (the farmer) might claim the reward of 25,000 lire (in gold) offered by the Germans and Italian Fascists for information leading to the capture of an escaped British PoW. Berzigotti readily agreed to do so, whilst having not the slightest intention of denouncing me, however tempting the bribe.

An intrepid youth, called Anacleto, assigned as my official guide to escort me from one hide-out to another, arrived one evening on his bicycle. With me perched precariously on the cross bar, we rode to the house of a priest three kilometres away to listen to the BBC news, a pastime forbidden by the authorities and severely punished if anyone was caught in the act. It was exhilarating to hear once again the voice of a BBC newsreader and to have reliable news of the progress of the Italian campaign.

Time weighed heavily and the days dragged by. I was not allowed outside during daylight hours. Only after dark could I venture out to stroll in the fields, being careful not to stray too far for fear of getting lost, or of meeting people from the village who were unaware of my existence. For more strenuous exercise I would sometimes chase the twins, Armando and Vittorio, round the haystacks and amongst the shoulder-high maize crop.

Apart from Nazarena's infrequent visits, there was little to relieve the sense of boredom and frustration, with no books and only an occasional newspaper to read: nothing to stimulate my rapidly degenerating mind. I did, however, use the time to brush up my Italian. And this I would do for hours on end, seated on my bed poring over school books lent me by the Berzigottis' delightful nine-year-old daughter, Guiseppa. These, I found, were filled with much heroic Fascist propaganda intended to instil into the minds of Italian children the might and glory of the erstwhile Italian empire. But they served my purpose ideally, being well illustrated and written in the simplest and most understandable style.

Two weeks into October and still no news from Jimmie; I was becoming restless and irritable, wondering what to do and how long to wait before making a move myself. This prolonged idleness, being cooped up day after day in a confined space, unable to venture outside except after dark, was deeply demoralizing. Moreover, it became clear from the BBC broadcasts and from the Italian papers, that the Allied advance up the peninsula continued to be painfully slow.

Following the successful invasion of Sicily, the landing on mainland Italy by the Allied Forces began on 3 September 1943 with the landing of British Eighth Army troops at Reggio di Calabria, followed, six days later, by the American Fifth Army, which included British troops, at Salerno. Although Naples and Foggia had been taken in early October, progress north had become bogged down by the deteriorating weather, the tricky terrain, and by the Germans' tenacious defensive fighting. Unknown to us, ahead of the Allied forces lay the monastery of Monte Cassino and the well prepared Gustav Line. Cassino did not fall until May 1944.

Assuming that something had gone seriously amiss and that Jimmie never turned up, there was no future in sitting tight and waiting for our troops to arrive. Soon, therefore, I would have to decide whether to stay put, and if so, for how long: or whether, with the help of my Italian friends, I should organize my escape, either by infiltrating through the front lines (the more dangerous option), or by sea.

Early on the morning of 17 October, I was trying out my Italian on Signora Berzigotti, in her stone-flagged kitchen, when the door burst open – and there stood Jimmie, a broad smile on his face.

'I've come to take you home,' he announced, slumping exhausted into a chair by the stove. 'I'm utterly bushed,' he added. 'We landed late last night at Gabicce, the other side of Pesaro, and Cagnazzo sent me straight here in a friend's car. It's been one hell of a trip!' Jimmie reached into a large pack dumped on the floor and produced a tin of fifty Players cigarettes, followed by a bottle of Johnny Walker whiskey. 'I hope these are worth waiting for!' he grinned. It was wonderful to see him again, and I was impatient to hear what had happened to him and Cagnazzo.

Over a large plate of steaming spaghetti, Jimmie proceeded to recount his adventures since leaving me eleven days ago. After an uneventful journey, the fishing boat had arrived safely near the port of Termoli. He and Cagnazzo went ashore and were promptly arrested by two RAF policemen from the nearby airfield. They suspected Jimmie to be a German spy. Protesting vehemently, they were marched to the Military Police headquarters where Jimmie was separated from Cagnazzo and locked up in a small ration store-room. From there he was taken under armed escort to Divisional Headquarters in Bari where he was interrogated at length. It must be said that at that time Jimmie did have certain lean Teutonic features; a strong jaw line, sallow complexion and close-cropped hair. Added to this his scruffy civilian outfit would have aroused further suspicion. Loudly protesting his innocence and demanding to see the nearest general, Jimmie was led outside to be marched a short distance to the local military detention centre.

He and his escort had gone a short distance when a distinctly Scottish voice called out, 'Good God! What the hell's going on, Jimmie?' It was an old golfing chum of Jimmie, Hamish Sandilands, from Kirkcaldy, Fife, who was astonished to see him being escorted by an armed military policeman through the streets of Bari. 'For Christ's sake, Hamish, tell this bugger who I am!' Jimmie yelled. 'They think I'm a German spy!' Shocked and incredulous, Hamish accompanied Jimmie and his by now confused escort to the military police headquarters. There he was quickly able to establish Jimmie's real identity and arrange for his immediate release.

Together Jimmie and his saviour, a staff major at GHQ, Bari, repaired to the officers' mess for a couple of stiff whiskies, which Hamish ordered while Jimmie disappeared for a quick wash and brush up. Thus fortified and refreshed, Jimmie was taken to meet a staff captain from A Force, the branch of M19 responsible for questioning and debriefing escaped PoWs.

Jimmie outlined, briefly, the purpose of his clandestine journey south. A band of Italian partisans, he said, based in the Apennines to the west of Pesaro, was willing and eager to undertake sabotage operations against German military installations and transport in the area. His own mission was, first, to arrange for supplies of Allied arms, ammunition, and other essential equipment to be parachuted to the partisans at regular intervals; secondly, to identify and pinpoint suitable dropping zones; thirdly, to establish radio communication between the partisans and our forces (bearing in mind that he, Jimmie, was an experienced officer in the Royal Corps of Signals); and lastly to liaise closely with neighbouring guerrilla bands to ensure that all clandestine activities in the region were properly co-ordinated. He and the colleague he had left behind, Captain Pat Spooner, would train and lead them, and act as the liaison link with the Allied forces and with any agents operating in the area.

The captain listened patiently until Jimmie had finished. Pausing to offer Jimmie a cigarette, and to light one himself, he rose from his chair and turned to face Jimmie. 'I'm sorry to disappoint you, old man, but I'm afraid it's just not on,' he said. 'As an escaped PoW you must, of course, be repatriated at the first opportunity.

We already have a number of others here, like you, waiting to be sent home by boat. There's absolutely no question of your going back into enemy occupied territory. Contrary to regulations, old boy, and quite unheard of!'

But Jimmie, stubborn by nature, was not to be so easily deterred. He insisted, once again, on seeing a more senior officer, preferably of general rank. Clearly taken aback, but swayed by Jimmie's forceful determination, the staff captain agreed, albeit reluctantly, to refer him to higher authority. That afternoon he was taken before the Colonel commanding the Divisional counter-intelligence unit to whom he outlined his plans even more vigorously than before. In reply, the Colonel said he had every sympathy with Jimmie's 'commendable proposals'. However, he was equally adamant that they were incompatible with the Allies' strategic plans. Notwithstanding this further setback, Jimmie remained fiercely determined to return, come what may, to Pesaro. 'Sir, with respect, I gave my colleague, Pat, my word that I would be back, and no way will I let him or our Italian colleagues down.'

Telling Jimmie to wait, the Colonel left the room abruptly and disappeared down the corridor. Half an hour later he returned. 'I've had a word with the BGS (Brigadier General Staff),' he said, 'You'll be glad to hear he's agreed to make an exception in your case and allow you to go back behind the lines with your Italian friend. However,' he added, 'there is one very important condition. We need you to contact two of our Generals and an Air Vice Marshal, who have escaped from a senior officers' camp near Florence, and bring them back here. You will be in charge of the operation and my organization will, of course, give you every possible help. It's a matter of the utmost importance that we get these VIPs back here safely and as quickly as possible.' He paused, looking intently at Jimmie, 'The choice is yours.'

Jimmie hesitated, knowing full well how bitterly disappointed Cagnazzo and his partisan friends would be to learn that their requests had been rejected outright. However, he also recognized that it was beyond even his persuasive powers to reverse what was so obviously a high level decision.

'I accept the conditions, Sir,' Jimmie said, after a momentary pause, adding, 'May I ask, who are these senior officers?' He was taken aback when the Colonel revealed their identities, namely,

General Neame VC, General O'Connor, and Air Vice Marshal Boyd. He then proceeded to recount their recent histories.

Lieutenant General Sir Philip Neame VC and Lieutenant General Sir Richard O'Connor had been captured together in the spring of 1941 near Derna in the Western Desert. General O'Connor had led the Western Desert Force in the victorious battles of 1940–41 in which it had utterly destroyed the Italian Tenth Army, many times its size. General Wavell, Commander-in-Chief in Egypt, considered him a brilliant commander and had recalled him from Cairo to take over from Neame as commander of the Desert army which was then in sad disarray. He arrived in the middle of a battle which was going badly. Wavell counted on O'Connor to salvage the situation and to win back the confidence of senior commanders, whose morale was at a low ebb.

On 6 April 1941 Neame and O'Connor were in a staff car, making their way across the desert. They were in a small column with other senior officers from Corps Headquarters. In the darkness they ran into another column of lorries and cars which turned out to be part of the 3rd German Reconnaissance Battalion, and the whole party was taken prisoner.

Air Vice Marshal Owen T. Boyd had been captured in 1940 when his plane was forced to land in Sicily while he was on his way to Cairo to become Deputy Air Commander-in-Chief, Middle East. He had held many senior air appointments, including Air Officer Commanding Balloon Command in England, responsible for the balloon barrage which proved so effective in preventing low-level attacks by German bombers.

Suitably impressed by the calibre of his charges, Jimmie had no doubts about the vital importance of his mission. This, in large measure, compensated for the bitter disappointment of failing to organize the delivery of arms and supplies so urgently needed by the Italian partisans.

Over the next twenty-four hours Jimmie was thoroughly briefed on his dramatic mission. A plan was evolved for the Royal Navy to pick our party up in a submarine off the coast, near Pesaro, at 10 pm on 3 November. Should this fail for any reason, back-up plans were scheduled, with alternative dates, times and rendezvous. Jimmie was required to memorize code names of other agents in the region, and told how to contact them in an emergency. He was fully briefed, too, on German counter-intelligence activities in the area.

Jimmie was fitted out with authentic Italian civilian clothes. And he and Cagnazzo (both now enrolled as official A Force agents) were issued with Italian lire, identity papers, escape packs (containing medical aids, pep pills, etc.), and a small supply of emergency rations and cigarettes.

They left Termoli early on the morning of 17 October in the same motorized fishing boat which had brought them there. The following night they made landfall, without incident, at Gabicce, a small fishing village near Cattolica. Thanks to the co-operation of his uncle, the harbour-master, their intrepid skipper, Guerino, had explained away (we never discovered how) the sudden arrival of his boat at Gabicce. Even more importantly, he had somehow managed to cover up its ten day absence from nearby Cattolica without arousing any official suspicions. Cagnazzo set off immediately to make contact with the generals, who had made their way, first by train from Florence to Arezzo, and then by coach to a Dominican monastery in the Apennines.

For several days the generals and the AVM had been moved around the mountains, in appalling weather, to avoid recapture by the Germans and Italian Fascists who, by now, had learned of their presence in the area. On 31 October, whilst billeted in the village of Straubatenza, they received word from the Prior General at Eremo Monastery that a British agent had been sent to rescue them. After a sleepless night in a cattle barn, they set off before dawn with their guide, Signore Maurizzio. It took them seven hours' hard marching on rough tracks, covering twenty miles across the mountains, to reach their destination, the monastery of Verna. Soon after their arrival, Cagnazzo turned up with three bicycles in the back of his car.

That same afternoon, although dog-tired, they cycled thirty-five miles, following Cagnazzo's car and passing groups of German engineers preparing bridges for demolition. Next day (2 November), they started at dawn and cycled another forty-eight miles, this time with a new guide, called Canestrade, who preceded them on his bicycle. They arrived, utterly exhausted, at a farm owned by a Signore Ruggeri near the village of Pozzo Basso, a few miles outside Pesaro. It was here, shortly afterwards, that Cagnazzo brought Jimmie and me to meet them.

Despite being worn out and dishevelled after their long and arduous journey, the three senior officers were in buoyant spirits. They were, of course, impatient to learn from Jimmie the plans A Force had made for their rescue by submarine the following night. Jimmie took charge firmly and efficiently, undaunted by the weight of responsibility resting on his young shoulders, and undeterred by the prospect of giving orders to two distinguished generals and an Air Vice Marshal. They listened politely as Jimmie outlined arrangements for the following evening and explained the back-up plans if things went wrong. He answered their questions without hesitation and they seemed satisfied.

Neame and O'Connor, in their mid-fifties, were not dissimilar in appearance: both were rather small in stature, lean and wiry, with bristly moustaches and greying hair. From the start, Neame seemed more sensitive than the others that Jimmie was in sole charge of the operation. To some extent, I suppose, this was understandable, given Neame's eminent career, highlighted by the award of the Victoria Cross, won for conspicuous bravery in France early in the First World War as a lieutenant in the Royal Engineers. In 1916 he won a DSO and, during the First World War, was Mentioned in Despatches five times.

O'Connor was dapper, with a soft Irish brogue and a warm, friendly smile. He, too, had distinguished himself in acts of gallantry in the First World War, having won the DSO and Bar, the Military Cross, and had been Mentioned in Despatches no fewer than nine times. But I was struck at once by his modest and self-effacing bearing; he was far less likely, I suspected, to throw his weight around.

Boyd was of medium height, slim, broad-chested and powerfully built, like a rugby wing three-quarter. The same age as O'Connor (fifty-four), he had graduated from Sandhurst and been commissioned into the Indian Army in 1909, transferring to the Royal Flying Corps in 1916. In the Great War he had won both the MC and AFC and was awarded the OBE in 1919. He was a quiet-spoken, gentle man who accepted without demur the fact that they were entirely in Jimmie's hands, and showed no sign of resentment.

We learned later that during their time 'in the bag', first in a camp near Sulmona and later in Vincigliate Castle, near Florence, two of them (O'Connor and Boyd) had made attempts to escape. O'Connor very nearly succeeded in July 1942 by scaling the walls of the castle, only to be spotted halfway down the rope by one of the sentries. Again, in March 1943, he and Boyd, together with four other senior officers (including the legendary General Sir Adrian Carton de Wiart, who had lost an arm and an eye in the First World War, and won a VC) had escaped through a tunnel which had taken six months to dig. The Air Vice Marshal was apprehended on the Swiss border at Lake Como, and O'Connor, after seven days' cross-country walking, was picked up by a carabinieri patrol on the Bologna plain, 150 miles from camp.

By all accounts, the generals and the AVM were a tough trio, game for almost anything. After more than two frustrating years in captivity they were more than ever fiercely determined to gain their freedom.

It was, therefore, a delicate task confronting Jimmie: to assert his authority on three such gallant and distinguished gentlemen, preferably without intimidating them. Another factor to be coped with in the coming weeks was a tendency on the part of the leaders of the Italian underground to defer to Neame, as the most senior of the three 'brass hats' rather than to Jimmie. But Jimmie managed admirably. He never appeared overawed and throughout our ensuing adventures he maintained a fine balance of respect, firmness and dogged determination.

One slight problem, for us, was that the generals and AVM were fairly fluent in Italian. O'Connor had served in Italy in the Great War and had been decorated by the Italians. They had spent much longer than us as PoWs and had devoted much of their incarceration learning the language. It was natural, therefore, that the Italians we came into contact with tended to communicate more freely with them than with us.

Early that first afternoon, Jimmie and Cagnazzo returned to Gabicce, where they hoped to borrow (or steal) a rowing boat to take us all out to sea to await the submarine.

Meanwhile, O'Connor, Neame, Boyd and I, led by our trusted guide, cycled into Cattolica and went straight to the house of a Major Gusto Tilloy, a former General Staff Officer in the Italian Army, who was also a well-known military historian.

Well aware of the death penalty for harbouring British prisoners, nevertheless, like many other brave Italians we encountered (from all walks of life), the Tilloys were prepared to risk their lives to help us. They had three young children who were kept up at the top of the house in case they should say something that would betray our presence, whilst we stayed downstairs and spoke only in whispers.

At 8 o'clock the following evening, 3 November, the generals, the AVM, our guide and I set off briskly on foot towards the sea. There was no moon and it was pitch dark. This made it difficult to find Jimmie and Cagnazzo who were waiting for us on the beach in the shelter of the pier. Quickly we boarded the rowing boat Cagnazzo had procured and rowed out several hundred yards beyond the pier. There we waited, and waited, tossed by the waves and drenched by the stinging, salty spray, while Jimmie signalled periodically with his shielded flashlight, carefully masked so that its beam could be seen only from the seaward side. However, there was no answering flash from the submarine.

At midnight, two hours after the appointed pick-up time, Jimmie decided to abandon the attempt. A blustery offshore wind had developed, and this, with the strong current, made rowing back to the shore very hard work. As a result, we landed some distance from where the rowing boat had been appropriated. What would happen, I wondered, when the owner discovered, a few hours later, that his precious boat was missing? At the very least he would report his loss to the police who would promptly investigate the boat's disappearance. This could seriously interfere with our plans for the following night, when a second attempt was to be made by the submarine to pick us up from precisely the same spot. But this was a risk we had to take. There was no alternative, no way at this late stage, in the absence of a direct radio link with A Force, of warning the Royal Navy to keep clear of the area.

To Tilloy's discomfiture, the bedraggled party returned to his house. And there we stayed for what little was left of the night, and throughout the next day. So ended the first of numerous abortive attempts to escape by sea.

After dark that evening we again gathered up our meagre belongings and trooped down to the beach. This time Jimmie decided to wait on the beach beside another rowing boat which Cagnazzo had that afternoon arranged to borrow. Huddled together for warmth, we sat in the bitterly cold, drizzling rain until the appointed hour, when Jimmie started flashing the agreed signals on his torch, the beam of narrow light piercing the darkness out to sea.

In the early hours of the morning we heard the throb of an engine out at sea. Convinced it was the submarine, Neame was upset to be contradicted by Jimmie who recognized the distinctive sound of an Italian patrol boat's engine. To make absolutely sure, he and Cagnazzo, at considerable risk to themselves, walked to the end of the pier and once again flashed the prearranged signals out to sea. As before, these went unanswered. Dejected and drenched through, we made our weary way back once more to the Tilloys' house, where the welcome we received was bleaker even than our shattered morale.

Some months later, O'Connor learned that on both occasions our submarine had been diverted, at the last moment, to 'another important mission elsewhere' – scarcely a satisfactory or indeed a flattering explanation.

Gusto Tilloy warned us that the Germans were setting up a new headquarters in Cattolica, and that there had been increased patrol activities along the nearby coast. It was clearly far too dangerous, therefore, for us to remain in Cattolica any longer. And in any case, it was all too plain that we had outstayed our welcome at the Tilloys' residence.

Luckily for us, a Signore Spada turned up unexpectedly at the Tilloys'; through him we were able to make fresh plans for our escape. Spada was a fanatical anti-Fascist political leader who, from humble beginnings, had done well in the textile trade before going into politics. He was a leading member in this province of the ULI (*Unione Laburista Italiana*), an organization that had given considerable help to British and other escaped PoWs in the way of clothes, food and money, all of which were unobtainable by normal means.

With the generals' agreement, we decided to split up into two parties for the time being. The situation looked bleak and the risks of recapture were growing daily, the more so if we stayed together in one group. Spada solved the problem by arranging for the generals and the AVM to be housed, as Swiss refugees, in a chapel on the estate of one Count Spina, while Jimmie and I were taken back to our old friends, the Terenzis, in Pozzo Alto.

For the next ten days the senior officers fared badly. The chapel was like a mausoleum, freezing cold and draughty. They had to sleep on the wooden pews, and indifferent if not unpalatable food was brought to them from a local café. After several days it was plain they had to move. Rumour and gossip were rife in the village, and the generals became increasingly concerned about Spina's motives, even suspecting him of playing a double game with the local Fascists.

At daybreak on 16 November, Spada arrived at Count Spina's chapel with four bicycles in the back of a small lorry. With Spada in the lead, the generals and Boyd set off along the main coastal road. After thirty-five miles they stopped for a meal in a restaurant, then continued cycling until they reached Cesena where an artist friend of Spada called Magnani, put them up for the night. Next day they cycled for over three hours to Forli, Benito Mussolini's home town. After two nights spent in two separate houses they were moved into a villa in the suburbs, owned by a Signore Spazzoli, where they spent the next seven days in reasonable comfort. Spada told them that the Germans had closed and occupied the port of Cattolica, so all hope of getting away from there, at least for the time being, was completely dashed.

Meanwhile, a certain Signore Bruno Vailati had courageously taken a hand-written note from Neame, addressed personally to Generals Alexander and Montgomery, through the German front lines. He had successfully delivered the note to the Allied HQ in Bari and returned safely with further plans for the generals' escape.

Jimmie and I met Bruno Vailati on 22 November, when he came to see us in Pesaro to discuss the new plans and offer his help. Our immediate concern was to rejoin the generals and the AVM in Cervia, forty-five miles up the Adriatic coast road, where a further attempt was to be made by A Force to rescue us by submarine. We decided to make the journey on bicycles, as this seemed to be the safest mode of travel. The majority of Italians moved around in this way so it attracted the least attention. Our cycling excursions were normally restricted to daylight hours as the curfew was strictly enforced.

Preceded by our guide, Anacleto, we set off early one morning on our trek northwards along the coast. There was no way to avoid the main road without taking a circuitous route, which would have prevented us from reaching our destination before dark. En route we had to pass through the port of Rimini. Approaching a main bridge across the River Marecchia, in the town centre, we saw civilian cars ahead of us being stopped by a German military policeman waving a stick with a red disc on the end. Anacleto had already crossed the bridge safely. Jimmie motioned to me to dismount while we decided whether to go ahead and take the risk, or turn back and wait until the coast was clear. The problem was that, without the guide, we would be lost: neither of us knew the precise location of our rendezvous in Cervia. So there was nothing for it but to continue, one by one, towards the bridge. I was in the lead; if I was stopped Jimmie could turn back.

As I drew near, to my consternation the German started to raise his red disc. My heart raced faster. Then a car passed me, slowing down, and I realized with profound relief that it was not I who was being stopped. So I pedalled on, looking firmly ahead, and reached the far end of the bridge. Jimmie soon joined me. Out of sight of the police guard, we put on a burst of speed to catch up Anacleto, knowing he would be unaware of the reason for our delay. We found him a mile down the road, waiting anxiously, and delighted to know we were safe.

Later, Anacleto stopped at a wayside restaurant for much needed refreshment and rest. We were saddle-sore, stiff and limp with fatigue and hunger, our throats parched with thirst. We had cycled non-stop (apart from the incident at the bridge) for forty-eight miles in just over six hours. The restaurant was packed with German soldiers, so Jimmie and I remained discreetly silent, leaving our guide to chatter away in Italian. We listened intently, understanding little.

That evening we met Bruno Vailati, the generals and the AVM, who had bicycled over from Forli, some twenty miles to the west, at the Osteria del Cacciatore, a former hunting lodge, a few miles north of Cervia. This was the rendezvous from which we were to launch our fourth attempt to escape.

As soon as it was dark we set off for the beach, although still exhausted from our bicycle rides. We walked in single file, with Bruno in the lead, over miles of marshland and flooded pathways. The going was terrible in the dark and it took us two and a half hours. We had to wade, sometimes up to our knees, through swamps and glutinous mud which all but sucked off our saturated shoes.

To make matters worse, the place chosen by A Force for our rendezvous with the submarine was, unknown to them, teeming with German military activity. We appeared to be walking slap through the middle of intensive German night manoeuvres. Flares streaked up into the moonless night sky, brilliantly illuminating the surrounding countryside. The squeal of tank tracks could be heard in the distance, mixed with the staccato crackle of small arms and machine-gun fire. Nearing the shoreline, we saw helmeted German infantrymen sharply silhouetted on the distant dunes, preparing to fend off some mock invasion. Fluid coastal defence was vital to prevent what the German High Command no doubt assumed (wrongly, as it transpired) would be Allied landings sooner or later on either side of the upper Italian peninsula.

Bruno came to an abrupt halt, and turning to Jimmie, who was immediately behind him, expressed his apprehension about going any farther. He was convinced we were in imminent danger of being discovered. The Germans were all around us, he argued, and it was only a matter of time before our ragged band ran into them. We had a hurried consultation with the generals, but they and the AVM were adamant about carrying on. We had come so far, Neame insisted, it would be senseless to abandon the attempt. So we struggled on, now less than a quarter of a mile from the beach.

Shortly after 10 pm, miraculously undetected, we finally reached our objective, a small wooden shack half-hidden amongst the sand dunes close to the mouth of the River Savio, where two fishermen were waiting for us. Leaving the rest of us in the hut, which reeked of rotting fish and musty nets, Jimmie and Bruno helped the fishermen put to sea in a small rowing boat, wading through the pounding surf before themselves scrambling aboard. Some way from the beach they weighed anchor; and there the four of them waited in the freezing cold, while Jimmie intermittently flashed the prearranged signals seawards. Over and over again he repeated the signals. There was no sign or sound of the submarine in the inky blackness.

At 3 am they returned disconsolately to the beach and rejoined us in the dank and smelly shack. Silently, Vailati led the party back to Osteria, reaching it at daybreak, each one of us cold, wet and dejected after yet another distressing setback.

Later that morning we were taken to an empty, unfurnished villa nearby. Bruno contacted a friend of his, Signore Sovera, who owned a hotel in Cervia. At that low point in our fortunes, Sovera proved himself a godsend. An assistant manager at Claridges in London before the war, he was a jovial, rotund little man with bright sparkling eyes, who exuded an air of bustling efficiency. He was also a very brave man.

Anxious to improve our creature comforts, Sovera contrived to move us next day into a modern, well-furnished villa which stood amongst thick pine woods on the outskirts of Cervia. This luxurious residence, ironically, was the summer home of none other than General Graziani, the commander in the 1940/41 desert campaign of the hapless Italian forces, which had been soundly thrashed by Dick O'Connor's brilliant strategy.

Rodolfo Graziani had served in the First World War and became the youngest colonel in the Royal Italian Army. When in 1935/36 Italy invaded Ethiopia, Graziani commanded the southern front and as a reward for his role he was made a Marshal of Italy. After the war, Graziani was made Viceroy and Governor-General of Ethiopia. In February 1937 he survived an assassination attempt, followed by a bloody and indiscriminate repression for which he became known as 'The Butcher of Ethiopia'. In the Second World War Dictator Benito Mussolini ordered Graziani to invade Egypt in September 1940. The Italian Tenth Army was soundly defeated by the British forces under General Sir Richard O'Connor and Graziani resigned. He ended his career as Minister of Defence for the Italian Social Republic.

Sovera was able to bribe the caretaker, whom he trusted to keep his mouth shut, and to take it in turns with his assistant, Spazzoli, to bring us hot food, prepared in the hotel kitchens, and masses of fresh fruit. He even provided whiskey and wine with our meals, and more important still, a radio on which we could listen to the BBC news.

Immediately opposite the Graziani villa lived an Englishwoman, Signora Tellesio, whose brother was an RAF fighter pilot. One evening she called on us and invited us to tea the following afternoon. Married to an Italian journalist, she was a charming lady who did everything she could to make us as comfortable as possible under the circumstances.

The next morning, however, we had a real scare. Jimmie was looking out of the sitting-room window when he spotted a squad of German soldiers riding slowly towards our villa on bicycles. The officer in charge stopped at our front gate and was about to open it when Signora Tellesio hurried across the road to intercept him. Soon after, the Germans left and she came to tell us that they were a billeting party. She had diverted them to another part of the neighbourhood where, she told the officer, the accommodation was far more suitable. She hustled us out of the back door with our bicycles, telling us to hide in the pine woods behind the villa, and to stay there until she gave us the all clear. It was dark before the Signora came to tell us it was safe to return to the villa.

We learned, much later, that soon after we left Cervia the Fascist police came to arrest Signore Tellesio and his wife. Neither was there, so they seized the baby and nurse as hostages. Signora Tellesio then gave herself up, whereupon she was thrown into a prison cell with fifteen male prisoners. She was continually interrogated about her husband's whereabouts. But despite threats to shoot her, they failed to get the information they wanted. She was released after a month of very rough treatment. When the British Forces arrived, Signore Tellesio became a liaison officer between the Allied HQ and the civil authorities. After many months' delay, his wife and baby were sent home to her mother in England, as her health had suffered badly from the brutal treatment she had received from the Italian police.

Our next escape attempt came on the night of 28 November. This time A Force was to send a motor fishing boat to pick us off the coast near Cervia. Yet again we made our way down to the shore, blessed for a change with favourable weather. Once more we spent the entire night on the beach, waiting and hoping. And once again, we were to be bitterly disappointed - not a glimmer of response to Jimmie's signals. Later, in London, we were told that intensive British naval operations in the Adriatic, involving the bombardment of Ancona, ninety miles to the south, had caused the cancellation of the rendezvous.

In his diary for 29 November, Signore Sovera describes the critical situation:

6 am. Once again the departure has not taken place. They are all wet, dirty and very dejected. I endeavour to cheer them up. As before, they are given food. We are back where we started!

In Cervia people are beginning to talk about my guests and we are not very happy about it. Bruno and Spazzoli leave to get instructions. We think they will be away about five or six days. I promise to come back at 12.30 pm with luncheon. At midday I am worried. I get the meal as quickly as I can and together with Mario, who helps me to carry the food; I reach the villa just in time to come face to face with a German sergeant and a billeting officer who, with skeleton keys are trying to force open the gate.

I recoil. A moment's delay and all would have been lost! I approach them and ask them what they want and they tell me they want to enter the villa to inspect it. I reply that my servant has the keys and that he will be returning at 4 pm. It seems they want somewhere with a garage. I then take them to the villa opposite where a friend of mine lives and show them the garage. My friend protests but I insist that they should be allowed to use his garage. He is annoyed with me. He doesn't know what is going on nor does he understand why I should be doing such a thing. Then the Germans go away but say they want to see the villa at 4 pm. In the end I take the food inside and decide to arrange for them (the generals' party) to leave in the afternoon. To remain in the pinewoods would be dangerous. I decide to send them to some trustworthy peasants. At 2 pm we leave the villa to fetch them from the pinewoods and later in the afternoon they start off for the country.

30 Nov. I send them supplies. Am informed by Baselli that the place is not safe. A Fascist has been killed and they are searching everywhere. My friends change their hiding place three times in three days. No news from Bruno.

1st Dec. Baselli comes to tell me that they cannot stay there any longer as rumours (of their presence) are spreading . . . And still no news from Bruno . . . I decide to move them back to Cervia again. O'Connor and Neame are entrusted to Spazzoli's care and Boyd comes with me. My hotel, meanwhile, is requisitioned and occupied by the Commander of the

Piazza Pillugari – a real Prussian. He occupies Room No. 27 and I put Boyd in No. 28 which has its own bathroom. This room has a communicating door into my flat from which I take his meals. Boyd is quite content. He had a wireless set and from his window he can see all the movements of the Germans without himself being seen. Every night, when my children are in bed, he comes into my flat. I give him some books to enable him to practise his Italian. Mrs Tellesio brings me novels. I go and see the others who are living in a small villa in Cervia and they are very comfortable. They don't want anything else. I send them tea and whiskey.

2nd Dec. I liaise with my friends. I visit them every evening. Have let Boyd have my pyjamas whilst his own are being washed and I have fixed him up with a stove. He is extremely courteous and it is a real pleasure to do something for him.

8th Dec. Bruno arrives: leaves again in the afternoon. What a man he is! Have found a taxi and take them to Riccione the same evening. We bid each other farewell . . . It was all very moving. We hope to have good news of them soon.

Sovera ends his diary account by noting that 'on the 20th January we hear – on the wireless – that they have arrived safely. We celebrate with champagne!'

While the Air Vice Marshal was enjoying Sovera's generous hospitality, Neame and O'Connor had been moved back into Cervia where they were billeted, in reasonable comfort, with a hospital nurse called Ida. The two generals shared a large bed and Sovera brought them a box of food each day. Before they left, Ida asked them to inscribe their names under the bed as a memento of their stay.

It was clearly unwise and dangerous for us all to remain together in one place for longer than was absolutely necessary. Nor was it fair on our Italian helpers and agents, who were already taking enormous risks on our behalf. Splitting up the party, too, reduced the chances of us all being caught together. And so Jimmie and I, again guided by the indomitable Anacleto, bicycled the fifty miles back to our old familiar farmhouse in Pozzo Alto. There we were to stay while Cagnazzo made strenuous efforts to procure a fishing boat to take the party down to Termoli, as he had successfully done for the first trip.

The skipper of the Cattolica boat, Guerino, had decided, wisely perhaps, not to tempt fate again so soon after the last voyage south. Considering the huge risks to himself and his family, he could scarcely be blamed for his reluctance. Indeed, it was astonishing to me that anyone would contemplate such a hazardous mission, however tempting the rewards.

By now things were becoming desperate. Official efforts to rescue us having failed dismally, we were now left very much to our own devices. Jimmie made several abortive attempts to contact other A Force agents in the area. I found it incredible that not a single agent had been in touch with us since Jimmie's return from Termoli. Surely, I thought, A Force would move heaven and earth to keep open whatever lines of communication were available, however slender, given the vital importance of getting the three senior officers back to safety.

I was puzzled, too, that Jimmie had not been issued with a two-way radio. For two simple reasons, he explained. First, they were in very short supply. And secondly, even the so-called 'portable' units were bulky and heavy, too cumbersome to carry around and hard to conceal.

It was a question of relying on our faithful Cagnazzo, or one of the other Italian 'helpers', to pull something dramatic out of the fire. Neame, in particular, was becoming fractious and frustrated; O'Connor and Boyd also were understandably restless. On the other hand, we were aware of the danger of relying too heavily on our Italian friends, however loyal and trustworthy their motives might be. There were ominous signs, too, of a jealous rivalry between the partisan factions, each vying for the honour and glory of helping the British VIPs to escape.

Cagnazzo, Spada and Sovera, we knew, had maintained close contact with resistance groups in the area: but the partisans' help, incalculable though it was, had been confined to the provision of 'safe houses', guides and transport. Indeed, had it not been for them, undoubtedly we would have long since found ourselves behind bars in Germany, or suffered an even worse fate.

Under these circumstances, Jimmie and I thought it prudent to move the generals and the AVM down the coast to Riccione as soon as arrangements could be made. Two days later, they were driven there in the same taxi that had brought Cagnazzo from Pesaro. The driver, Signore Lisotti, was blissfully unaware of the identity of his passengers for the hundreds of miles he was engaged as their chauffeur. It was not until the very last journey that the secret was finally revealed. Perhaps this explains why he drove them so nonchalantly through four German checkpoints on the way to Riccione!

Lisotti took them straight to the house of Signore Pietro Arpesella, a wily young Italian, proud of his business acumen and financial manipulations in the real estate market. His shrewdness came to light over the loan of the 100,000 lire (about £800) which we needed to pay, in advance, to the fishing boat captain who was prepared to take us down to the Allied lines. No fool, Arpesella was willing to lend us the money on condition the IOU, signed by Neame, was repayable in pounds sterling, and that he received a letter of commendation from Neame. Not surprisingly, both conditions were agreed with alacrity.

The fact that Arpesella's house was situated next door to the German headquarters appeared not to bother him at all. He even encouraged his British guests to venture out after dark to walk the streets which were crawling with German soldiers. The danger was not so much from the Germans, but from the chances of being stopped by an inquisitive Fascist or an alert Carabinieri patrol.

The next day, 7 December, Cagnazzo turned up at our farmhouse in Pozzo Alto with the grim news that the Germans had seized and impounded the fishing boat we were to use. Their suspicions had apparently been aroused: how, we never knew. Thwarted yet again, our spirits plummeted to an even lower ebb.

Cagnazzo then suggested sending the generals and the AVM to a place called Cingoli, some eighty miles farther south, where a band of partisans under a General Ascoli claimed to be in radio contact with Allied headquarters in Bari. O'Connor and Neame both endorsed the idea on the grounds that to do anything faintly constructive was preferable to prolonged inertia.

On 10 December, Lisotti drove the three men down to their new place of refuge near Cingoli without mishap. There they spent three uncomfortable days in primitive lodgings, sleeping above stables which stank abominably. They were all suffering from heavy colds and nasty coughs. Neame, we heard, was in a particularly bad way, showing signs of a fever and the possible onset of influenza. This presented a serious problem. Thanks to the ministrations of a local doctor, however, he recovered with commendable speed.

General Ascoli readily agreed to transmit a message from Neame to General Montgomery, asking him to send a naval craft to Porta Civita Nuova, south of Ancona, to rescue us. Being Jewish, General Ascoli had gone into hiding and was himself trying to get out of the country. While the generals were in Cingoli he was tragically killed. He was being chased by the Fascist militia when his bicycle skidded over the side of a steep bank and he suffered a fatal fracture to his skull.

Yet again the generals were moved, this time to a small flat in Cingoli itself, rented by Cagnazzo. One night the police conducted a thorough search of the town. Whether they had got wind of the generals we never discovered. It was, in any event, time for them to move from an area which had become increasingly hazardous.

On 16 December the generals were driven back to Riccione, once more passing all the German checkpoints without any problems. Neame was angry at being made to move yet again. He had wanted to wait in Cingoli for a reply from General Montgomery. In the event this never materialized. Jimmie and I strongly suspected that the much vaunted radio link was a myth dreamed up by the partisans to impress the generals.

Meanwhile, at Jimmie's suggestion, Vailati contacted Ezio Galluzzi, the fishing-boat owner who had arranged Jimmie's and Cagnazzo's trip south the previous month, and who had stoutly offered to repeat the process, using the largest boat in his fishing fleet. We trusted him implicitly. But Jimmie sensibly insisted on Galluzzi meeting the generals and Boyd first, to make sure that they, too, were happy with his credentials. After a brief meeting, Neame expressed their joint approval and confidence in him. This was just as well, for we were running out of time. Tempers were increasingly frayed. Moreover, the weather was becoming problematical for a voyage in a fishing boat down the Adriatic, which, we were warned could be dangerously tempestuous in winter.

Bruno Vailati arrived on 13 December with the welcome news that Galluzzi had agreed to take us south himself, sailing out of the port of Cattolica. He was influenced in his decision by two very strong motives: to prevent the 'flagship' of his fishing fleet being seized by the Germans or damaged by Allied bombing of the port. Also, he asked to be allowed to take his wife, as he was unwilling, for obvious reasons, to leave her behind on her own. This presented no problem and was readily agreed.

There still remained the critical question of laying our hands on the money to pay Galluzzi. This now being a matter of top priority, Jimmie sent an urgent message to Arpesella. Two days later, to our immense relief, he obligingly turned up with the required 100,000 lire in cash. This was immediately handed over to Galluzzi on the understanding that, all being well and weather permitting, he would be ready to leave in the next day or so.

An urgent meeting was arranged with the generals and Boyd, at which both Cagnazzo and Vailiti were present. It was essential to plan the embarkation in detail so that everything went smoothly for what was to be our eighth and, hopefully, final escape attempt. None of us was under any delusion as to the risks and difficulties we faced. Timing, for instance, was a crucial factor; much depended on us all getting down to the boat speedily, unobtrusively and on a tightly controlled schedule.

It was already dark, on 18 December, when Vailati went off in Lisotti's taxi to pick up Father Leone from the monastery in Pesaro, where Jimmie and I had spent several days in hiding. Father Leone had been heavily involved over many months in helping escaped PoWs and was now forced to flee from the Fascist regime. Vailati then went on to collect Jimmie and me from the Terenzis' farm in Pozzo Alto. From there he drove by a circuitous route, carefully avoiding the main roads, to the outskirts of Cattolica. There we met our skipper, Galluzzi, who was to guide us on foot down to the port area. At 8.30 pm we crept silently and stealthily along the quayside for a hundred yards or so, until suddenly we found ourselves following Galluzzi up a short gangplank onto his fishing boat. Cagnazzo and his wife, together with Signora Galluzzi, had already been smuggled aboard; also a South African corporal, named Macmullen, who had had the good fortune to encounter Cagnazzo the previous day.

The unflappable Vailati then went off, again in Lisotti's taxi, to fetch the generals and the AVM from Riccione. He found them waiting, nervously impatient and anxious. The agreed pick-up time was 6.30 pm. So for two hours they had become increasingly fearful that, yet again, things had gone wrong. Against Vailati's advice, Neame insisted on taking with him a bulky suitcase containing his precious diaries and the draft of his book on the desert campaign.

They left Riccione at about 9 pm, only half an hour before curfew. Just outside Cattolica they were halted at a German control post. Their papers were examined but miraculously passed muster and they were allowed to proceed. Half a mile from the port they met Skipper Galluzzi at the same place where Jimmie and I had stopped. An emotional scene followed. Lisotti, their stout-hearted driver, embraced the generals and Boyd and, somewhat to their embarrassment, kissed them each on the cheek. We heard later that he had been betrayed and arrested soon after our escape. He was tortured by the Gestapo but remained silent. Tragically, he died soon after the arrival of the Allied armies as a result of his brutal treatment.

With Galluzzi leading the way in the pitch dark, they moved slowly, in single file, down the canal path towards the little harbour, and along the narrow jetty to where the boat, rocking gently on the evening tide, lay moored. Scarcely daring to breathe, they crept on board and joined the rest of us below decks. The time was 10.25 pm.

All night we were battened down in the cramped bowels of the sixteen-metre vessel, huddled together in what Neame likened to the Black Hole of Calcutta. The hold was dark, damp, very hot and stuffy, and smelled strongly of fish. Conditions were scarcely conducive to sleep, desperately tired though we all were.

The night seemed interminable, each of us lost in his own thoughts – and fears. I doubt that I was the only one praying fervently, as even the bravest atheist is prone to do when faced with real danger. Nightmarish thoughts leap to mind at such times. Could the owner of the boat really be trusted? Here we were sitting ducks, an enviable prize for the Germans. What was there to stop him taking the 100,000 lire from Arpesella and handing us over to the Germans for a further reward, except perhaps the certain knowledge that he would face the vengeance of our partisan friends? Might not the German guards search the boat before allowing her to sail? And so we waited, and waited, increasingly apprehensive, tension mounting as the minutes ticked by, inexorably, through the night.

At 5.30 am, while it was still dark, we heard heavy footsteps on the gangway, of men coming aboard. Were they crew members? Were they German or Fascist harbour police? Had we been betrayed? Moments later we heard muffled voices – Italian voices – the skipper giving orders to his crew, followed soon after by the reassuring sounds of a boat getting underway, the diesel engine starting up and ticking over, the clanking of chains, the casting off of ropes, the gentle easing away from the quayside, and the movement of the boat as it chugged slowly towards the mouth of the harbour. By decree, all boats were compelled to stop at the German pierhead control to be given official clearance to leave port. On no account were fishing vessels permitted to leave harbour before dawn: and they had to return to the same harbour one hour before dark. Any infringement of this strict edict was severely punished.

Then came the moment of truth, and a collective holding of breath, as the boat slowed, engines in neutral, waiting to be checked out of the harbour entrance. The Skipper yelled out a password: '*Sessanto otto*' (sixty-eight), '*Dux!*' (the name of the boat), followed immediately by an unintelligible, guttural response from the German guard at his pier head post . . . a brief pause . . . then, we heard the sound of the engines being revved up as the boat gathered speed and, unimpeded, made for the open sea. The noise of the engines, now at full power, became almost deafening. And suddenly we found ourselves rolling and pitching violently as the boat battled her way out into the wild waves of the Adriatic.

Dick O'Connor, eyes gleaming, shook hands all round, exclaiming: 'We've done it! We've done it!' somewhat prematurely, I felt, since we still faced a hazardous sea trip.

The skipper, taking no chances, insisted we remain below deck during daylight hours, doubtless a sensible precaution. Nevertheless, it was pure purgatory for his human cargo, cooped up in the confined quarters of a smelly, foetid hold. The weather was worsening and with one exception we were all horribly and continuously sick. Jimmie somehow survived the entire voyage without any apparent ill-effects. That evening he generously offered me some greasy fried fish which he himself was devouring with great relish. I declined, none too gracefully.

The stormy conditions and poor visibility, on the other hand were in our favour, since we were less likely to be spotted from the shore or from an enemy aircraft or patrol boat. Towards nightfall the weather improved. The wind fell, the clouds cleared away, and soon the boat was bathed in bright moonlight. Now we were in danger of being spotted by an aircraft or patrol boat out searching for us, or even by a lurking submarine.

The seas became calmer, and to our immense relief, we were allowed up on deck. In the early hours the skipper altered course to the southeast. An hour before dawn we suddenly saw, westward towards the Bay of Pescara, signs of a fierce battle raging on the coastal plain: flashes of opposing artillery batteries, tracers streaming wildly in parabolic curves, occasional Very lights. Urgently, Jimmie told the skipper to alter course again and head back out into the Adriatic. An hour later, by now well clear of the battle zone, the skipper edged slowly back towards the coast line. We now knew, for certain, that when we made landfall it would at least be on the Allied side of the lines.

As dawn broke we were greeted by the gloriously welcome sight of Allied aircraft flying low overhead. Our Odyssey was nearing its end. With mounting excitement we approached the coastline. Passing close by the Islands of Tremiti, we chugged slowly in towards a town with a sizeable harbour which Jimmie recognized as the port of Termoli, near where he and Cagnazzo had landed on their previous trip.

It was 11 am on 20 December 1943. As the boat drew alongside an empty space on the harbour pier, two armed guards raced down the quayside and arrested us as we disembarked. O'Connor asked to see their commanding officer. When he arrived O'Connor was surprised and delighted to find that the man had been on his staff when he was a Brigade Major. The poor fellow was utterly astonished and immediately took us all to the officers' mess where we were invited to wash and shave before being given a hearty English breakfast.

Jimmie immediately contacted the local Brigade Intelligence officer who, in turn, alerted the A Force commander. Both these gentlemen reached the mess with remarkable speed, prompted no doubt by the unheralded arrival of the generals and the AVM on their doorstep, and particularly in view of A Force's signal failure to rescue them.

Meanwhile, a message was sent to General Alexander at his headquarters in Bari. Back came an immediate reply congratulating the generals and the AVM on their safe return and inviting them to dine with him that evening.

With mixed feelings of jubilation, relief and mental and physical exhaustion, we foregathered in the lounge of the hotel requisitioned by the local Allied command as their officers' mess. We were joined by Cagnazzo and Vailati for a celebratory drink of Italian champagne. The mood was exuberant. The generals and Boyd were properly lavish in their praise for the bravery of our Italian colleagues on whose selfless help their successful escape had largely depended. Shaking each of them warmly by the hand, they vowed to return to Italy after the war to visit their homes and families, and to thank personally the other courageous people who had so readily risked their lives on their behalf.

Then, after thanking Jimmie and me equally profusely, O'Connor, Neame and Boyd were driven off to General Alexander's headquarters in Bari where they received a hearty welcome. At dinner with General Alexander that evening, still dressed in their filthy, ragged Italian civilian clothes, they were joined by none other than the Supreme Commander of the Allied Forces in Italy, General Eisenhower himself, who was paying Alexander an official visit. Next day they were given new uniforms, put on a plane and flown to Tunis where they were met by Air Chief Marshal Tedder.

At this time the Prime Minister was in Tunis, but confined to his bed convalescing from a bout of pneumonia. Churchill had sent a message to say that he wished to see the generals and the AVM, and that they were invited to dine at the mess at Supreme Command HQ, which was where he was staying. In his memoirs, O'Connor recounts the historic meeting as follows:

> Directly after dinner, we were ushered into the Great Man's bedroom by Lord Moran (Churchill's personal physician). There he was, like an old Buddha, sitting up in bed. The first thing he said to me was: 'Why did you allow yourself to be taken prisoner?' And then, after a moment he added: 'But you are forgiven.'
>
> He then went on talking to us for nearly an hour and a half,

hardly pausing to draw breath . . . He really brought us completely up to date . . . we sat there completely spellbound.

On 22 December they were flown to Algiers. Bad weather delayed their departure for England, so they stayed the night and dined with Harold Macmillan. Next day, they flew over the Atlas Mountains to Marrakesh in Morocco. There they changed planes for their final flight to Prestwick, arriving in Scotland, safe and sound, on Christmas morning.

On the whole they had survived their ordeal remarkably well, considering they were well into middle age. At times, Neame had proved difficult to deal with, betraying an underlying resentment that he, a full blown lieutenant general (and a VC) was not solely in command. On the other hand, O'Connor, who was of equal rank, and Boyd only slightly less senior, had given Jimmie and me their wholehearted and ungrudging support, and had been consistently friendly and gracious towards us.*

Jimmie and I, meanwhile, had been taken to a transit camp in Bari where we were issued with new battledress uniforms, boots and sundry other immediate necessities. To our dismay, this was the very same PoW Camp where we had spent several months on our arrival in Italy; the same walled and barbed-wire enclosures, dreary huts, wash rooms, cook house and parade ground. Ironically, there was even a guard (albeit British) on the main gate, supposedly to keep out unwelcome Italian intruders. And, unbelievably, we had to have a pass to leave the camp to go into the town. We met other escaped PoWs awaiting repatriation who shared our resentment at finding themselves cooped up behind barbed-wire so soon after their first taste of freedom.

However, we were in no mood to sit around waiting to be shipped home by sea. After all, the generals and the AVM, whom Jimmie and I had risked our lives to help rescue, were already halfway to England. 'Why,' Jimmie asked scathingly, 'should we have to kick our heels indefinitely in this God-forsaken dump?' A fiercely determined man, Jimmie was not easily deterred once he

---

* Notes on what happened to Neame, O'Connor and Boyd appear at the end of this chapter.

made up his mind, as he had so amply demonstrated over the previous weeks. Next day, Jimmie made his views known, in no uncertain terms, to the Major in charge of the Transit Camp, having cannily first sent a message seeking the support of the A Force Colonel. Thus it was that Jimmie and I found ourselves, on Christmas Eve, the sole passengers on a military plane winging its way to Algiers.

That night we celebrated in style, devouring long-forgotten delicacies, drinking ourselves into a state of semi-oblivion, and ending up in Algiers' most convivial night club. Christmas Day was spent recovering from a serious hangover, sipping endless cups of black coffee interspersed with glasses of fiery French brandy.

Three days later, having sampled the delights of Algiers to the full, we became restless and anxious to complete the final stage of our homeward journey. Once again, Jimmie prodded the authorities to good effect. We were told to report to the RAF base and await a flight to the UK. At dusk we boarded an RAF transport plane and, moments later watched the glittering lights of the city falling away below us as we headed west into the night. We took turns to go up into the cockpit where the squadron leader pilot explained our route, which took us 200 miles or so to the west of the Bay of Biscay before turning north, beyond the reach of German fighter patrols.

As dawn broke we could just make out, far below on the distant horizon, the faint outline of the English coast. It was indeed a memorable moment for us both. Soon afterwards we landed at the RAF base at Hendon, just outside London. It was 29 December. We had finally arrived Home.

It is impossible to describe our feelings as the taxi cab took us through the suburbs of north London, past Golders Green, Hampstead and St John's Wood, then along Park Road into Baker Street. We could see anti-aircraft guns in Hyde Park as we drove down Park Lane, and barrage balloons shimmering in the leaden sky above. Nor could we fail to notice the bomb damage, the boarded-up building sites, the sandbagged doorways, the scarcity of private cars, the long, patient queues at the bus stops. And yet, somehow, the people in the streets seemed unchanged, any war-weariness well concealed from casual observation.

The cab dropped us off at my Club, The Overseas League, in

Park Place just off St James's Street. There, luckily, we found rooms for the night, and immediately telephoned our families. Since that day, whenever I entered this Club, I was reminded of that historic call and my mother's ecstatic reaction when she heard my voice. She had received a telegram on Christmas Eve which read: 'Officially reported Captain A. P. Spooner arrived British lines in Italy. Letter follows shortly. Secretary, Military Department, India Office.' So my call was not entirely unexpected.

Later in the morning, Jimmie telephoned a number we had been given at the War Office to report our arrival. The staff officer he spoke to instructed us to present ourselves at the Mayfair offices of MI9 at 3 pm on New Year's Eve for a thorough debriefing. Jimmie, a Scot through and through, was not, however, about to celebrate Hogmanay anywhere other than with his family in Scotland. And the slightly bemused staff officer was so advised, politely but firmly. To his credit, he accepted Jimmie's explanation with seasonal good humour, and agreed to postpone our visit to the War Office until early in the New Year.

After dinner, Jimmie and I wandered out of the Club's solid Edwardian buildings into Park Street, and strolled up St James's Street in the unfamiliar blackout. At the top we turned right into Piccadilly and joined the milling throng heading for Piccadilly Circus and beyond. Without knowing (or really caring) where we were bound, we found ourselves in Glasshouse Street, outside the Regent Palace Hotel. Entering the crowded lobby, we made our way to the bar, finding it packed with Allied officers, and servicemen and women, wearing uniforms of diverse nationalities – British, Free French, Polish, Dutch, American, Canadian, Belgian . . . and many others.

Suddenly, a bell clanged loudly and the air raid sirens sounded. Jimmie and I looked at each other nervously. But no one took the slightest notice. There was no mass exodus for the safety of an air raid shelter; not a single person left the bar. This, we realized, was war-time, blitz-hardened London, its residents, native or otherwise, blithely unconcerned that high explosives were about to rain down on the metropolis.

An hour or so later the all-clear went. We staggered out into the cold night air and the darkened streets, and groped our way uncertainly back to The Overseas League, with the clanging of bells and the wail of sirens from ambulances and fire engines ringing in our ears.

Dog tired, that night we slept soundly through yet another air raid, unaware of the blockbuster bomb that badly damaged an office building round the corner in Pall Mall, as we were told, in a calm, matter-of-fact manner by our waitress at breakfast next morning.

After a late and leisurely breakfast, Jimmie rang for a taxi to take him to Euston for his train to Edinburgh. It was difficult to realize, all of a sudden, that our journey had really ended, that our trials and tribulations were over. We were not to know that, within a few months, we would be together again, working as a team for E Group, the MI9 organization in Southeast Asia corresponding to A Force in Italy, and engaged in clandestine activities behind the Japanese lines in the jungles of Burma.

When Jimmie left I had an hour or so to kill before catching a train to Stewkley in Bedfordshire, where my mother, bombed out of her Wimbledon home, was staying for the duration. I walked slowly down past St James's Palace, along Marlborough Road, crossing the Mall into the peace and tranquillity of St James's Park. I followed the path that leads to the ornamental lake and stood, as I had so often before, on the iron suspension bridge and watched the ducks and geese swimming round in circles below me, ever hopeful for a crumb. From here one could see, to the west, the Queen Victoria Memorial, and beyond, the august façade of Buckingham Palace, for more than a hundred years the Sovereign's London home.

Turning about, looking eastward through the barren wintry trees, there in the distance were the familiar twin Towers of the Royal Palace of Westminster, the Victoria Tower of the House of Lords, and, further to the left, 'Big Ben', overlooking the House of Commons. How truly remarkable, I mused, that from this hub of the nation's capital, the hum of traffic barely audible, almost no other signs of human habitation could be seen, even now in the depth of winter.

At that moment, I vowed that, henceforth, whenever I returned from far off places, I would first make a pilgrimage to this very spot – it would become my very own, private Mecca.

As I stood there, absorbing the serene beauty of this magical scene set in the heart of England's teeming metropolis – a million miles from Camp PG 19, Bologna – I saw a flock of Canada Geese wheel in a graceful curve over Duck Island and land in perfect formation at the end of the lake. Had they, too, I wondered, flown from afar – and found their 'other Eden'?

NOTES

Lieutenant General Sir Philip Neame VC KBE CB DSO DL was appointed in 1945 to be Lieutenant Governor of Guernsey and the Channel Islands where he remained until 1953. His autobiography *Playing with Strife* was published in 1946. Throughout his career he was a keen shot (big and small game, rifle and revolver) and was appointed a Vice President of the National Rifle Association and President of the North London Rifle Club. On his retirement he lived in Faversham, Kent and in 1955 was made a Deputy Lieutenant of the County. In his later years his main recreations were gardening and fruit growing. He died on 28 April 1978, aged eighty-nine.

General Sir Richard O'Connor KT GCB DSO MC was chosen by Field Marshal Alan Brooke (later to become Sir Alan Brooke) to command VIII Corps, then in training for the Normandy invasion. He assumed command on 21 January 1944, exactly one calendar month after landing at Termoli, a tribute to the will-power and courage with which he overcame so rapidly the effects of three years' captivity. During the winter of 1944 O'Connor led his forces with great skill and determination against the Germans and helped to secure the Allied advance towards the Rhine. Then, in January 1945, he was appointed GOC-in-C Eastern Army, India, the most important of the four major commands in India. There he remained until the following November when he took over Northern Command, India with its Headquarters in Rawalpindi, and was promoted to full General. In July 1946 he was appointed to be Adjutant General to the Forces, the second highest army post after the Chief of the Imperial General Staff, who by then was Field Marshal Montgomery. He retired in August 1947 at the age of fifty-eight, and he and his wife, Jean settled in Rosemarkie, near Inverness. For four years he was Colonel of the Cameronians

(Scottish Rifles) and for ten years the Lord Lieutenant of Ross & Cromerty. General O'Connor received his final honour on 3 July 1971 when he was installed as a Knight of the Thistle by HM The Queen at St Giles Cathedral, Edinburgh. He died on 17 June 1981, aged ninety-one.

Air Vice-Marshal Owen Boyd CB OBE MC AFC fell seriously ill on his return to England and died eight months later, on 5 August 1944, aged fifty-five.

Chapter Five

Undercover in Burma

The trauma of the past year or so in Italy as a guest of Mussolini culminating in our escape took its toll on Jimmie and me. There was an initial period of anticlimactic reaction, followed by morose depression, which I found hard to understand or explain. We were granted indefinite leave, Jimmie with his family in Scotland, I with my mother in Bedfordshire where she had been evacuated following incendiary bomb damage on her house in Wimbledon. I recall sitting in the drawing room of my aunt's grand manor house in Stewkley, struggling to describe our exploits and the privations Jimmie and I endured whilst on the run in the Italian countryside.

Psychologically and physically I felt completely drained. Talking to anyone, even my mother, was a huge mental effort. In those days there was no remedial treatment for soldiers returning from active service, such as now exists for battle-weary personnel back from Iraq or Afghanistan. One was expected to thank one's lucky stars, pull up one's socks and get on with life as best one could.

The best antidote, I decided, would be to spend my army pay saved while in captivity on a few wild flings in London. A friend of my mother's was in charge of a 'Hut' at the Bletchley Park Establishment near Stewkley. This was where German secret coded signals were decoded with the use of the Enigma machine which, unknown to the Germans, the British had procured. The lady in question introduced me to a succession of 'bright young things' who relished the idea of a night out in London. Hand-picked by Bletchley Park for their brains if not their beauty, the girls adamantly refused to divulge under any circumstances the nature of their work. My playful efforts to extract information from them proved fruitless, even under the influence of copious gins and tonics. Charming, excellent company, and anxious to please, they

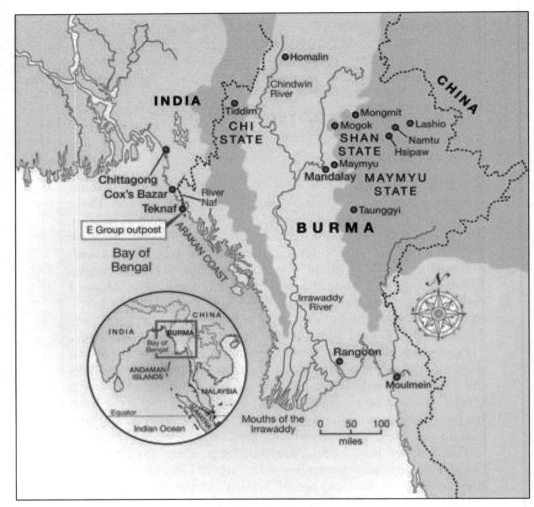

Map 3 – Burma

did much to boost my morale. It was not until long after the War that the critical importance of Bletchley Park became public knowledge. Indeed, it is no exaggeration to say that had it not been for their remarkable efforts we might well have lost the war.

Following dinner in a West End restaurant we repaired to 'The 400', an exclusive night club in Leicester Square. It opened at 10 pm and closed around 4 am. It was known as a 'bottle club'. This meant that instead of serving single drinks the member would buy a bottle of whatever alcohol they chose. You paid separately for the 'mixes'. At the end of the evening the waiter would seal the bottle and mark the level of the remaining liquid on a strip on the side of the bottle. It would then be kept for your next visit.

The club was small, intimate and dimly lit. The only lights came from table lamps with dark red shades and a single spotlight on the dance floor. Two bands took it in turns for sessions of three hours each, so dancing was continuous. They played all the old favourites such as *Begin the Beguine* and *Smoke gets in your Eyes*. The atmosphere was subdued and romantic, a perfect setting for anyone bent on subtle seduction. Couples on the crowded dance floor moved closer and closer together as the night wore on, blissfully oblivious to others around them.

So soundproof was the club that bombs could be dropping close by and no one inside would know. Early one morning, as dawn was breaking, my partner and I emerged from the club to see fires burning in buildings on the opposite side of Leicester Square. By now, Londoners had become so used to air raids they no longer rushed to shelters at the first sound of the air raid sirens. I was astonished at the apparent air of complacency. People carried on regardless of the danger not only from bombs but also from anti-aircraft shells, since what goes up must come down.

On another occasion I was in a theatre when the sirens sounded. The actors on the stage carried on as if nothing had happened. Instinctively, I looked for the emergency exits and started to move out of my seat. No one else budged an inch so I stayed put. The true grit and calmness of the audience put me to shame. I thought, 'Who am I to talk of bravery 'on active service' when for months on end civilians in our capital city bear the brunt of these savage attacks and ignore the very real prospect of being blown to bits at any moment?'

One morning I was coming out of the Green Park underground station on Piccadilly when I heard the sound of an approaching aircraft. Looking up I saw a strange object streaking low down just above the roof tops. At first I thought it must be a German plane hit by ant-aircraft fire. Then I saw flames coming from its tail and the next moment it disappeared from view, followed by a loud explosion. Puzzled, I went on my way. Next day, the papers headlined a story about a 'mystery plane'. Later, examination of the wreckage revealed that this was the first 'buzz bomb' or 'doodlebug', Hitler's secret weapon designed to wreak havoc on London and create panic amongst its inhabitants. Thousands were launched in the months that followed. Many were shot down over the south coast by RAF fighters and ack-ack fire. It was certainly unnerving to hear these missiles approach. If, before it reached you, the engine cut out, you ducked for cover. If it was overhead when the engine stopped, you knew you were safe.

Jimmie telephoned one day to announce the receipt of his marching orders sending him back to India in early April. Instead of joining the Indian Signal Corps, he had been 'headhunted' by a clandestine organization called E Group. He promised to fill me in with more details once he found out what they did.

My leave came to an end on 30 April. After four months of comparative indolence I was ready to get back to work. As instructed, I reported to a Movements Officer at an hotel in London to be told that I was to take charge of a batch of young officers and escort them to India. During the voyage I was to lecture them on India and the Indian way of life, teach basic Urdu and generally prepare them for what lay ahead. Three weeks later the troopship (a converted P&O liner) reached Bombay.

My orders were to report to a Jungle Warfare School in Dehra Dun. Once again, the army had decided, in their infinite wisdom, that an officer with active service experience confined to the desert would be best qualified to instruct other officers in the art of fighting in the jungles of Burma and Malaya. My experiences in Iraq had taught me to accept such incredible ineptitude with the cynicism it deserved. Meanwhile, Jimmie had persuaded E Group to ask the Commandant of the Jungle Warfare School to release me for transfer to the E Group establishment. The request was duly granted, much to my relief.

So it was that I found myself in New Delhi, India's capital, being interviewed by the CO, Colonel 'Joey' Jackman. He agreed that Jimmie and I should establish a base in the Arakan from which to conduct clandestine operations behind the Japanese lines in Burma and Malaya.

E Group was an operational intelligence organization in the MI9 family. Our main headquarters for the East was in New Delhi, with

Advance HQs in Calcutta and Colombo where there was also a jungle school. The Group's principal tasks were to make contact with Allied prisoners of war in enemy hands, to advise members of the three services on how to avoid capture, to rescue any who were trapped behind enemy lines (shot down air crews, for example), and to advise all personnel on what to do if taken prisoner. This included how to withstand interrogation (a tall order), how to escape from a Japanese PoW camp (an even taller order) and how to evade recapture. Hence the E stood for 'escape/evasion'.

Members of the Group were seconded from the three services and were made up of British and Commonwealth officers and senior NCOs, many of whom had themselves escaped. Among these was our CO, 'Joey' Jackman, who had effected a dramatic escape from a Shanghai camp in 1942. Units and individuals were parachuted behind enemy lines, or (as in our case) landed by sea on enemy-occupied coastal regions. It was undoubtedly a hazardous occupation, for reasons which became all too apparent.

E Group also boasted a 'toy' department which produced and distributed (mainly to air crews) escape kits comprising such handy devices as a map of the relevant area printed on silk, a miniature compass, a hacksaw, local currency and a small silk handkerchief on which was printed, in several languages/dialects, a message offering a reward to anyone helping the holder. These and other equally ingenious escape aids were sometimes sewn into the airman's uniform. The officer in charge of this secret department was none other than the great Jasper Maskelyne, an internationally famous magician. I was a keen amateur conjuror myself, having been inspired at an early age by an uncle, a member of the Magic Circle, who had introduced me to some of the mysteries of legerdemain. Most of my precious pocket money had been spent on conjuring tricks and on holiday visits to the mind-boggling Maskelyne and Devant magic show at a London theatre. I had even become rash enough to perform before audiences, having built up a modest repertoire over the years and used it to alleviate boredom during wartime periods of inactivity. Gurkha soldiers in particular, being of a childlike disposition, were flatteringly appreciative of my efforts to amaze with amateurish wizardry. Whether this weird talent made me, in their eyes, a better officer I do not know. It certainly helped me to establish a rapport with them which must have been to our mutual benefit.

After a thorough briefing, Jimmie and I set off for Calcutta. There we reported to Colonel Clague, CO of E Group's Advanced HQ, who had himself escaped from a camp in Hong Kong. Briefed again, even more thoroughly, and kitted out for jungle operations, Jimmie and I picked up an American jeep and drove down the coast road, through Chittagong and Cox's Bazar, to our destination in the Arakan.

Our base was to be an abandoned Burmese Forestry Commission basha (hut) in the jungle on the north side of the River Naf, and close to its mouth which was about half a mile across at this point. The nearest village was Teknaf. We had been briefed in Calcutta that Japanese forward troops were somewhere on the south side of the river, diametrically opposite our base. To launch an attack across the river the enemy would need sizeable forces and risk being bombed and strafed by the RAF in the process. Both sides used reconnaissance patrols and the likelihood of a Jap patrol arriving on our doorstep was very real. This made us particularly sensitive to nocturnal noises, caused possibly by monkeys, or possibly not. It was known that the Japanese had developed a system of signals made by imitating monkeys. One night we heard shots fired coming, it seemed, from a few hundred yards away, in the general direction of the river. Jimmie radioed the HQ of the nearby Commando Brigade to be told that units were engaged in night exercises in our area. Jimmie suggested politely that, in future, it would be nice to be given advance warning.

Our living quarters were primitive, to say the least. They consisted of a basic wooden platform, raised ten feet off the ground on sturdy stilts to deter snakes and other undesirable creepy crawlies and to keep the occupants dry during the heavy rains and in the monsoon period. There was one large room doubling as an office and bedroom, and a small veranda for us to sit on in the cool of the evening, sipping drinks. The walls and roof were made of wooden slats reinforced with rattan (palm tree leaves with long stems) and wickerwork. Simple wooden furniture with wicker chairs provided a modicum of comfort. The hut stood in a small compound surrounded by a six-foot wickerwork fence – no barrier to unfriendly intrusion. A hundred yards away, in a clearing, was a larger bungalow which housed our motley crew of Indian and Burmese soldiers, plus a Burmese cook who provided our meals, and one or two Burmese agents. We were well stocked with fresh food, emergency rations, bottles of very strong Jamaican rum and tinned cigarettes, plus spare arms and ammunition.

Early contact was made with the Brigade Major of the Commando Brigade which had set up shop further up the river. Consisting of four battalions (1 and 5 Army Commandos, 42 and 44 Royal Marine Commandos) their task was to send fighting patrols by land and sea into enemy-occupied Burma, and to harass the enemy at every opportunity, using Motor Torpedo Boats provided by the Royal Indian Navy. Jimmie, as the nominal CO of our unit, obtained the Brigadier's agreement to provide us with back-up personnel from the Commando's Special Boat Section (SBS), should we ever need this. The SBS were only too glad to help: we even detected a sense of jealousy of our independent and challenging role.

Jimmie's professional knowledge as a Signals Officer proved invaluable. We kept in continuous wireless touch with our HQ in Calcutta, and were poised for our first operation.

During this waiting period we made furtive sorties across the river in the motor-boat, late in the afternoon as the sun was going down. Apart from a small village, we saw no sign of habitation or of the Japanese. One day we heard a commotion coming from the Indian compound. Investigating, we found that the Indian officer in charge had been bitten by a snake. Alarmingly, this turned out to be a krait, one of the deadliest snakes in Asia, many times more potent than a cobra's venom. The poor man was in great pain. I will never forget seeing him writhing in agony on the ground, suffering from acute cramps, tremors and spasms. We took him immediately to the Commando HQ where he was promptly seen by a doctor and treated with a serum, just in time to save his life. Death from paralysis of the diaphragm is almost inevitable if the victim is not treated within six to twelve hours. It transpired that there was a nest of kraits in the hollow space beneath the bungalow.

Our first operation was to take two Burmese agents some 120 miles down the coast in a Motor Torpedo Boat, land them and fix a rendezvous for their collection at a prearranged date and time. The agents were fully briefed on their mission, which was to find two aircrew survivors of an RAF bomber shot down over their target and believed to be in hiding in the jungle near the coast. The agents were supplied with local currency, small packets of opium, lengths of brightly coloured cotton material for making into *lunghis*, loose-fitting skirts worn by both sexes (including Jimmie and me in our jungle lodge), and other items that could be used to obtain information and assistance in the Japanese-occupied territories.

A week later, we returned to the drop-off area, disembarked from the MTB into a canoe provided by the SBS and paddled towards the shore. It was just after dawn and as we approached the beach and navigated the surf I thought I saw movement amongst the sand dunes. Was I hallucinating? If these were Japanese alerted by the agents, following their capture and torture, our fate was sealed. We wouldn't stand a ghost of a chance. We had no option, however, but to go ahead and land the canoe. There was no turning back. Jumping into the shallow surf, we cocked our sub-machine guns, ready to fight back if this was indeed an ambush, and flung ourselves onto the sandy beach. After a minute or so, we realized there was no one else on the beach, got to our feet and made for the thick bushes beyond where we stayed for some time to make sure the danger had passed.

We made our way cautiously to the rendezvous. The possibility of betrayal was still uppermost in our minds. On arrival, there was no sign of the agents. We waited all morning, hidden from view. The MTB was anchored out at sea, waiting for our return. If we failed to turn up by a certain time they would return to base. This had been agreed with the captain. Reluctantly, we made our way back to the beach, recovered the canoe and paddled out to sea. Safely on board, we gladly accepted a stiff drink and went below to recuperate.

It was impossible to know what happened to the agents. The temptation to profit from the 'bribes' given to them may well have proved to be too great.

Soon after this I went down with a bout of malaria, the first of no less than nine attacks which occurred with regular frequency, a month or so apart. The initial stages were very unpleasant; shaking uncontrollably, perspiring profusely, with nausea, delirium and a burning sensation behind the eyes, one wanted to creep into a corner and die. This lasted twenty-four hours, followed by twenty-four hours of apparent recovery, only to be hit with the same symptoms all over again. There were three cycles of this particular type of malaria, leaving one completely drained. My second attack was worse, so Jimmie insisted on taking me to an Advanced Dressing Station some thirty miles back up the coast. This was a tented hospital where nurses from the QAIMNS (Queen Alexandra's Imperial Military Nursing Service) did sterling work, mopping fevered brows and much, much more. It was rumoured that Commando personnel had been sent to the beach opposite the hospital for rest and relaxation. No one told them there were nurses nearby so they swam in the sea naked as the day they were born, until the Matron appeared, horrified, and blazing with fury and righteous indignation!

Once, visiting Calcutta for a briefing, a malaria attack came on suddenly as I was returning to the HQ on a motorbike. I barely had time to park the machine and stagger into the building before collapsing on the floor. An ambulance took me to a Military Hospital. While there I had a surprise visitor, General Sir Richard O'Connor, who, since January 1945, had been General Officer Commanding-in-Chief, Eastern Army, India, the most important of the four major commands in India. He spent an hour by my bedside reminiscing about our escapades in Italy. To top it all, he invited me to convalesce at his house in Calcutta where I spent several delightful days with the General and his charming wife.

As part of my E Group training I was sent on a parachute course at Rawalpindi, preparatory to being dropped into Burma, Siam or French Indo-China. Flying from Calcutta to New Delhi, I started shivering feverishly, betraying the onset of yet another bout of malaria. Seated on the opposite side of the plane was a Japanese officer, captured in Burma. He was being escorted to the Red Fort in Delhi for interrogation, it being rare for a Jap officer to be caught alive. Noticing my condition he leant over and, in perfect English, asked me what was the matter. I told him I was in the early stages of malaria, whereupon he smiled and said, 'We know all about that. Many of our troops have suffered in the jungles of Malaya and Burma, in fact more than those killed or wounded'. I was surprised, knowing that the Japanese-occupied areas of Asia where quinine, the oldest and most famous anti-malarial drug, was available in abundance. Anti-malaria precautions were rigidly enforced by all British and Commonwealth troops in the jungle areas. This included regular doses of Mepacrin, a less potent drug than quinine, and making sure the body, legs in particular, were always well covered. Infringement of these regulations could result in a court martial.

On arrival at New Delhi, I telephoned my cousin who lived there, and was invited to stay at their house while I recovered. I was able to postpone my parachute course, which I was determined to go through with, come what may. Unfortunately, I contracted another dose of malaria en route by plane to Rawalpindi. This time the pilot radioed ahead for an ambulance to meet us at the airport and take me to the Military Hospital. There I met a major from whom I bought a miniature dachshund called Bungy, which I fell for in a big way and decided to take back to Calcutta. Having made a full recovery, and although a bit groggy, I checked in to the Parachute School for the course. I hired a bicycle and put Bungy in a basket strapped to the back of my bike. During the training periods I arranged for Bungy to be cared for by a chirpy corporal.

The course lasted two weeks, the first spent entirely in the gym, learning how to roll forwards or backwards on landing, depending on how one was swinging when the feet hit the ground. We graduated from a mat on the floor of the gym to jumping from a mock-up of a plane door some six feet up. Finally, we had to jump off a twenty-foot-high platform in a harness attached to cords similar to those on a parachute. This swung backwards and forwards as it descended to the matted floor, necessitating a quick decision as to which way to roll on landing.

Then dawned the day of our first jump. Together with a dozen other students I boarded the RAF transport plane at the nearby airfield. We sat facing each other on either side of the cabin, parachutes strapped to our backs. As we neared the drop zone we stood up, hooked the rip-cord to the sliding rail fixture above us, and shuffled slowly aft. A sergeant instructor, standing by the exit door, waited for the red light to warn us to get ready. Once over the drop zone the green light came on and the sergeant banged the first jumper on the back and yelled 'GO!', whereupon the jumper disappeared out of the door and the second man took his place. When my turn came I found myself remarkably calm, collected and quite resigned to my fate. I felt a thump on my back . . . 'GO!' I jumped out, arms firmly clasped to my sides as we had been taught. I felt the blast of air, saw fleetingly the tailplane, and started to drop like a stone. Within seconds I heard a loud bang, saw the 'chute opening above me and felt myself floating gently and soundlessly earthwards. Jumping at 600 feet there was, sadly, little time to enjoy the scenery. Much too fast I saw the ground coming up to meet me. I landed on my feet, rolled onto my back and lay winded but highly elated.

We did seven daylight jumps and one at night, the latter being more scary, not being able to see the ground in the dark. On the last night there was a celebratory dinner in the mess when the School Commandant pinned a parachute badge on each proud chest.

And so back to Calcutta and then to rejoin Jimmie in our jungle 'hideout'. I had been warned that the RAF banned taking animals on their planes, so I wrapped Bungy in a blanket which I carried, under my arm, onto the aircraft. However, an RAF officer spotted a tail wagging out of the blanket and Bungy was confiscated on the spot. A sad end to an otherwise happy relationship.

In Calcutta, Duggie Clague told me that, before returning to the Naf river base, I was to undertake a special operation in the Andaman Islands. This involved working with an RAF Catalina Squadron to land on remote uninhabited islands and lay dumps of food, water and other emergency kit for use by aircrew unable to make it back to their base in Calcutta or India. This news softened the blow of being told that my history of malaria would very likely prevent me from accompanying Jimmie on a parachute drop into north-east Burma with the objective of contacting British and Commonwealth PoWs on the infamous Burma–Siam Railway.

Chapter Six
Clandestine Catalinas

Early in 1945, in the final stages of the campaign to drive the Japanese out of Burma, the Royal Air Force decided to lay dumps of food, water and other survival kit on a number of remote uninhabited islands off the coasts of Burma and Malaya.

The purpose of these dumps was to provide our bombers and fighters, hit by Japanese anti-aircraft fire or enemy aircraft en route to or from their target in Burma or Malaya, and thus unable to return to their base in India, with a convenient 'half-way house' where they could crash land on an island beach, having first signalled their position. Nearby, hidden in the undergrowth, in stout wooden boxes, would be a cache of canned food and water, first aid kits and signalling devices. They would then have a sporting chance of being rescued by an RAF Catalina flying-boat operating from an Indian airbase.

I was the British officer assigned to the task of laying the first of these dumps. As mentioned before I was an operational intelligence officer seconded to E Group (a branch of MI9).

I had spent several months operating from a remote 'hide-out' on the Arakan coast of Burma, near Akyab, working with the Special Boat Section of the Royal Marine Commandos. With the help of motor torpedo boats supplied by the Royal Indian Navy, our task was to land on the Burmese or Malayan coast, behind enemy lines, and make contact with ditched RAF aircrew, using Burmese agents. These agents, however, were unreliable and tended to vanish without trace after being dropped at the landing point. Nor could they be trusted not to alert the Japanese to our pick-up rendezvous in return for a monetary reward. For this reason, our operations on the Arakan coast were not entirely successful.

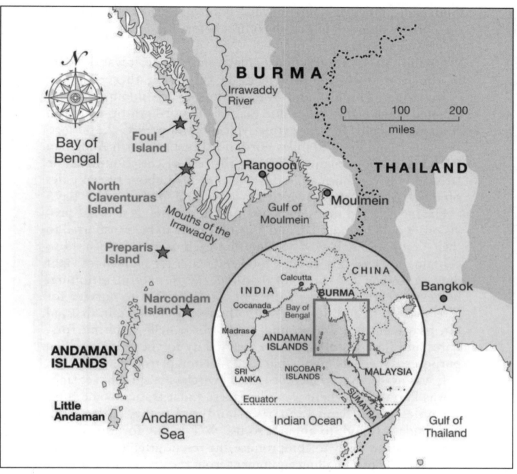

Map 4 – Andaman Islands

The dump-laying scheme was a novel idea, never before attempted. Our E Group HQ in Calcutta, working closely with the RAF HQ, decided that the area to focus on would be the Andaman Islands, located in the Bay of Bengal and forming the western perimeter of the Andaman Sea. The 572 islands of the archipelago are swathed in thick forest. It was known that only thirty-six of these islands were inhabited (still true to this day).

Following the fall of Singapore, the Japanese had occupied the

Andamans, previously under British control. At the end of the war they briefly returned to British control before becoming part of the newly independent state of India.

On the basis of information available at the time, it was decided, in the first instance, to select the following three islands: Narcondam, Preparis and Foul Islands. Narcondam Island is situated some eighty miles due east of the northern tip of North Andaman Island. It is an extinct volcano and rises to 2,600 feet. Preparis Island lies 120 miles north northeast of North Andaman Island and about eighty miles south-west of the mouth of the Irriwaddy River, Burma. Foul Island is located about fifteen miles off the coast of Burma to which it belongs, and south of Mayo Bay.[1]

Having selected the islands, the question arose as to what provisions would be required, and how they were to be transported to their destinations. It was decided that each cache would need to contain, in sealed tins, enough food and water for six men for eight days, allowing for three meals a day. With careful rationing, however, there would be sufficient for eight men to survive for three weeks. In addition, the dump boxes would contain first aid kit, two identification ground strips, three heliograph mirrors, flares and flare pistol and three heavy duty torches for signalling purposes, as well as maps, solidified fuel and petrol lighters.

It was agreed not to include a W/T (wireless/telegraph) set since it was known that there was a Japanese radar station some fifty-six miles away from Preparis Island and eighty miles from Narcondam Island: to attempt to use W/T in any form would be dangerous and likely to compromise any rescue attempt. Likewise, the salvaging of signalling equipment from the abandoned aircraft would serve no useful purpose. The aircraft best suited to this operation was the Catalina flying-boat, named after an island off California. First developed in 1933 by the Consolidated Aircraft Corporation, it was by far the most successful and versatile flying-boat ever built.

The Catalina served with distinction throughout the Second World War in virtually every theatre. After Pearl Harbor, US Navy Catalinas became very active in the Pacific, ranging from bases in Alaska down to the South Pacific. They specialized in night attacks against the Japanese, and operated from the UK, Iceland and bases in North Africa and Gibraltar.

Two Catalina captains were awarded the Victoria Cross. The first was earned by Flight Lieutenant John Cruickshank of 210 Squadron, RAF Coastal Command, for his successful attack in July 1944 on a German U-boat near the Shetland Islands. The second VC was awarded to Flight Lieutenant David Hornell of 162 Squadron, Royal Canadian Air Force. In June 1944, he attacked a surfaced German submarine off the Scottish coast, which was sunk with depth charges. Considerably damaged by a withering flak barrage, the Catalina was ditched and rapidly sank. So, too, was Cruickshank's Cat and one member of his crew was killed while he, and two others, suffered wounds. Although wounded seventy-two times, Cruickshank brought the aircraft back safely.

Earlier in the war, the Catalina had become famous for an event which involved a Catalina from 209 Squadron RAF tracking the German battleship *Bismarck*, shadowing her to a position some 700 miles west of Brest. As a result of the Catalina's contact report the battleship was sunk by the Royal Navy. Searching for the Japanese navy off the coast of Ceylon in April 1942, a Canadian squadron leader, captain of a Catalina patrolling the area, sighted the enemy ships and reported their position. The aircraft was badly damaged by anti-aircraft fire and ditched in the sea. Following battles at sea and in the air, an invasion of Ceylon was prevented. Churchill was reported to have said, 'We were saved from this disaster by an airman on reconnaissance who spotted the Japanese fleet'.

It was decided to use the headquarters of the Catalina flying-boat squadron based at Cocanada (now Kakinada) on the east coast of India (16.93 degrees North – 82.21 degrees East) as our base, albeit some 800 miles from Narcondam, the nearest island. There I spent ten days' intensive training with the men assigned to me, an Indian VCO (Viceroy's Commissioned Officer), two troopers lent by 42 Royal Marine Commando, based in Burma, an Indian NCO, and a corporal wireless operator, all experienced in clandestine operations. Between us we established procedures, on a trial and error basis, for loading the two deflated rubber dinghies and the dump boxes onto the Catalina, inflating the dinghies on a wing and launching them into the water under varying sea conditions. Then came the tricky task of loading the heavy dump boxes into the dinghies, and fixing the outboard motor onto the lead boat. The party would then board the dinghies and motor as fast as possible towards the shore, careful to avoid being swamped in the surf which could sometimes be heavy. The landing drill was practised relentlessly; those few moments after landing on the open beach in broad daylight were critical: the boxes had to be offloaded, the dinghies deflated and all equipment hidden in undergrowth with lightning speed. Training completed, the party flew back to Calcutta to prepare for the ensuing operations.

The original ETD (Estimated Time of Departure) from Bally, Calcutta, was the night of 18/19 February. Owing to bad weather conditions at Narcondam Island reported by the Met Department, the operation was delayed at the eleventh hour. By midday on 20 February a Met report stated that conditions were now favourable.

The party, consisting of myself, Troopers Sage and Golder, Royal Marine Commandos, Corporal Lewis, Royal Signals (W/T operator), Jemadar (equivalent to lieutenant) Saidbaz, Indian Army, and Naik (equivalent to corporal) Gul Mohamed, Indian Army, left HQ at 9.30 pm. The stores and miscellaneous kit had been previously stowed in the Catalina. We boarded the aircraft at 11.30 pm and were airborne at half-past midnight on 21 February.

Conditions on board were extremely cramped. Catalinas were not designed to accommodate six additional bodies, plus their equipment, four heavy wooden crates, digging tools, and the two deflated dinghies. The crew consisted of the squadron leader captain, a co-pilot, a navigator and a flight engineer. Aft of the cockpit bulkhead was the navigator's table on the port side, and the radio/radar operator's position to starboard. Beyond this, the flight engineer sat in a confined space in one of the two 'blisters', each of which housed a 0.5-inch machine gun and were the main point of entry to the hull.

For the take-off, the captain ordered my men to move as far forward as possible, I, myself standing between the pilot and co-pilot giving me a ringside view of the take-off procedures. As the aircraft gathered speed, the spray from the floats increased dramatically until it seemed that the strong plumes of water must damage the fuselage, particularly in the 'blister' area.

For some seven long hours I lay curled up under the navigator's table, unable to sleep, while the Catalina, cruising at no more than 110mph, driven by two 1,200hp Pratt & Whitney air-cooled radial piston engines, slowly made its way to the target area, a sitting duck for any Japanese aircraft patrolling the area.

We reached Narcondam Island at 7.15 am, where weather and sea conditions were found to be too bad to land. It was overcast and clouded and there was a heavy swell. The captain, a New Zealand squadron leader, decided to fly on to Preparis Island where weather conditions were slightly better, although the swell was still bad. The aircraft circled the island at a low altitude and the air-gunner in the port blister reported having seen smoke along the beach on the east coast. (This was later found to be a slight haze.) The aircraft landed successfully 300 yards off the west coast at 8.45 am.

Rain and swell made the inflation and loading of dinghies extremely difficult, but the co-ordinated efforts of all concerned overcame this. Both dinghies were loaded up and ready to move off at 9.15 am.[2]

The heavy swell helped to carry the dinghies in to shore, where the surf was negligible, and a successful landing was made on the beach at 9.30 am. Corporal Lewis signaled the letter 'B' to confirm that we were safely ashore, then the letter 'K' and the aircraft left to return to base.

Whilst dinghies were being beached and unloaded, I made a quick recce, and found a small clearing in the jungle off the beach opposite our landing point. All stores, equipment and dinghies were carried to the clearing and dumped. There were no signs of any 'foreign bodies', and as it was still raining hard the first problem was to find a dry place for the stores, etc.

A small space was cleared under trees a short distance away in the jungle. Both dinghies were turned upside down and suspended at a height of ten feet above the ground, thus forming a reasonable waterproof shelter.

At 11.30 am the party was split up for a quick recce to make sure that the area in the immediate vicinity of our HQ was clear of Japanese or locals, and to find possible places for burying the dump. The jemadar remained at HQ to act as guard and ensure that all stores were kept as dry as possible. In case of trouble the alarm would be given by firing three rounds in rapid succession.

At noon the two parties returned to HQ. No signs of Japanese or locals. No suitable place for dump. Thick jungle encountered in interior.

At 12.30 pm Sage and Mac brewed up tea. One twenty-four-hour emergency ration tin was issued between each pair. At 1.30 pm Golder and I set off on a recce of the beach to the north of HQ, while the rest prepared the dump stores for the move to the chosen spot.

About 500 yards along the beach we came across two lone coconut trees on the fringe of the jungle at the entrance to a dried up riverbed. I chose a suitable place for the dump near the second tree. We also found a pool of water, tested it and found it brackish but drinkable. I sent Golder back to HQ with orders to keep within the fringe of jungle off the beach and to return with the carrying party the same way.

An hour later the party arrived with the first load plus digging tools. Golder reported that, owing to the density of undergrowth, it had not been feasible to return through the jungle and he had had to use the beach. The heavy weight of the boxes had made it hard going on the soft sand. The party returned to HQ for the remaining stores and we started on digging the dump trench.

1600 hrs: Party returned and boxes lowered into prepared trench. (Rough dimensions: depth – 4 ft, length – 6 ft, width – 3 ft.) Spaces between boxes filled in and the whole covered with 6-inch layer of soil (surface being left uneven). Five medium-sized stones placed on top of mound and area re-covered with dead leaves to blend with surroundings. Finally, a branch about six feet long was cut from a tree, one end of which was embedded in loose soil under centre rock with the other end resting diagonally in the fork of a tree stump to one side.

The rain had stopped at about 3.00 pm, but all clothes and personal kit were still saturated. Party returned to HQ at 6.00 pm. The W/T operator reported that no signals had been picked up between 4.00 and 6.00 pm. (Arrangements had been made before leaving No. 1 Advance HQ E Group, Calcutta, that any important messages would be transmitted from HQ between these times.)

Preparations were made for the night. After a meal, jungle hammocks were slung between trees all around the improvised shelter of upturned dinghies.

A sentry roster was made out covering the period from 7.00 pm to 5.30 am. Orders issued to sentries were:

To patrol camp area and keep moving

To avoid making any noise

To open fire on anyone approaching without calling out precautionary 'Halt'

Not to use a torch unless absolutely necessary

Last man on guard to rouse all personnel (at 5.30 am)

If any signs of trouble, sentry to waken me

The night passed without event. The next morning, at 5.30 am after a mug of scalding tea, all stores and kit were packed up and No. 2 dinghy deflated. No. 1 dinghy was taken down to the beach and loaded up. This was completed by 7.00 am.

Half an hour later, as there was no sign of the returning aircraft, I sent Sage and MacLaughlin off along the beach to the south on a quick recce of the dump to see whether it had been disturbed during the night. Accompanied by the W/T operator and Golder, I did a recce of the beach to the north. Both parties were to return immediately the aircraft was sighted and recognized.

By 8.00 am there was still no sign of the aircraft, so I decided to carry on round to the east side of the Island and inspect an abandoned vessel identified in aerial photos.

We reached the wreck at about 11.00 am, boarded her and carried out an extensive search. It was a medium size fishing vessel, seemingly blown onto the beach in a severe storm. Like the famous *Marie Celeste*, there was evidence of her crew having abandoned the ship at short notice, leaving everything untouched – a cooked meal in the small galley; clothing lying around; bedding in bunks unmade; fishing tackle neatly stowed on deck. There was no sign of arms or ammunition. I realized that the crew might well be hiding somewhere on the island, awaiting rescue, possibly by a Japanese naval ship. So we would need to be extra cautious and keep a sharp lookout for them on our way back to the dump area. In the event, we saw no sign of the fishermen. It was likely that they had been swept off the boat in the storm before it was hurled up onto the beach

The recce of the ship concluded, I decided to continue round the island. The going was hard owing to the fact that it was necessary to walk sometimes on the soft sandy beach, sometimes on the jagged rocks and where there was no beach we had to wade waist deep in the sea amongst the coral reef. Added to this we were carrying no water and had had no food before starting out as the original intention was to be away from HQ one hour at the most. As a result we were suffering from extreme exhaustion. By 4.30 pm the whole party was safely back at HQ, the total distance covered being nearly twenty miles.

At 6.00 pm a meal was prepared and eaten, after which a fresh sentry roster was made out covering the period from 10.00 pm to 5.30 am, the W/T operator and Golder being excused guard after their long day's march. The orders to sentries were in no way relaxed, despite the fact that it could be safely assumed that there were no 'foreign bodies' on the island. The night passed peacefully enough, except for the unceasing antics of large numbers of indigenous rodents which quite obviously (and naturally) strongly objected to our presence and, moreover, appeared eager to relieve us of the little that remained of our rations.

I was roused at 4.00 am to take over guard duties from Sage who insisted on staying up to assist in the preparing of breakfast at 5.00 am. After breakfast, kit was repacked and No. 1 dinghy loaded up, ready for the return of the aircraft, which was due to arrive between 7.00 and 7.30 am. It was decided that No. 1 dinghy would be unable to take all kit, plus No. 2 dinghy, plus the whole party in one go, and that a double trip would be necessary.

At 7.00 am an aircraft was heard in the distance and everyone took cover in case it happened to be an enemy plane. As soon as the Catalina had been recognized the letter 'C' was signalled ('we are returning to aircraft'). Although there were no clouds and little wind the swell was very heavy, and the flying-boat had great difficulty in landing.

Leaving Sage, the W/T operator, Golder, MacLaughlin and the naik on the beach, the jemadar and I embarked on No. 1 dinghy and set out for the aircraft. The dinghy was badly swamped getting through the heavy surf. Once beyond the surf the motor was started up, but the safety line became entangled in the propeller, and had to be cut free. On nearing the aircraft I noticed that it was a different Catalina with a different crew, but was greatly relieved to see Squadron Leader Harrod on board. Several abortive attempts to come up alongside were made before success was finally achieved.

The dinghy was made fast and all stores were offloaded into the blister. I reported to the squadron leader who said that he had received a Met report the previous evening giving indications of bad weather conditions in this area. He had decided to take one of the other aircraft down to the Island and drop food and water in containers, and also a message explaining the situation. On arrival at the Island he picked up the signal flashed from the beach and decided to risk landing, despite the adverse conditions

The squadron leader volunteered to accompany me on the return trip to the shore. So, leaving the jemadar on the aircraft, the dinghy was taken back to pick up the remaining personnel. By this time the state of the surf had worsened considerably and the dinghy was swamped time and time again, filling it almost completely with water. When the time came to return to the aircraft the motor refused to function, seawater having flooded the carburettor and other vital parts, which meant the dinghy had to be rowed.

With great difficulty the dinghy was manoeuvred up close to the port blister, a line was thrown and it was hauled up alongside. All except Sage and I embarked on the aircraft, which had meanwhile drifted dangerously close to the shore. To avoid any risk of her fouling rocks, the aircraft was taxied out to sea, but the wash caused by so doing swamped the dinghy which all but capsized. Eventually No. 1 dinghy was in a position to be hauled up onto the blister. This done, it was deflated, re-rolled and stowed away.

At 8.30 am the aircraft taxied round to the east (leeward) side of the island where it was more sheltered, and the swell, though heavy, was not so great. It was an anxious moment for all when the aircraft moved forward for the take-off, slowly rising up on the step beneath the floats. As she gathered speed the Catalina bounced heavily across and at right angles to the rollers until sufficient speed was reached to make her airborne. Squadron Leader Harrod, who was piloting the plane, told me later that it was touch and go, and had he not managed to gain enough airspeed, forcing the stick (column) back by using every ounce of his strength, 'the Cat would have nose dived into the drink, and it would have been "curtains" for all of us'.

At 9.30 am the aircraft set course for base and Coconada was reached safely at 3.00 pm on 23 February. The second part of the operation was delayed owing to bad weather conditions in the area of the Andamans. By midday on 26 February the weather had cleared sufficiently to be able to proceed with the Narcondam operation. During these few days of waiting all arms and ammunition had been thoroughly cleaned and overhauled by the RAF armourers who were extremely obliging and did everything they could to help. This applied equally to the Marine Craft Section who inspected and cleaned the outboard motor. The bolt on the clamp had jammed as a result of corrosion caused by seawater and this was dealt with and rectified by the Naval Workshops.

All personnel kit was dried out and repacked, this time keeping the jungle hammocks separate. No. 1 dinghy was dried and re-rolled. Cloth caps were made for the party by an RAF tailor, with a KD attachment for protection of the neck and back against the sun, which were found to be very useful. Preparations were made to leave on the night of 26 February, and all boxes and stores, etc., were loaded into the aircraft in the morning.

After a final briefing and inspection of air photos, we embarked at 11 pm, and were airborne at 11.30 pm. At 7.30 am we reached Narcondam Island where the weather was perfect and the sea like a millpond. The aircraft circled the island and landed on the south-west side. She was then taxied round to the east side where a suitable beach had been sighted. I conferred with the squadron leader and we decided to land at the northern end of the longest beach. The aircraft taxied to within 200 yards of the beach. While the aircraft was still taxiing, No. 1 dinghy was inflated on the port wing without any difficulty.

It was decided to increase the load on No. 2 dinghy by the addition of two dump boxes. When No. 2 dinghy was ready I ordered Golder to row off towards the beach, as the distance was so short, and indicated an approximate landing point. The current proved to be stronger than anticipated and No. 2 dinghy landed 200 yards lower down beach. When No. 1 dinghy was ready, I informed the squadron leader who expressed a desire to accompany the party ashore and remain with them on the island in order to gain first-hand knowledge of the methods employed by the Army party for the actual laying of the dump. I readily agreed to this proposal.

We landed on the beach at 8.30 am, and as there were no signs of any Japanese or locals, the 'OK' was signalled to the aircraft which took off and left for Cocanada. All being well, the Catalina would return the following morning to pick us up.

All stores and dinghies were dumped off the beach under cover and camouflaged. As mentioned above, this was vital at this stage when the danger of being spotted by low-flying aircraft was considerable. Friendly planes were just as liable as enemy planes to strafe anything that appeared in the least suspicious. The W/T operator, Sage and McLaughlin set off on a quick recce of the north end of beach, while the squadron leader, Golder and I recce'ed the beach to the south.

After a strong brew of tea, the jemadar and naik were sent on a recce for water. They returned an hour later having found no water but had succeeded in shooting three hornbill birds and unearthed an old skull. The former were duly cooked and produced for lunch, and eaten with relish by the jemadar and naik.

At 11.30 am I carried out a lone recce along the beach, and discovered an ideal place for the dump less than fifty yards away from the camp. It consisted of a lone tree that had been blown down and lay across and at right angles to the beach. Behind, and close to the end of this tree, stood the tree stump, which was about ten feet high and five feet wide. I returned to the camp and detailed a carrying party to transfer the boxes, etc., to this chosen spot. The dump was laid in the curved niche on the north-west side of the stump, the ground being first levelled out. The boxes and tins were placed side by side in this niche and finally completely covered over with pebbles and rocks taken from the beach

The dump took one and a half hours to lay and was finished by 1.30 pm. Photos were taken of it from every conceivable angle.

At 2.00 pm Sage, MacLaughlin, Golder and I climbed the hill behind camp. We found it very hard going, owing to the density of jungle and the steepness of the hill, and after three-quarters of an hour we returned to camp. Back at camp, Golder and MacLaughlin had sighted a herd of goats on the cliff nearby and shot one with a carbine. It was cooked and eaten as part of the evening meal. This indicated the presence of fresh water but, being mountain goats, this water may have been fairly high up the mountain.

At 1 am an aircraft passed close to the Island. It was a Catalina, probably on reconnaissance or air sea rescue work. Otherwise nothing unusual occurred during the night.

At 6.30 am two RAF Liberators appeared on the scene, circled the Island two or three times, then made off in a south-westerly direction. (Narcondam Island was frequently used as a 'turning off point' by long-range bombers, etc.)

This time we decided to use both dinghies, and they were loaded up ready for the arrival of the aircraft. The Catalina duly landed at 7.15 am and within fifteen minutes the party had re-embarked on the aircraft. No. 2 dinghy was deflated on the wing and No. 1 between blisters. Soon after we were airborne and arrived back safely at Coconada at 4 pm on 28 February, our mission successfully accomplished.

On this last operation the landing and pick-up procedures went without a hitch. At the same time, many lessons were learnt: for example, (a) don't send dinghies ashore independently if it could be avoided; (b) it was better to use both dinghies when returning to the aircraft, rather than either over-load No. 1, or make a double trip; (c) ensure that there was a means of securing the outboard motor when it was tilted forward on nearing the beach, otherwise it had to be held in position which was very tiring and unnecessary; (d) don't on any account move about if any aircraft approached the Island – keep well hidden and observe; (e) get all stores, dinghies, etc. under cover as soon as possible after landing; and (f) last, but not least, don't rely on having any dry clothes to change into.[3]

NOTES

1. It was decided that Foul Island was too close to the Burmese coast and therefore the idea of placing a dump there was abandoned.
2. I learned later that the navigator had been awarded the Air Force Cross for his remarkable achievement in finding the two targets with such unerring precision.
3. Later on, dumps were laid at North Claventuras Island, Oyster Island and South Chance Island. The number of dump boxes varied and where fresh water was available, no tinned water was included.

Chapter Seven

Sunset in South-east Asia

The lumbering RAF transport plane slowly circled the airfield and made a bumpy landing on the sun-scorched runway. The flight to Bombay from Colombo, Ceylon, had been uneventful. I was glad to be on the move again after a welcome spell at E Group's 'rest and relaxation' base, a spacious if rather dilapidated bungalow facing the beach at Mount Lavinia, a few miles out of Colombo.

Months of nervous tension close to the front lines on Burma's Arakan Coast, with occasional brief spells behind the Japanese lines, had made me appreciate life's uncomplicated pleasures. Here was a sandy beach, cooled by sea breezes, to laze on by day, and a sprung bed (devoid of mosquito net) to luxuriate on at night. Here were offered regular meals, prepared with loving care by an inspired Goanese cook, who surpassed himself on Sundays with his soporific curry lunches, inducing lengthy siestas lasting into the early evening. Here one could indulge oneself, with relative impunity, in post-prandial forays to sample the bright lights of the nearby city; and perchance to share, for a few brief hours, the company of some young lady, maybe even one of the many naval uniformed maidens employed at Admiral Lord Louis Mountbatten's Colombo head-quarters.

One memorable evening a colleague and I celebrated his birthday at the Galle Face Hotel, a rambling, old-fashioned Edwardian edifice on the city's seafront. Having dined and wined rather well, and undaunted by competition from handsome, smart, and suave staff officers who frequented this particular hostelry, my companion and I lured two fresh-faced, fair-haired Wrens (Women's Royal Naval Service) onto a crowded dance floor on the terrace overlooking the harbour. Bathed in moonlight, this was indeed a romantic setting. Somehow we persuaded them to desert their party and join us at our

115

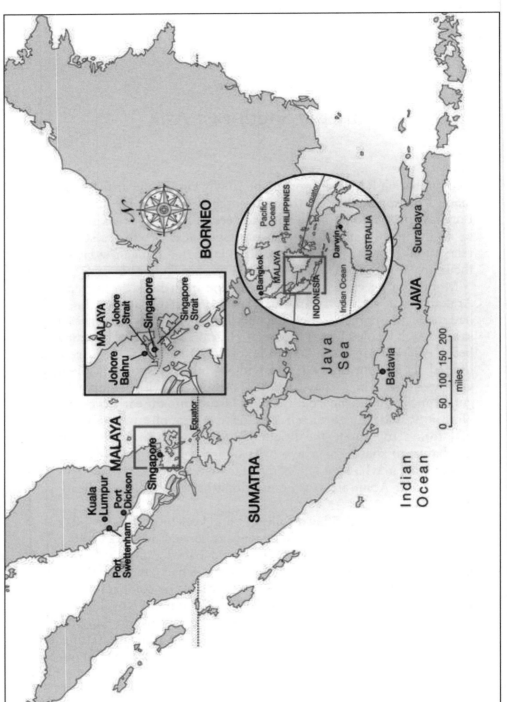

Map 5 – South-east Asia

The Grand Entrance to Old College, Royal Military College, Sandhurst. (Now the Royal Military Academy Sandhurst).

Bayonet training, India.

Vickers machine-gun training, School of Infantry, Saugor, India.

The Author.

The Author with his shotgun prior to a
big-game shoot in nearby jungle.

The Author on his charger before a Quetta meet.

Gurkha soldiers in the author's Machine Gun Platoon in Iraq, 1942.

Gurkha soldiers in the Western Desert. (Gurkha Museum, Winchester)

Author's 'mug shot' as a prisoner of war at PG21 PoW Camp, Chieti, February 1943.

Author demonstrating method of escape over the wall from Camp PG19, Bologna. This photograph was taken after the war.

The Author on the camp wall, also after the war. At the time of the escape a 4-foot barbed-wire fence topped this wall.

The Monastery at Fonte Avellano where the monks gave us refuge.

The farmhouse outside the monastery.

The Monastery courtyard. We escaped from the top floor, third window from right, when a German search party arrived unexpectedly.

The Berigotti family, one of many families who sheltered us on their farms during our escape.

Captain Jimmie Ferguson, who shared the author's adventures.

Lt Gen Sir Richard O'Connor, AVM Owen T. Boyd and Gen Sir Philip Neame VC, the VIP party whom the author and Jimmie Ferguson helped escape from behind German lines in Italy. (Imperial War Museum: CNA 2378)

The hunting lodge in Cervia where the author and Jimmie Ferguson rendezvoused with the two generals and the AVM.

Signor Terenzi, his wife and daughter.

Signora Cognetti-Fratini.

Delpiccalo farmyard, watching out for a German foraging party approaching the farm.

Bridge at the port of Rimini on the Adriatic coast. En route to Cervia the escape party cycled across this bridge.

The escape party hid in this house in Cervia. It was owned by Marshal Graziani, the Italian Minister of Defence.

Cattolica, the port from which the party eventually made its escape in a fishing boat.

Preparing for parachuting in India.

A Consolidated Catalina flying-boat alights on the water. It was in a Catalina that the author flew to the Andaman Islands to establish supply dumps for shot-down aircrew. (Photo courtesy Mike Stroud Collection)

Alongside a moored Catalina, training to load and remove boxes from the aircraft. It took a considerable amount of skill as well as patience to load equipment and material into a Cat. Considerable practice was required.

No 1

No 2

JX 32!

The side observation blisters could be used to load dinghies. Here Catalina Mk IVB JX325 of No. 212 Squadron, the unit that undertook the special duties flights to the Andaman Islands, is being used for training.

Battling through the surf from the flying-boat to the shore. The surf was the biggest obstacle. As always, there was a right way to do this – in this case, nose first as someone has written on the photograph. Narcomdan and Preparis islands were both used to establish secret dumps but Foul Island was considered too close to Burma to be used safely.

Unloading equipment from the dinghies on dry sand. This photograph was taken during training at Calcutta.

A silk handkerchief issued by E Group to aircrew operating in the Burma/Siam area. The handkerchief was sewn into the uniform and the message, which was printed in several languages/dialects, offered a reward to anyone who helped the holder.

Members of No. 2 War Crimes Investigation Team (WCIT) at Batavia airport: from left Sqn Ldr Bill Pitts, Capt Godfrey, Lt Cdr Gaunt, the team's secretary, Lt Van Der Weg and three British NCOs

A Japanese war crimes suspect, Lt Soni, being escorted from Batavia to Singapore to stand trial for crimes committed whilst he was commandant of the men's PoW camp at Batavia. He is escorted by (L to R) Capt Godfrey, Capt Lewis and Lt Van Der Weg.

The staff of No. 2 WCIT outside their HQ in Surabaya. The author is fifth from right and on his right is Lenka.

Vladimir Trechikoff, the White Russian portrait painter, in Batavia.

The author in the uniform of his regiment, 8th Gurkha Rifles.

candle-lit table for iced champagne and supper, interspersed with increasingly uninhibited dancing. We abandoned ourselves unashamedly to the wild, hedonistic pleasures that presented themselves so unexpectedly. Later, returning them in our jeep to their cloistered quarters, we found ourselves taking a circuitous but richly rewarding route via a secluded moonlit beach. As the popular saying went, 'Up with the lark. To bed with a Wren'.

It was early August 1945. The Americans had all but obliterated two of Japan's largest industrial cities. The first atomic bomb was exploded a thousand feet above Hiroshima on 6 August, the second over Nagasaki three days later. The shock waves reverberated around the world. A few days later, while I was enjoying a long, cool drink in the bar of the Taj Mahal Hotel, Bombay, news came of Japan's surrender. The celebrations lasted well into the small hours – until, in fact, the bar ran dry. At midnight a spectacular fireworks display lit up the harbour and drew thunderous cheers from the tens of thousands thronging the surrounding streets and the waterfront around the 'Gateway to India' monument, Bombay's Marble Arch.

My orders (irrespective of Japan's capitulation) were to prepare a small unit of E Group for the invasion of Malaya. I immediately set about acquiring, from the Special Services section of an ordnance depot nearby, the equipment needed for our operations. This included maps, compasses, Malayan currency, American dollars, weapons, ammunition, emergency rations and protective clothing – all the paraphernalia needed to keep us going under what might still prove to be fairly rough conditions, even though the war had ended. Clandestine units such as E Group were given carte blanche choice in the selection of equipment. I took full advantage of this top priority treatment.

In the meantime, the other members of my team were arriving in Bombay, jubilant to a man that the war was over, but excited nevertheless at the prospect of further adventures in the jungles of Malaya.

Despite Japan's timely capitulation, we were told that the 'invasion' (code-named ZIPPER) was to go ahead as planned. Convoys being assembled in Calcutta, Ceylon and Bombay would converge on the west coast of Malaya where the landings were to take place. Even after six years of 'real' war, it all sounded adventurous and exciting if, under the circumstances, somewhat redundant.

On 30 August we embarked on a troopship and joined a flotilla anchored a mile or so out in the Bombay Roads. There we sat for four frustrating days, half hoping, half expecting to be disembarked once the futility of the operation finally dawned on the High Command in Delhi. At night the lights on the waterfront sparkled and beckoned enticingly. Memories of pleasurable evenings spent in the fleshpots of Bombay only increased our feelings of frustration.

Then suddenly, early one morning, we were conscious of slight vibrations and found ourselves moving slowly out to sea. The ship was overcrowded, as troopships invariably were; there was little room for exercise or indeed any other form of recreation. We spent the daylight hours enjoying whatever amenities there were – eating, drinking, sunning ourselves on the cramped decks, playing cards, reading, chatting and, of course, sleeping. Mindful of my responsibilities, I gathered my team together to brief them on the sealed orders that had arrived on board just before we sailed, disclosing the precise destination of the task force and its operational plans. The E Group unit's main task was to make early contact with prisoner-of-war camps in central Malaya and to organize the supply of food and other vital necessities, preferably from local resources.

The convoy steamed steadily south to Ceylon, then eastwards into the Bay of Bengal. One week later, passing between the Indian islands of Andaman and Nicobar, we sailed south-east into the converging Straits of Malacca, between Sumatra and Malaya.

It was just as well the Japanese had surrendered. The landings on D-Day, 10 September, on a stretch of the west coast of Malaya, midway between Port Dickson and Port Swettenham, were little short of catastrophic. Right from the start, it was transparently obvious that there had been little (if any) training for an amphibious exercise of this magnitude and complexity. When the first wave of troops, heavily laden with weapons and other accoutrements of war, began to scramble down the nets into the bobbing landing craft below, there was a strong sense of impending chaos. Had the landings been opposed, even lightly, there would have been a bloody massacre – no less. Whatever intelligence had been gathered on conditions prevailing on that particular stretch of the Malayan coastline proved totally inadequate. When the tide receded, landing craft, stuck fast on submerged sandbanks, were left high and dry, like beached whales. A 3-ton lorry, off-loaded into soft sand, had slowly subsided until only the tilted superstructure remained visible, providing yet another hazard for following waves of landing craft heading for the shore. As it was, my own group was fortunate to reach land more or less intact, after ten long hours cooped up in cramped conditions on a landing craft before wading onto the beach through five feet of water, struggling to keep arms, ammunitions and equipment dry.

Next day, having successfully browbeaten a quartermaster sergeant into handing over to our safekeeping a 15cwt truck and a jeep, we made our way to Kuala Lumpur, a hundred miles or so inland. Just outside the town we reached our first objective, a PoW camp containing more than 2,000 Indian prisoners, most of whom were in a shocking condition. Emaciated, weak, half-starved and suffering from a variety of debilitating diseases, many were scarcely able to stand upright. And yet, having somehow learned of our coming, an almost immaculate guard of honour, provided by the Gurkha contingent, greeted our arrival. At that moment I was prouder than ever before to have served in the Gurkha Rifles.

We established our headquarters in a private house provided by a wealthy Chinese businessman who overwhelmed us with his welcome. This palatial dwelling was fully furnished and complete with electric lighting, fans, running water and sprung beds. We were even able to enjoy the luxury of iced drinks, thanks to a large American refrigerator proudly shown us by the owner and, miraculously, in working order.

The Chinese had been treated atrociously by the Japanese occupation forces and so were even more overjoyed to see us than the Malays themselves. They rallied round enthusiastically to offer practical help of every kind. Within a very short space of time I was able to requisition from the Japanese some vitally needed transportation with which to convey food and other supplies to the relieved PoW and internee camps in the area, including a Chevrolet saloon, an ambulance, an elderly Austin Ten and a rather rusty MG.

The day after our arrival in Kuala Lumpur I had the satisfaction of attending a ceremony to mark the formal surrender of the Japanese Army in Malaya. This was accepted by our Corps Commander, Lieutenant General Ouvry Roberts, a brief, simple yet dignified ceremony in the city's central park. General Roberts had been Commander of 20 Indian Infantry Brigade in Iraq in 1941. This was part of 10th Indian Division (otherwise known as PAIFORCE) and had included my battalion, 2/8th Gurkha Rifles, in which I had served as Machine Gun Officer, before becoming a Brigade Intelligence Officer in the Western Desert.

A few days later I celebrated my twenty-fifth birthday by having the pleasure of personally disarming a large group of Japanese soldiers and relieving their commanding officer of his sword. Ceremoniously, the officer unsheathed his sword, knelt down, kissed the polished blade, and then rose slowly to his feet. He bowed low three times and handed the sword to me, his face impassive and betraying none of the emotion he doubtless felt.

To those who had first-hand experience of Japanese tenacity in battle, their ferocity in the face of hopeless odds, their willingness to be killed rather than face capture, it was astonishing to witness the calmness and resignation with which they accepted their ultimate and total defeat. There were, of course, isolated exceptions, of which the following is a simple example. A Japanese officer in charge of a working party detailed to shift a rubbish dump objected vociferously when I approached to take a photograph. Ignoring his protestations, I promptly went nearer and took several close-ups, much to the delight of a crowd of Malayans enjoying the humiliation of their erstwhile tormentors.

Meanwhile, an organization known as RAPWI – Release of Allied Prisoners of War and Internees – had been established by Admiral Lord Louis Mountbatten, Supreme Allied Commander, who recognized the urgent need to repatriate the tens of thousands of men, women and children who had suffered so terribly at the hands of the Japanese. Thus, RAPWI was set up with commendable speed, using the combined resources of all the clandestine forces which had been operating in this theatre, such as the one to which I was attached, and whose specialized covert services were now superfluous.

Having received orders to report forthwith to Singapore, I set off from Kuala Lumpur on 20 September by road, a 400-mile journey through Seramban, down the coastal road, via the port of Malacca, through Muar, Bata Pahat and Johore Bahru, and finally over the causeway that joined the Malay mainland to the Island of Singapore. Down this same road hordes of Japanese soldiers had pedalled their bicycles southwards in their relentless drive on Singapore in February 1942.

On the way I encountered parties of armed Japanese troops

moving into concentration areas – mostly, it seemed, under their own steam and without supervision. As I passed, these little men in their drab uniforms dutifully bowed and saluted. Many of the Malay *kampongs* had erected an archway over the main road, festooned with flowers and colourful paper decorations, and sometimes super-imposed with a large banner proclaiming 'WELCOME TO OUR LIBERATORS'. We had seen press pictures of our victorious troops driving through the streets of liberated towns in France; nubile girls scrambling to kiss the victors, showering them with floral tributes, champagne, wine and confetti; bands playing, people dancing in the streets and other displays of ecstatic jubilation.

Here, whilst the Malays appeared generally glad to see the back of the hated invaders, their jubilation at the arrival of Allied forces was markedly more restrained. The return of colonialism in any form obviously was not regarded with huge enthusiasm. In the final stages of the war, the first signs of Communism had appeared ominously and were spreading rapidly through the jungles of the Malayan peninsula. Already, gangs of guerrillas, armed with weapons supplied during the hostilities by our clandestine forces, or abandoned by the Japanese, were raiding villages, ambushing trains and generally causing severe disruption. Many of them had infil-trated from Communist China during the last few months, setting up scattered pockets of agitators and organizing supply dumps in the depths of the jungle. These same bandits were to occupy the attention of an entire British army corps over the next several years.

I could not help reflecting, as I crossed the famous causeway over which Japanese forces had swarmed on 15 February 1942, in the final assault on what had been foolishly considered an impregnable fortress, how close I had been to ending my war, if not my life, either in Singapore itself or somewhere in Malaya.

As described in Chapter 1, in April 1940, following a period of mobilization and intensive training in Quetta, Baluchistan, on the north-western boundary of India, my battalion had been equipped and prepared for active service in Malaya. Indeed, together with the rest of the Brigade, we had embarked at Karachi, all set to sail to Singapore, when sealed orders arrived on board diverting our entire Brigade to Iraq where the country's leader, Rashid Ali, seemed hell-bent on encouraging the Germans to occupy Iraq and deny its vital oilfields to the British. Convinced of a German victory, and with promises of German help, he had seized power in Baghdad only to be thwarted in his evil intentions by the timely arrival of 10th Indian Division, which rapidly took control of all the vital strategic points.

Unwittingly, Mr Ali had done us a good turn. Instead of sharing the hideous fate of Commonwealth forces captured at the fall of Singapore, we spent a year chasing around the deserts of Iraq, with sporadic sorties into Syria and over the Persian borders. The Division joined Eighth Army in the Western Desert in May 1942 and, shortly thereafter, I was taken prisoner and spent the next fifteen months languishing in various prisoner-of-war camps in Italy – a singularly tedious and unrewarding experience.

On arrival at E Group headquarters in Singapore, I reported to Lieutenant Colonel Leslie Pritchard who told me not to bother to unpack as I was to fly to Batavia, Java the following morning. 'Not to worry, old boy,' said Leslie cheerfully, as he guided me con-solingly towards the makeshift bar and poured me a stiff *chota peg* (whiskey and soda). 'At least you'll have the honour of being one of the first British Officers to enter the Dutch East Indies since the Japanese packed it in.' I thanked him politely, if unenthusiastically.

Leslie explained that I was to head up an investigation team to collect evidence of atrocities committed by the Japanese and Koreans in Java. We would question released Allied prisoners of war and internees, as well as Indonesians, and, wherever possible, identify informers and collaborators. I was to make my own arrangements with the incoming British forces headquarters for accommodation, rations, transport and anything else I needed, and to liaise closely with the field security section and the divisional intelligence units when they appeared on the scene. 'I'm sure you will have a warm welcome. So long as you explain that you are not Dutch,' he added hurriedly. How right he proved to be – if not quite in the way he meant it.

The next day I flew to Batavia and found myself a room in what had been Java's leading hotel, the Hotel des Indes, and which now looked rather the worse for wear after prolonged occupation by the Japanese. Such staff as existed succeeded in making themselves conspicuous by their absence; and, when they did materialize, they were none too friendly, no doubt suspecting me of being an advance guard of the returning Dutch colonials.

As soon as the RAPWI Control Staff arrived in Batavia I contacted their second-in-command, Major Eggleton, and explained my mission. Seriously understaffed themselves, he was not sympathetic to my request for the transfer to my command (as agreed by Colonel Pritchard in Singapore) of Captain Godfrey, Royal Marines, an E Group Officer who had been seconded to RAPWI. Admittedly, RAPWI faced the Herculean task of taking care of the immediate needs of the tens of thousands of half-starved prisoners of war and civilian internees discovered in the numerous camps in Java at the cessation of hostilities and organizing their rapid repatriation. However, despite the urgency of RAPWI's task, and since Admiral Mountbatten had decreed that the investigation of war crimes must be given the highest priority, 'Godders' duly joined my small but growing body of sleuths, now known officially as No. 2 War Crimes Investigation Team.

Politically, the situation in the Dutch East Indies was critical. The Indonesian Government was in disarray and totally unable to control the militant elements seeking to prevent the return of Dutch colonial rule. The Japanese had long since promised the Javanese their independence, once the war was won. They had stirred up a bitter resentment, bordering on hatred, towards the pre-war Dutch rulers. Now that the Japanese had been defeated and were unable, therefore, to fulfill their promises, a nationalist movement erupted, first in the urban areas and slowly spreading throughout the country, encouraged and supported, no doubt, by the vanquished Japanese. There was evidence too, that military equipment abandoned by the Japanese, including large supplies of arms and ammunition, was being handed over to the nationalists who had every intention of using it in their fight for independence.

Armed gangs now roamed the streets. 'MERDEKA' (Freedom) and other nationalist slogans began to appear on walls and banners all over the city. The situation rapidly became so critical, with disturbances often turning into riots, that Admiral Patterson, Commander of Allied Forces in the Netherlands East Indies, ordered that all Japanese forces must, for the time being, remain armed. We even found ourselves in the ironic situation of being unable to venture outside the gates of our hotel without an armed Japanese escort. British military personnel, so easily mistaken for Dutch, were obvious targets for the insurgents, so had to be protected by their former enemies. This weird state of affairs was likely to last at least until the arrival of stronger British forces, which was not expected before mid October at the earliest. Moreover, during the hours of darkness, a strict curfew was imposed.

I continued to search for suitable accommodation for my unit. Admiral Patterson issued a decree that all buildings under Japanese control were to be taken over by the Allied forces in the first place. Until then they were to be kept in proper repair by the Japanese. 'The return of houses to their former owners will be done exclusively through the Headquarters of the Allied Forces to which owners should apply.'

At last I found a large, comfortably furnished bungalow in what had been a fashionable residential section on the west side of the city. Number 23 van Heutsze Boulevard offered sufficient if somewhat cramped space for our offices and living accommodation. The owner, a well-to-do Chinese merchant, had fled to greater safety in the hinterland, since the Javanese had always resented the Chinese for their commercial acumen, and this, together with the antipathy of the Japanese, had made life increasingly intolerable for them during the occupation. Having traced his whereabouts and let him know that we had appropriated his home and would take good care of it, he expressed profound relief that his property and what remained of his possessions were in safe hands and gave us his blessing to use it as long as we wished. Apart from its isolation, it was ideally suited to our purposes. Like most middle-class suburban dwellings, there was a small guest bungalow at the back of the garden, which was happily taken over by the NCOs.

We learned of a Eurasian family nearby who had suffered badly at the hands of the Javanese. Like the Chinese, Eurasians as a minority group were generally unpopular with the natives who tended to treat them with disdain. The mother assumed the post of general house-keeper, supervising with admirable efficiency the Malay servants she recruited for us. They were a wonderfully cheerful bunch, smiling and giggling as they went about their chores – cooking, washing, mending and keeping the bungalow spotless. We drew our rations in the normal way as a military unit, and supplemented them with fresh fruit, eggs and vegetables from the market. Japanese currency, in the form of virtually worthless paper money, was still in use as the new currency was not yet in circulation. Much of the trading, for this reason, was conducted by means of barter.

The most notorious of the prisoner-of-war camps in Java was located on the outskirts of Batavia. Known as Cycle Camp it housed some 2,300 PoWs, 1,100 of them British and the rest made up of Dutch, Australian, Asian and other mixed nationalities. I had made early contact with Wing Commander Alexander, the Senior British Officer, who did everything possible to assist in gathering evidence of atrocities committed by the Japanese and Korean guards. In the time that was available before the camp was evacuated, Alexander and other camp leaders compiled a written record of crimes committed, not only in that particular camp, but also in other places where inmates had been incarcerated since their capture. Horrific stories came to light, too, of conditions experienced in transit on the high seas, where some of the worst crimes were perpetrated, with prisoners crammed into the stinking holds of rickety cargo boats, without food or water for days on end.

One of the Australian officers in the camp, Squadron Leader Bill Pitts, offered to stay behind to help collect evidence of crimes committed against Australian PoWs, and permission for him to do so was speedily obtained. He proved a valuable addition to our team, quite apart from being a wonderfully cheerful personality despite the privations he had suffered during the previous two and a half years.

In those early days one needed a certain imaginative flair to tackle the grim task of investigating war crimes. Understandably, perhaps, there had been thus far scarcely any guidance on the subject from our masters, either in India or Singapore. Caught short by the sudden and unexpected ending of the war with Japan, they were unprepared for the need to switch, almost overnight, from conducting clandestine operations behind enemy lines to the less dangerous but more challenging business of apprehending war criminals. Teams, like ours, were being set up and assigned sizeable slices of South-east Asia, briefed only to gather evidence, from whatever sources were available, of the ill-treatment of Allied service personnel and civilians, and to prepare cases as best we could against the accused.

Obviously, witnesses were important but in many instances extremely hard to track down: as, for example, in the case of torture carried out in a *Kempeitai* headquarters. These were the notorious secret police, the equivalent of the Gestapo, whose methods were somewhat similar to their German counterparts, but even more inhumane and brutal.

In the absence of any precise definition of what constituted a 'war crime', therefore, we were compelled to rely on our common-sense in determining which of the numerous reports of ill-treatment to pursue, and in what order of priority. Those of us with intelligence training had been taught how to interrogate captured enemy personnel. And most officers had been involved at some stage in their career with the conduct of a military court martial. We were vaguely familiar with the basic legal requirements pertaining to the Rules of Evidence: that is to say, what was or was not permissible, or accept-able, in a military court of law. For the time being these tenuous guidelines had to suffice. Nor did the lack of knowledge seem to interfere unduly with our ability to function effectively as war crimes investigators.

One of the chief culprits at the Cycle Camp in Batavia, it appeared, had been a certain Sergeant Mori, otherwise known as 'Bamboo' Mori, a particularly nasty specimen who strutted about the camp with a bamboo stick which he used frequently, and at the slightest provocation, to belabour anyone unfortunate enough to come within striking distance. It was well known that his aggressive behaviour increased in relation to the phases of the moon. When it was full he was apt to behave, like a true lunatic, in a totally irra-tional and dangerous manner. The evidence we collected against Sergeant Mori, our first prime suspect, was overwhelming and he was duly dealt with by a war crimes court and sentenced to a lengthy prison sentence, lucky to have escaped the death penalty.

I had served long enough in a 'cloak and dagger' organization to know that such units were inclined to be regarded with slight suspi-cion, sometimes tinged with jealousy. We were somehow 'beyond the pale'; because of the secretive nature of our activities no one quite knew what we were up to. Even so, one could detect a grudging respect amongst senior officers who usually succumbed to our polite requests for 'special' equipment, non-standard weaponry, priority passes and such like. I had learned from Jimmie Ferguson that if you want something badly enough you must 'go to the top'. A tough Scot, some six years older than me, Jimmie had on several occasions convincingly demonstrated the efficacy of this forthright philos-ophy; now seemed the right moment to put it, once again, to the test.

I needed to get things moving quickly and could not afford to sit around waiting for the imminent arrival of a divisional headquarters and the inevitable red tape this would bring in its wake. With a flourish of unaccustomed bravado, therefore, I signalled Admiral Patterson requesting an early meeting. Within the hour, much to my astonishment, I received an invitation to join him that same evening on board the cruiser HMS *Cumberland*. Arriving at the naval docks, I parked my jeep on the quayside and mounted the steep gangway, wondering apprehensively if I should have sported a tunic and tie rather than the informal, open-neck khaki bush shirt I was wearing. I was greeted by a petty officer and escorted to the Admiral's presence in his state cabin. Admiral Patterson welcomed me aboard and quickly put me at my ease, offering me a drink and a seat in a comfortable leather armchair.

'Well, Spooner, I'm glad you've come. As I'm sure you know the Supreme Commander wants war crimes investigations to be given top priority. You have a hell of a job on your hands, so you can count on my full support and co-operation.' Turning to an officer seated alongside him, he added, 'This is Lieutenant Commander Wheen, my Private Secretary. He will act as a liaison officer between us. Anything you need – within reason, of course – let him know.'

He cross-examined me thoroughly on my plans and, much to my relief, seemed satisfied that I knew, more or less, what I was doing. I promised to keep him informed of our progress, and was about to take my leave when, to my surprise, he invited me to stay the night on board so that our discussion could continue over dinner. I readily accepted, of course, realizing that such an opportunity was unlikely to recur. The very idea of wining, dining and sleeping on one of His Majesty's heavy cruisers, as the guest of a real live Admiral, was a considerable boost to my ego.

Admiral Patterson was a charming man and an excellent host. He brushed aside my apologies for the way I was dressed. 'My dear chap, you are still on active service. Can't expect to be all dolled up when you have to cope with a ruddy revolution, on top of everything else!' I had mentioned in passing how restless the natives had become since our arrival, and the pot shots that were liable to be taken at anyone remotely resembling a Dutchman.

At dinner, served in the Admiral's elegantly furnished stateroom, I was introduced to his other guests: Mr van de Plasse, who had been Governor of Java before the occupation; General N. L. W. van Staten, the senior Dutch officer in Java, who had just arrived from

Ceylon, and his ADC, Colonel Voorens, a former prisoner of the Japanese. I told the General that I badly needed help with the questioning of non-English speaking Dutch personnel in the camps. He readily agreed to second two Dutch officers to my Team and appointed Lieutenant van der Weg and Lieutenant Roselaar, both English speaking, the former to interrogate Dutchmen in the Cycle Camp and the latter to do likewise in the camps in Bandoeng (the capital), where there were reported to be about 17,000 civilian internees, and in Samerang, where 2,810 Service PoWs of mixed nationalities, had been imprisoned.

Before disembarking the next morning, I prepared a letter, which the General signed, authorizing Lieutenant Roselaar to requisition transport 'as he is engaged in work of vital importance'. Both officers reported for duty two days later, and the following morning Roselaar flew to Samerang to begin his first assignment.

I discovered, quite by chance, a Japanese map showing the locations of the PoW and internee camps in Java. This was a useful find and indicated that these contained some 5,000 PoWs and more than 62,000 civilian internees, according to Japanese records. Whether or not this was accurate and reliable information remained to be seen. Soon after this, the Red Cross appeared on the scene and took over the task, in close conjunction with the RAPWI staff, of determining precise numbers.

In the early days of their occupation of Batavia, the Japanese had rounded up all the Dutch and other alien women and children and herded them into a suburban residential area which they then designated as a civilian internment camp, surrounding it with barricades of barbed-wire and fencing, with guard posts at intervals around the periphery. The area they chose contained rows of poorly built bungalows previously occupied by Eurasian and Chinese families who were summarily turfed out and forced to find somewhere else to live.

I visited Tjidang Camp soon after my arrival in Batavia. Accompanied by Lieutenant Klaas van der Weg, I went to the main entrance of the camp and asked to see the camp leader. We were ushered into a tiny office and there met Miss Roorda van Eysinga, who was in charge of more than 9,500 Dutch women and children, and Miss Nicolich, who looked after some 150 British women internees. The tour of the camp was an experience which became indelibly imprinted on my memory. We saw the appalling conditions under which these wretched women and children had miraculously managed to survive for more than three long years. In one four-room bungalow I counted no less than thirty-two women and children, all of them emaciated and haggard. Over the years, many had died from starvation and malnutrition: undoubtedly many more would have suffered the same fate had the war not ended when it did.

Now a small team of doctors and nurses were working around the clock to help those in urgent need of medical help. Lorry-loads of food supplies – rice, bread, fresh vegetables and fruit – brought immediate relief to the starving inmates. But there was the inevitable problem of organizing the issue of these food supplies so that no one, least of all the children, suffered from the harmful effects of premature over-indulgence. The RAPWI staff were even obliged to impose a form of rationing, each person's intake being gradually increased under strict medical supervision, over a period of several weeks.

It was heartrending to see the pitiful state of these hapless people, many of whom were in such a dazed state that they scarcely realized their ordeal had ended. It was as if they had lost all sense of feeling, almost paralyzed by a numbness induced by months of total despondency and absolute despair.

Questioned about the treatment they had received at the hands of their Japanese guards, Miss van Eysinga and Miss Nicolich both insisted, much to my surprise, that although the Japanese had been consistently harsh, to the best of their knowledge there had been few cases of extreme brutality. Yes, they had suffered from a starvation diet: but then, they pointed out, acute food shortages had been experienced by the entire civilian population throughout the occupation. There had, however, been several instances of women being assaulted, in particular by a vicious officer called Soni. Such cases, they promised, would be documented and full details handed over to us.

That same afternoon, Klaas and I visited Struiswyk, another civilian camp in Batavia, containing some 1,300 Dutch women and children. Conditions there, too, were lamentable, but nothing to compare with Tjidang.

A few days later Major Nick Read-Collins joined my merry band. Admiral Patterson had given permission for him to be transferred from RAPWI, having once again decided that my needs were greater than theirs. Nick had been amongst the first British officers to arrive in Batavia, with the specific task of organizing emergency air supplies to PoW and civilian internment camps throughout Java and Sumatra. He, too, had been horrified to see the shocking conditions of the women in Tjidang, Kramat and Struiswyk camps. He agreed that Tjidang was the worst.

> I shall never forget the utter revulsion I felt when I saw those wretched women and children crammed into totally inade- quate and filthy dirty bungalows and shacks. Their entire existence seemed to revolve around acute hunger and the urge to possess trivia, such as string, bits of paper, old tin cans, torn clothing. Most were suffering from deficiency diseases, such as oedema and beri-beri, and many were so weak from dysentery and malaria that they could scarcely stand.

He told me they subsisted largely on a diet of sour black bread made from tapioca flour and almost the only vegetable was obi leaves.

Evidence of war crimes started to accumulate, with information now pouring in to our office as a result of the publicity we had obtained locally. For example, a diary kept by a Warrant Officer Reich had been found at St Vincontuis Hospital in Batavia giving the names and other details of Japanese who had mistreated patients. Because of shortage of staff, however, I decided to concentrate all our efforts, in the early stages, on the PoW and internee camps before they were evacuated and it was too late.

Since all efforts to obtain reinforcements from E Group Singapore or from the Dutch were unavailing, I had little choice but to make the best of what staff I had, despite the mounting work load. I did manage to take on three Dutch ladies from the Tjidang camp, who had volunteered to do secretarial work. Although still weak from their privations, they rapidly gathered strength and were a great asset to the unit. Up until then Sergeant Bryce had carried out the secretarial chores, but I needed him for more productive fieldwork and he was only too glad to be relieved of these onerous duties. In addition, the Australian ex-PoW, Wing Commander Bill Pitts, had joined us and I sent him off to liaise with Colonel Havercamp in the capital, Bandoeng, in central Java.

I met the former Chief Advocate, Batavia, Mr P. J. Brugman, at the Hotel Tjikini. He was investigating the mistreatment of civilian prisoners by the Japanese and handed over copies of statements incriminating, in particular, the Kempeitai. The Admiral sent word that Lord Mountbatten, the Supreme Commander, wished to know how things were progressing on the war crimes investigations front in Java. Rashly, I promised to produce an interim report within the week or no later than 4 October. Once again, he invited me to spend the night on board HMS *Cumberland*, but this time, due to pressure of work, I declined regretfully.

The Americans had sent a small unit of their Office of Strategic Services (OSS) to Batavia. I was informed that a Captain Shaw would be arriving next day to 'deal with war crimes' and would contact me. I found this rather puzzling; to the best of my knowledge there had been no American military serving in Java. There were, on the other hand, quite likely to be Americans amongst the civilian internees, although we had not, as yet, encountered or heard of any.

On 30 September E Group was officially made responsible for the investigation of war crimes in South-east Asia. There would be a forward headquarters in Singapore with teams operating in Java, Sumatra, Singapore and Malaya. Other teams would be located in Burma, Siam and Indo-China, under a forward headquarters in Bangkok. This was welcome news: with my own colleagues running the show I felt less likely to be messed about.

I heard through the grapevine that Mountbatten's entire Allied Headquarters staff of some 2,000 was being moved from Ceylon to Singapore where, as the newly formed South-east Asia Command (SEAC), they would be housed in the Cathay Building, Singapore's sole skyscraper. They duly arrived on 22 November after a fairly unpleasant (by all accounts) six-day voyage on the troopship *Devonshire*. Nearly 700 staff officers had been compelled to suffer the indignity of 'travelling hard', with brigadiers and above berthed in the iron cots of the Mental Sick Bay, and colonels in quarters normally occupied by seamen gunners. Officers of the rank of major and below had to be content with hammocks slung on the troop mess decks.

In early October, 5th Indian Division, commanded by Major General Mansergh, arrived in Java and set up its headquarters in

Batavia, where the primary task of 1 Indian Infantry Brigade was to maintain law and order in by far the largest urban community in the country. The situation had deteriorated during the previous month, with clashes and street battles becoming more frequent. Bands of Indonesian nationalists roamed the streets, looting, setting fire to shops (those of the Chinese in particular), and generally causing considerable mayhem. The Japanese, we discovered, had handed over arms and ammunition to the Indonesian rebels, in blatant disregard of explicit orders issued by the Allied Command. As a result of this gross and deliberate intransigence Lieutenant General Nagano, Commander of the Sixteenth Army in Java, his Chief of Staff, Major General Vamamoto, and Major General Makimura, Commander of the Japanese forces in Central Java, were arrested, transferred to Singapore and put on trial.

Despite the 10 pm curfew, rigidly enforced, the sounds of sporadic small arms fire echoed across the rooftops throughout the night. Isolated as we were in the suburbs, and feeling distinctly vulnerable, I set up a nocturnal sentry system, each of us taking turns to mount a two-hour armed guard. Doors and windows were reinforced with sandbags and extra supplies were laid in against the possibility of a siege. We became accustomed at night to the sounds of naked feet padding along our boulevard, but not to the bloodcurdling shrieks of '*Merdeka*!' ('Freedom!'). There was a feeling of eerie uncertainty which kept our nerves constantly on edge, not quite knowing what to expect, and wondering whether we would be attacked in the dead of night by a mob of fanatical young nationalists.

From the early part of the seventeenth century much of the Indonesian Archipelago was under Netherlands rule. This included Java, Sumatra and a string of islands which sprawl across the Equator, encompassing an area of more than half a million square miles and a population well in excess of 100 million. In the years immediately preceding the Second World War a strong nationalist movement had developed, led by Doctor Soekarno, a Javanese intellectual, who was gaoled by the Dutch for political agitation and then freed by the Japanese to head their puppet Government in Indonesia. He had even been to Japan and received a decoration from Emperor Hirohito for all the help he had given to the Japanese cause in Southeast Asia.

The British Government was anxious to arrange a meeting

between the Dutch Lieutenant Governor, Dr van Mook, and Dr Soekarno in the hope that law and order could be restored with the least possible bloodshed. This proposal, however, was categorically rejected by Sutan Shamir, the Indonesian Premier. No Indonesian leader would take part in any meeting attended by the Dutch authorities. This outright rejection of Britain's attempt to solve the political differences between the two main parties in the dispute meant that British forces would continue to bear the brunt of the hostile behaviour of the Indonesian rebels, not just in Batavia but throughout the country.

Meanwhile, alarming reports were coming in from Soerabaya, the main port in eastern Java. Gangs on the rampage had mutilated and dismembered Indian soldiers who had had the misfortune to fall into their hands, set fire to houses containing women and children, and attacked hospitals clearly marked with the Red Cross. Europeans were being rounded up at random and either released after questioning or handed over to frenzied mobs who slaughtered them mercilessly.

RAF Thunderbolts and Mosquitoes, carrying out bombing attacks on the rebel Indonesian headquarters, were fired on by an anti-aircraft gun inherited from the departing Japanese, along with armoured vehicles the Indonesians used to support their attacks. After several days of stiff fighting, troops of 5th Indian Division succeeded in clearing most of the port and naval base of extremists. However, they were still engaged in fierce fighting in the centre of the city, capturing the main post office against heavy machine-gun fire, supported by an artillery battery which shelled their machine-gun nests and strong points. Part of the city quickly became a shambles, and our advancing troops found the streets littered with scattered remnants of furniture, crockery, assorted clothing and other miscellaneous impedimenta looted from shops and houses.

The civil disturbances that continued to disrupt life in Batavia failed to prevent courageous attempts to return to more normal peacetime conditions. Cinemas opened their doors and even a few restaurants lured customers inside with seductively lingering smells of Indonesian cuisine, the delights of which we had so far had little chance to sample.

Early in November, my staff and I were invited to a piano recital at the Hotel des Indes given by a thirteen-year-old Chinese girl called

Lee San San. She was the prodigy of a Dutch lady concert pianist who had recognized her remarkable talents. Having managed to avoid internment, she had coached Lee daily for the past three years. It was at this concert that I was introduced to a remarkable White Russian artist, Vladimir Trechikoff, who had escaped from Singapore shortly before the Japanese arrived. Afterwards, he and his girlfriend, Lenka Salomonson, invited me to join them for supper at her house.

Born in Russia in 1913, Trechikoff grew up in Vladivostok, Manchuria where he showed early signs of his outstanding artistic talents. At the outbreak of the Second World War he was working as a cartoonist for the *Straits Times* in Singapore and also for the Ministry of Information, illustrating anti-Japanese propaganda posters and pamphlets. When the Japanese attacked Singapore, his English wife, Natalie, and young daughter, Mimi, escaped by boat to India, making their way eventually to South Africa where they spent the rest of the war in total ignorance of his fate. Trechikoff managed to embark on one of the last ships to leave Singapore. Having survived several bombing attacks, his ship was intercepted by a Japanese cruiser and passengers were ordered to take to the lifeboats before their ship was sunk. Several days later, the forty-one survivors landed on the island of Sumatra. After a while Trechikoff's luck ran out. Captured by a Japanese patrol, he was held with thousands of other refugees in a converted cinema in Serang, western Java. He was later released on parole, having convinced his captors that, as a Russian, he was 'neutral', since Russia was not then at war with Japan, wisely omitting to mention that he had become a British citizen in Singapore.

Under house arrest in Batavia, Trechikoff was forced to work for a well-known Japanese artist called Kano, whose job it was to record the success of the Japanese occupation of Java. Surreptitiously, he was able to earn a modest living painting the portraits of Swiss, Germans, Russians, well-to-do Javanese and Malays living in Batavia, and of Dutch women who had escaped internment. The proceeds of a single portrait covered his expenses for a whole month. Sometimes he was paid in kind – butter, milk, eggs and other commodities in short supply.

In his autobiography *Pigeon's Luck* Trechikoff describes the day he met, quite by chance, the girl who was to become the model for some of his most famous paintings.

I found myself gazing into the eyes of the most striking girl I had seen in Java. She was Eurasian, about my height with fine black hair to her shoulders. Her dress was immaculate, a surprise for wartime Java . . . But what riveted me to the spot were her eyes, jet black and with pupils so big they looked like burning coals.

Her name was Leonora Moltema and she was married to a Dutch Air Force Officer, called Salomonson, who had been evacuated from Java with the rest of the Dutch forces just before the Japanese arrived but was later taken prisoner. Extremely intelligent and very determined by nature, she had done well for herself before the war, becoming the only woman in Java to qualify as a chartered accountant. She lived comfortably in her own spacious bungalow situated in a pleasant, tree-lined boulevard, not far from the Presidential Palace. Trechikoff soon joined her, using the separate studio in the back garden to carry on his work in relative peace and with Lenka (as he nicknamed her) as his delightfully convenient model.

Over the next two years, Trechy (as she called him) was prolific with his paintings, covering huge canvasses with the fiery tropical colours of Bali, Java and Sumatra, many infused with the redolent mysticism of the east. Some of the paintings created during this period became world-renowned, such as 'Lady of the Tropics', the most famous of them all, featuring a nude Lenka with a background of brilliant red cannas; 'Madonna of the East'; 'Javanese Half-Caste', with Lenka's Dutch father and Malay mother in the background; and 'Lady of the Orchids', one of his most luxuriously exotic creations. These, amongst others he has since painted, are to be found as framed lithographs in millions of homes throughout the world.

Late one night, Trechikoff was picked up and taken to the head-quarters of the Kempeitai, where he was questioned about his contacts in Java and Singapore and held in solitary confinement for several weeks. Somehow he succeeded in satisfying his interrogators that he was innocent of any subversive activities and was released. Lenka, too, had been closely cross-examined and her house thoroughly searched on several occasions. They found nothing incriminating, however, as she had carefully hidden anything remotely significant, such as photographs of her Dutch husband, his clothing and his private papers.

I visited Lenka's house often and saw Trechy at work in the studio. I watched him put the finishing touches to 'The Blind Beggar', a life-size painting of an elderly Javanese man in rags, head tilted back, staring sightlessly at the sky, leaning on a long stick and with his right hand stretched out in front of him, palm upturned in silent supplication. Depicted in the background was the blackness of a void, the utter darkness of his world. It was the most poignant picture I had ever seen, and one that made a deep impression on me, as it must have on many others.

One day, Lenka was told that her husband was alive and returning home from the Philippines where he had been held prisoner. Reluctantly, Trechy moved out of her bungalow and went to stay with friends. A week later he received a letter from a friend in Singapore with the news that his wife and daughter were living in Cape Town, South Africa. I was having supper with them the evening Lenka gently but firmly persuaded Trechy to return to his family. His innately volatile Russian temperament caused Trechy to react violently to the very thought of leaving her. He became highly agitated, distressed and emotional and, to our acute embarrassment, started to weep copiously. Lenka tried to soothe him by pointing out how lucky they were to have enjoyed a near-idyllic existence together for so long but he refused to be so easily consoled. Torn between, on the one hand, a moral obligation to return to his family, and on the other, an overwhelming desire to stay with the delectable Lenka, of whom he had grown seriously fond and to whom he owed so much, the wretched Russian was obviously suffering acute mental anguish. Lenka, after all, had made it possible for him to continue his painting, almost undisturbed, in an oasis of relative peace and tranquility. Moreover, not only had she looked after him in every way, but for more than two years she had been his main, if not his sole source of inspiration. It was indeed a tough decision over which he fretted indecisively for several days.

Fortunately for me, as things turned out, his conscience prevailed, and shortly afterwards Trechy bade Lenka a tearful farewell and flew off to Singapore, en route for South Africa, taking with him his precious paintings encased in a special zinc cylinder. From Singapore he travelled on the troopship *Oranje*, intending to disembark at Suez whence he was to fly to South Africa. Unfortunately, having no valid papers, he was forced to continue to England, and it was nearly a year before he was finally able to reach Cape Town.

Reunited with his family, Trechy struggled hard, in alien surroundings to re-establish himself. Gradually his fame as a creator of popular art began to spread through South Africa, Canada, the United States and Britain. In London, more than 200,000 people visited his first exhibition at Harrods. Up to 1973, when *Pigeon's Luck* was published, over two and a half million people flocked to no less than forty-three exhibitions. His name soon became a byword, despite the condemnation of critics and purists who dismissed his work contemptuously as mere 'chocolate box art'. Trechy's success brought him wealth enjoyed by few artists in their lifetime.

Not long after Trechy's departure, I was enjoying a quiet evening at Lenka's when there was a loud knock on the front door. Opening it Lenka was startled to find her husband standing on the porch. This might have been an embarrassing moment for us both had he not calmly announced that he was there only to collect a few of his belongings before returning to the Philippines to marry a young girl he had met and fallen in love with after his release from captivity. Scarcely concealing her relief, Lenka helped him to pack his bags and saw him off the premises within the hour. Theirs had been a singularly unhappy marriage, Lenka told me, and this unexpected turn of events suited her admirably. She was so elated, in fact, that she promptly produced a bottle of champagne to celebrate her marital freedom and told me firmly to forget the curfew. Such an invitation was hard to refuse, nor was I in the frame of mind to do so.

Next morning Lenka asked if she could help in my office. Not surprisingly, I accepted the invitation with alacrity, not for a moment realizing the long-term implications. So it was that Mrs Lenka Salomonson joined the staff of No. 2 War Crimes Investigation Team as my 'personal assistant'.

A signal came in from Singapore ordering me to go to Soerabaya, at the far eastern end of Java, to have a look round with a view to moving my Team there. So, on 20 November, I flew to Soerabaya with Sergeant Sinclair, Royal Signals, and went immediately to the headquarters of 5th Indian Division to meet General Mansergh, who had led the Division during the last months of the fighting in Burma. I was given a bunk in the senior officers' quarters where I spent a sleepless night, interrupted by the incessant heavy gunfire from a nearby battery of 3.7s pounding Indonesian strongpoints in the southern part of the town. Shells from the rebel artillery fell harmlessly in the open ground near the Mess or into the harbour. The odd mortar bomb, the rattle of automatic fire and the occasional rifle shot added to the deafening noise which, at times, was almost continuous and scarcely conducive to peaceful slumbers.

The following morning, bleary-eyed but fortified by a hearty breakfast, I had a meeting with the senior staff officer (GI) and the staff officer in charge of Intelligence (GSO(I)) who briefed me on the current situation. In their opinion the Indonesian rebels, up against troops with modern weapons and seasoned by months of continuous fighting in the jungles of Burma, were rapidly running out of food and other essential supplies and would soon capitulate. At the same time the seriousness of the situation was not underestimated. Only a few days before, a large gang of bandits had carried out a well-planned attack on an ammunition dump guarded by a Japanese detachment. The assault would have succeeded had not a company of the Seaforth Highlanders come to the rescue. No contact had yet been made with the main Japanese garrison in Soerabaya, however, as this was in a part of the city still occupied by the rebels.

It was ironic, if not an unmitigated tragedy, that our troops, both British and Indian, who had fought so gallantly in Burma and had survived the hardships and dangers of that fierce campaign, should now have to risk their lives in a political struggle that was of absolutely no direct concern to them. They had been brought to Java for the specific task of disarming the defeated enemy forces and rescuing European women and children from Japanese camps. Instead they found themselves having to deal with a bloody insurrection which was rapidly getting out of hand, and causing casualties (some fatal) amongst their ranks. The irony was deeply compounded by the need to consort with the very enemy they had been fighting so recently and so bitterly in order to uphold the political interests of a foreign government.

Major Wilson, the GSO (I), took me to the main camp which held civilians interned during the occupation and who had not yet been able to return to their homes because of the intensity of the fighting. Into this same camp streamed a continuous flow of refugees carrying on their backs the remnants of belongings salvaged from their homes. They were mostly terrified women and children, many half-starved and in a wretched condition – altogether a pitiful sight.

The Camp Leader told me that several cases of brutality had been reported to the Field Security Service from whom I later collected the sworn statements they had taken. Included amongst these were one or two relating to mistreatment perpetrated by Indonesian guards in Kalisofok Prison.

It seemed clear from what I had been told by commanders on the spot, and learned from other sources, that there was more than enough work for us in Soerabaya to justify moving my Team there as soon as the situation was more firmly under control. Up to then, movement had been severely restricted in and around the city. Contact with the Japanese was impossible; there were restricted facilities for setting up our wireless transmitter; and the few remaining ex-internees were in such a state of nerves that obtaining coherent statements from them had proved very difficult. For the time being, therefore, no useful purpose would be served by remaining in Soerabaya, so Sergeant Sinclair and I returned to Batavia, leaving the Camp Commandant to let me know as soon as he had found suitable accommodation for my Team.

Early in December I received a glowing note from Colonel Francis Minshull-Ford, who was then in charge of the war crimes set-up in Singapore, thanking me profusely for all my efforts and loyalty, and regretting that E Group and all its happy associations were drawing to a close. He also mentioned that my promotion to the rank of lieutenant colonel had been confirmed by New Delhi, much to my surprise and delight.

Meanwhile, the terrorists had stepped up their activities in Batavia, with a considerable increase in sniping at our military transport, making daylight journeys even more hazardous than before. One of my staff, a petty officer, got caught between two fires in a jeep on his way to collect rations. With exemplary presence of mind he drove rapidly into an empty garage, slamming the doors behind him, and emerging an hour later when the shooting affray had subsided. Recently arrived Dutch troops had been forced to open fire on a mob attacking the Wilhelmina Barracks. The sounds of gunfire could be heard all round our bungalow throughout the day, dying down towards evening when heavily armed patrols kept the rebels off the streets during the curfew hours, from 10 pm to 5.30 am.

On Christmas Eve, 36 Indian Infantry Brigade arrived in Batavia, to reinforce 23rd Indian Infantry Division. It was not until many years later, when I read the official history of my Regiment, 8th Gurkha Rifles, that I discovered that the 1st Battalion had been part of this Brigade, the other two battalions being the 8/13th Frontier Force Rifles and the 5th Jat Regiment. Their first tasks were to restore law and order, to protect some 8,000 RAPWI, and to concentrate and disarm all Japanese forces in the Buitenzorg area. This was some thirty miles south of Batavia in the foothills of the central mountain range. Whilst carrying out searches for rebel leaders, the Gurkhas discovered an arms factory in which iron piping was being turned into primitive grenades. They also recaptured the vital waterworks which supplied Batavia. A month later they were moved back to Batavia for a brief period of patrolling, guarding camps and combing out suspected areas of the city, jobs heartily disliked by the professional soldier, before being assigned the role of protecting the lines of communication between Batavia and the capital, Bandoeng, some 150 miles to the south-east. The main road connecting the two cities passed through areas dominated by the terrorists, and convoys, some containing truckloads of women and children, had been subjected to vicious attacks resulting in heavy casualties.

The official history of 1/8th Gurkha Rifles records an encounter with the rebels, which gives an idea of what our troops were up against. One company had been deployed to guard a key bridge thirty miles out of Bandoeng and had been in action almost daily. On 30 March they made a sortie to open the road towards Bandoeng along which 36 Brigade, its task in the city completed, was moving. The company met with opposition and 'Fierce fighting ensued. The Indonesians were the fanatical 'Black Buffalo' irregulars. They hurled themselves on our men, slashing with dahs.'

However, the Gurkhas' kukris and bayonets were more than equal to the task. In the end, seventeen of the enemy were killed and two captured. It was a small-scale but vicious action, noteworthy for the sheer fanaticism of the enemy, who preferred to engage in suicidal hand-to-hand fighting, rather than their more usual hit-and-run ambushes.

The country lent itself to ambushes and the terrorists took full advantage of this at every opportunity. The strain on the troops was considerable and there were no regrets when fresh Dutch forces arrived and the Brigade sailed for Madras on 6 May breathing a collective sigh of relief.

The following month, 4/8th Gurkha Rifles, which had served with great distinction in the Arakan and Burma campaigns, after brief spells in Siam and Malaya joined 37 Indian Infantry Brigade which was guarding the Batavia area. The Battalion carried out a number of highly successful operations in and around Batavia until mid November, when it returned to Malaya prior to final disbandment.

We badly needed to publicize our existence so that anyone wishing to report a war crime would be able to get in touch with us. I held a press conference and invited representatives to help us in our task. The results were encouraging and articles appeared in the Dutch newspaper *Hat Dagblad* (Daily News), the *Evening News*, published in Batavia, and in various military broadsheets such as *SEAC*, the services newspaper of South-east Asia Command, Singapore, *The Fighting Cock*, a daily paper for troops of 23rd Indian Infantry Division, Batavia, the *Batavia Sapper*, put out by the Indian Engineers, Batavia, and *5th Indian Division Dispatch*, published in Soerabaya.

Although there was no dearth of evidence from victims of war crimes, we were faced with two major problems. The first, and by far the most important, of course, were the identification, location and arrest of suspects involved in these crimes. Identifying camp guards was particularly difficult, many of the worst offenders being Koreans. Rarely were any of the guards' proper names known: most were referred to by their nicknames, such as 'Blue lip', 'Baggy Trousers', 'Brown Bomber' and 'Man with the Evil Eyes'. Witnesses could hardly ever give more than a hazy description of the culprit. Where his rank and the period when he was at the camp were known, and the approximate date of the incident, there was an outside chance that he could be traced. It was no surprise that the Japanese themselves were infuriatingly obstructive and unhelpful. Tracking down these suspects was infinitely harder than the gathering of evidence. There were even reports, doubtless not entirely apocryphal, that when the Japanese surrendered many of the dreaded Kempeitai had at once donned Red Cross armbands and thus had been amongst the first to be repatriated to Japan.

Evidence, to be of any real value, had to be both reliable and corroborated. Hearsay evidence was inadmissible, as was the case in an English court of law. This made the gathering of such evidence an immensely difficult task. Often the witness or witnesses who could have supported the accusations of the victim had either died or moved elsewhere. This applied more particularly to crimes committed outside the camps. Obviously, we did all we could to question PoWs and internees before they were repatriated. This was not always feasible, however, and in such cases the individuals concerned were given forms on which to provide sworn statements which were admissible in court.

Yet another frustration was the shortage of Japanese interpreters and translators. This made the interrogation of Japanese prisoners difficult and, on occasion, quite impossible, thereby causing even further hold-ups in our investigations.

Thanks to Lenka's undoubted administrative abilities and general efficiency, she developed a recording and filing system which worked extremely well, and an office procedure to suit our growing needs. None of us had had the remotest experience of war crimes work, so it was a question of using our collective initiative and making the best of it. Here we were, a heterogeneous group of people thrown together in a foreign land, comprising members of the Royal Navy, Army, Royal Air Force and Royal Marines, of mixed nationalities and widely varying ages. We had, it was true, a strongly emotive common purpose – the bringing to justice of as many war criminals as possible within a reasonable period of time. There was no lack of incentive; one had only to reflect on the enormities of the crimes committed.

But no matter how many dossiers one examined, how foul the deed, one could never become immune to the ghastliness of it all. Nor could the unbelievable cruelty inflicted by the Japanese and Koreans be explained as a phenomenon of modern times. Throughout the ages, fearful deeds had been perpetrated by men on their fellow human beings. Examples are legion of what the poet Robert Burns described, in 1786, as 'Man's inhumanity to Man'. Consider, for example, the iniquitous Spanish Inquisition, an ecclesiastical court whose officials used the rack, thumbscrew and other diabolical tortures to punish heretics who dared to dispute the authority of the Church of Rome. Visit the 'Chamber of Horrors' at Madame Tussaud's in London and see the gruesome, lifelike recreations of human agony suffered through the ages. Delving further back in history, recall for a moment how the Romans treated their Christian slaves, how they allowed them to be torn limb from limb by half-starved lions to provide macabre pleasure for cheering crowds in a blood-soaked arena. The infliction of such barbaric public cruelty on innocent people beggars the imagination.

Our daily newspapers are filled with stories of gross inhumanity carried out in so-called civilized societies (some, like Northern Ireland, quite close to home) for religious, political or other sectarian reasons, sometimes with no particular motive. But whatever the reason, whether it be drug-related, social deprivation, feudal retaliation, religious or political fanaticism, there can never be any valid justification for inflicting deliberate and calculated physical or mental pain and suffering on fellow human beings.

Not being signatories to the Geneva Convention, the Japanese were completely impervious to what we in the West considered, by contemporary standards, to be civilized behaviour relating to the treatment of captured personnel, whether they were men, women or children, whether in the fighting forces or civilians. The Japanese commandant of a civilian internment camp, when approached by one of the inmates about the lack of medical facilities, retorted, 'You are not even prisoners of war. You are mere civilians, like paper cuttings chased by the wind. It is of no consequence to us if you die.'

In Japanese eyes it was the ultimate disgrace to allow oneself to be captured alive, whatever the circumstances. It was not entirely surprising, therefore, that they treated prisoners with such contempt. This, of course, explains why it was rare for a Japanese to be taken prisoner. On matters of discipline, too, their code of conduct differed considerably from our own. For example, it is a court martial offence for a British officer, or non-commissioned officer, to strike a subordinate, regardless of rank. In the Japanese forces this criterion did not apply. During the course of our investigations several cases came to light of a Japanese NCO in the Kempeitai striking, with absolute impunity, a Japanese officer on the camp staff, with consequent loss of face to the latter. The practice of beating up PoWs at the slightest provocation was, to them, a logical extension of the way they treated their own people. In no way, however, could such conduct be condoned on the grounds that it was accepted behaviour amongst themselves.

After Christmas Major Ross Lewis, my second-in-command,

together with Petty Officer Dodgson and Sergeant Cummins, flew to Soerabaya to set up our new headquarters there. Meanwhile, I decided to take a few days' leave in Singapore before tackling what was likely to prove a period of intense activity in Eastern Java.

It was a welcome change to be able to walk about the streets of Singapore without the danger of being shot at, and to enjoy whatever nocturnal entertainment the city had to offer without having to worry about a curfew. The headquarters of the war crimes organization, including the legal department, had by now been well established in the Goodwood Park Hotel which, although a pale shadow of its former glory, and rather overcrowded, still managed to offer adequate creature comforts to its residents and visitors.

This brief respite reminded me of the occasions when I had returned to Calcutta after a spell of operations in the Arakan, or after laying a dump of stores on some remote island off the Burma Coast. There was a feeling, however modest, that one was 'back from the front', so to speak. One sensed the realization amongst the headquarters staff that 'things must be fairly rough over there in Java', a tacit acknowledgement that we were functioning under conditions tantamount to active service. Of course, one didn't complain. It would have been a waste of time to do so. Many of the headquarter staff were themselves veterans of Burma campaigns and well entitled, therefore, to feel they had 'done their bit'.

In the three months since its liberation Singapore, struggling hard to shake off the effects of the Japanese occupation, was slowly coming back to life. This gradual resuscitation process manifested itself, for instance, in the famous Great World Amusement Park, a sprawling conglomeration of theatres, cinemas, dance halls, restaurants, funfairs and side shows where the young (and not so young) Singaporeans, Chinese, Eurasians, Malays and others would gather after dusk to let their hair down and enjoy themselves, at very modest cost. Here, too, British and Commonwealth troops, on leave or off duty, were able to dance with 'taxi' girls in exchange for a 25-cent coupon, watch a traditional Chinese play in an open-air theatre, or listen to live bands playing non-stop jazz. In this lively fairground atmosphere, a festive spirit prevailed, enhanced by the strings of multi-coloured lights that bedecked the buildings.

The final months of the occupation had seen the currency then in use, known in local parlance as 'banana money', become almost worthless. As in Batavia, most of the shops had had to close their shutters. Prices were still exorbitant, and with the influx of Allied military personnel, flush with savings accumulated in the jungle, combined with the scarcity of goods, prices spiralled even higher.

On New Year's Eve, I went with the E Group doctor to the first performance of the London Ballet which we both enjoyed immensely. My last visit to the ballet had been in Calcutta, to see the ballerina Alicia Markova and her equally famous partner, Anton Dolin, who toured India entertaining the troops with a small but lively group of dancers. They had come to our E Group HQ for a Sunday brunch, followed by strenuous games of badminton in the garden behind our offices. I seem to recall partnering one of the young ladies and being surprised at how uncoordinated she was, how ungraceful her movements!

After the performance we adjourned to the Phoenix Club in the Cathay Building where we were joined by Pamela, a girl I had known in England who was now working as a FANY in Singapore. (FANY stood for The First Aid Nursing Yeomanry which was formed in 1907. In the First World War they ran field hospitals, drove ambulances and set up soup kitchens and troop canteens, often close to the battle areas. In the Second World War they also acted as female agents in occupied France, three of whom (including the well-known Odette) were awarded the George Cross (equivalent to the Victoria Cross) for gallantry.)

Pamela came off duty at 10.30 pm armed with a bottle of gin which helped us to see in the New Year in proper style. On the last evening of my leave I splashed out and took her for dinner with all the frills, and dancing at the posh Tanglin Club, then on to Prince's, a cosy but overpriced nightclub, before returning her to her quarters in the small hours. After a couple of hours' sleep, I caught an early flight to Palembang in Sumatra and thence to Batavia, physically exhausted, but mentally refreshed.

By the end of 1945, some 51,000 internees as well as evacuees from other parts of South-east Asia had been processed by the RAPWI organization and were either on their way home or being cared for in temporary rest centres. From all accounts, RAPWI had done a magnificent job under the most trying of conditions. Within three weeks of their arrival in Singapore the vast majority of the

32,000 Allied PoWs and internees found on Singapore Island alone had been evacuated.

The disarming of Japanese forces had also proceeded with quiet efficiency. By the end of January, fewer than 120,000 troops remained to be deprived of their weapons and shipped back to the land of their forefathers, out of the three quarters of a million stationed in South-east Asia at the time of their surrender.

Meanwhile, the British Government, increasingly concerned about the worsening situation in Java, arranged to send a top flight diplomat to Batavia to attempt to achieve 'an amicable and satis-factory agreement'. The Dutch Government had little choice but to agree that Sir Archibald Clark, the British Ambassador in Moscow (before that in Peking) should use all his diplomatic skills and expe-rience to effect a solution, without himself appearing to arbitrate between the Dutch and the Indonesians. It was patently wrong to allow British forces to continue operating indefinitely in such a volatile environment, as pawns in a political context which was of little or no concern to Britain. The sooner our troops could be with-drawn from Indonesia the better.

The first of the British war crimes trials in South-east Asia opened on Monday, 21 January, at the Supreme Court Building in Singapore. Ten Japanese officers and NCOs were charged with the ill-treatment of Indian prisoners of war. This was a newsworthy event, covered extensively and in minute detail by the Singapore press, and greeted with immense relief and enthusiasm by the local populous who had suffered so much and for so long at the hands of the Japanese occupation forces.

Special municipal courts were also set up to deal with cases of collaboration committed by civilians who had passed information to the Japanese police resulting in the torture, imprisonment and sometimes even death of the victims. For political reasons, the British authorities shied away from uncovering, much less trying, cases of treason committed by ex-Indian Army troops who had sworn oaths of allegiance to the Japanese Emperor and joined special units dedi-cated to the overthrow of the British in India.

On arrival in Soerabaya, I found Dodgson and Sinclair comfort-ably installed in a large bungalow which, like the one in Batavia, belonged to a wealthy Chinese family who had moved away from the city when the Japanese arrived. Number 50 Kajoon was located in a pleasant part of the city which had so far escaped the attention of marauding terrorists. The rooms were spacious and cool, with high ceilings from which large electric fans were suspended, and colourful mosaic tiled floors. It was reasonably well-furnished and at least the former Japanese occupants had not desecrated either the contents or the building itself, as they had in so many other requisitioned premises.

To my surprise and carefully suppressed delight, Lenka Salomonson agreed to join the unit in Soerabaya. Without undue difficulty I was able to obtain the necessary authority for her to do so. After all, our work had to be given top priority, and Lenka had already proved an invaluable member of our Team. She duly arrived on 16 January and immediately set about organizing the office with considerable relish and zest. My staff now consisted of two British officers, Major Ross Lewis, formerly with Force 136 (another clandestine organization with which E Group had worked closely in Burma and Malaya), and Captain John Walker, Petty Officer Dodgson RN, and two sergeants, Sinclair and Cumming. Also assigned to my unit were three Dutch officers and a Dutch sergeant, an Indian supervisor, two translators and three Indian clerks. And, of course, the indomitable Lenka herself, who added more than just a touch of glamour to the surroundings.

It was Lenka who suggested throwing a party to celebrate the opening of our new office. To this house-warming we invited the entire key 'brass' from the headquarters of 5th Indian Division, including the GOC himself, General Mansergh, Brigadier Denholm Young, Commander of 123 Indian Infantry Brigade, and Mr van der Plasse, former Governor of Java. The evening was a huge success. Somehow we managed to acquire sufficient quantities of alcohol to satisfy the needs and quench the thirst of our guests. Thanks to a highly successful scavenging operation by Sergeant Sinclair, there was an abundance of delicious food. An Ambonese band played incessantly and with unabated gusto. A large stock of emergency candles procured in case the lights failed were happily not needed. With singular initiative and ingenuity, Ross Lewis had placed several imposing signs on doors at strategic points around the building, such as 'Special Investigators', 'Translators', and 'Records Office', all designed, of course, to impress on our guests that we were highly organized and extremely efficient.

One minor incident, however, somewhat marred what would otherwise have been Soerabaya's most successful social event. Towards the end of the evening I imprudently invited two lance corporals of the Military Police, who had been on duty outside, to join us in the Mess for a beer. To my consternation one of them rapidly became inebriated and was insolent to the General who was on the point of departure. Understandably angry, the GOC ordered me to have the culprit placed under close arrest. The next morning a messenger arrived hot-foot from Divisional HQ with a terse memo to me from the senior staff officer relaying the General's displeasure and demanding an explanation as to why I had allowed two non-commissioned officers to drink whilst on duty and, moreover, in an officers' mess. Presumably my apology was accepted, as I heard no more about the matter. In fact, I later learned that the General had much enjoyed himself. For a good part of the evening, it seemed, he had been well looked after and entertained by Lenka, who had performed her duties as my unofficial hostess with disarming charm and grace.

One day we had a surprise visit from the wife of the American novelist Ernest Hemingway, who was on an extensive tour of Java, writing articles for *The New Yorker* and *Collier's Weekly*. She quizzed me relentlessly for a solid three hours, demanding gory details of the most blood-curdling case histories. By then we had accumulated thirty-eight sworn statements involving more than a hundred suspected war criminals accused of horrendous barbarities, such as the infamous water torture, suspension upside down from a bamboo pole for long periods, punctuated by brutal beatings, cigarette burns on vital parts of the body, to mention but a few examples. Mrs Hemingway left to all intents and purposes well satisfied.

Early in February, I heard from Wing Commander Bill Pitts that the recently appointed new head of the War Crimes HQ in Singapore, a full colonel by the name of Bevis Lambe, had paid a visit to the Team in Batavia. 'We gave him a story of considerable hardship and perseverance in the face of great odds,' he wrote, 'and I think he was suitably impressed. Whether or not he takes any action remains to be seen, however. ' He complained of the lack of transport which severely inhibited movement of staff, which had increased to nine. He also said that a new Team (No. 3) was in the process of being formed in Batavia, with its headquarters in Orange

Boulevard, commanded by Squadron Leader McKinnon. The volume of work was certainly piling up fast in Java, and we in Soerabaya were putting in twelve to fourteen hours a day as the only way to keep abreast of the mounting backlog of cases.

I, too, had reported some of my problems back to Singapore. I remained the only legitimate member of No. 2 War Crimes Investigation Team, and still awaited confirmation of Lewis's and Walker's posting to the unit. I had applied for Walker's promotion to major, to replace the legal representative on our official establishment (who, I was reliably informed, was never likely to materialize), but so far to no avail. Colonel Lambe had, however, promised to send me two former Shanghai police officers who had been interned and were now offering their services to help with the war crimes investigations. Moreover, I had succeeded in persuading the authorities to agree to Lenka's appointment to the rank of staff sergeant, with commensurate pay and allowances, much to our mutual satisfaction.

Breaks for light entertainment were few and far between. It was dangerous to venture out unarmed, even in broad daylight, and even then only within a clearly defined area under our control. Lenka, I discovered, shared my fondness for classical music, and together we attended Sunday afternoon concerts given in the Officers' Mess by a motley group of musicians proudly calling themselves 'The NAAFI Palm Court Orchestra'. It made a welcome break from the distasteful business of listening to recitals of horror stories, and enabled one to regain for a fleeting moment, a modicum of sanity.

I woke up one day to the interesting realization that we were a mere 130 miles from the romantic island of Bali, the first of a long string of islands stretching for hundreds of miles to the east of Java. Sometimes called the 'Jewel of the East', Bali was known for its lush tropical splendour, for the delicacy of the Balinese arts and crafts and, not least, for the titillating beauty of the bare-breasted Balinese girls. By all accounts it was an entrancing place, an earthly paradise as yet unspoiled and rarely visited by Europeans because of its remoteness. Realizing that there would never again be the same opportunity, I arranged with an American pilot to hitch a ride on his next trip en route to pick up supplies from Darwin.

At dawn on 4 March, I arrived at the air base filled with eager anticipation. I was told there would be a slight delay due to a minor mechanical defect – the port engine had developed an untimely hiccup and required some attention. Three times I reported back to the control room, each time to be told that the mechanics were still 'working on it', and would I please return in an hour's time. Finally, I was advised that the problem was more serious than they had realized, and that the aircraft was going nowhere that day. Perhaps I could come back the following morning? So, I made my way back to my headquarters where a slightly surprised and unusually sombre Lenka handed me a signal from Singapore. It contained instructions for the immediate move of No. 2 War Crime Investigation Team to Burma. My impulse was to 'mislay' the signal and proceed with the planned visit to Bali next day. No one would have been any the wiser, except Lenka who could be trusted not to reveal my indiscretion. Somewhat reluctantly, however, I allowed military discipline to prevail over the strong temptation to seize this once-in-a-lifetime opportunity. My instincts warned me to comply with orders or face the possibility of serious repercussions. As a Regular Army officer, however unconventional, I could ill afford to take this risk.

An exchange of signals revealed that 'moving my Team' meant taking Ross Lewis and Johnny Walker, and possibly one of the sergeants, but leaving everyone else behind, including Mrs Salomonson who, by now, had made a deep and lasting impression on me.

The next ten days were fairly frantic. Having gone to such lengths to establish a close working relationship with the divisional headquarters and other local units, during the course of our brief stay in Soerabaya, closing down our unit was a painful process. Despite all the problems we had faced, particularly in having to operate under active service conditions, we had nevertheless managed to make considerable headway with our investigations. It was, therefore, hard to contemplate giving it all up, and to face the prospect of having to start all over again 2,000 miles away (as the crow flies).

I decided to go ahead to Rangoon as soon as possible to learn more about our new area of operations in Burma, leaving Ross to organize an 'orderly withdrawal'. Lenka made it abundantly clear that not only was she prepared to join us in Burma but that she certainly did not expect to be left behind. I had already discovered how fiercely determined she was when she made up her mind about something. Quite apart from this commendable trait there was no doubt that she possessed an exceptional talent for organizing, quite effortlessly, the considerable flow of paper we seemed to generate, in addition to setting up all the indexing and cross-indexing of hundreds of names of suspects, witnesses, interpreters, as well as a myriad of other contacts. With a little persuasion from Ross and Johnny, I proceeded to move heaven and earth to 'fix' Lenka's official transfer from Java to Burma. This proved rather more difficult than the initial move to Soerabaya, but I felt confident that somehow it could be arranged. If I failed in my approaches to local staff officers I would have no hesitation or compunction in applying once again the 'Ferguson principle' and going all the way to the top – if necessary to the Supreme Commander himself.

I explained to a disconsolate Lenka, who seemed disinclined to share my confidence, that I was doing everything possible to arrange for her to remain with the unit, and that perhaps in the meantime it would be best for her to return to Batavia and await word from me.

I left Soerabaya on 14 March 1946, and after brief stop-overs in Batavia and Singapore, arrived in Rangoon three days later.

NOTES ON TRECHIKOFF

Born in Russia in 1913, Trechikoff grew up in Manchuria and, at the outbreak of the 1939 war, was working as a cartoonist for the *Straits Times* and for the British Ministry of Information in Singapore, illustrating anti-Japanese propaganda posters and pamphlets. When the Japanese attacked Singapore, his wife Natalie and young daughter Mimi escaped by boat to India and thence made their way to South Africa, where they spent the rest of the war, ignorant of Trechikoff's fate. Trechikoff himself managed to board one of the last ships to leave Singapore before the Japanese arrived. Having survived several bombing attacks his ship was intercepted by a cruiser from the Japanese Navy and all passengers were ordered to take to the lifeboats before their ship was sunk. With forty-one other survivors, Trechikoff's lifeboat made for Sumatra, where they landed several days later. After many hair-raising adventures, Trechikoff was captured by a Japanese patrol and held with thousands of others in a converted cinema in Serang, Western Java. Eventually he was released on parole when his captors realized that, being a Russian, he was 'neutral', since Russia at that time was not at war with Japan. He made his way to Batavia, Java's largest city and the country's main port, where, under house arrest, he was forced to work for a well-known Japanese artist called Kano, whose job it was to record the 'success' of the Japanese occupation. On the side, Trechikoff was able to earn a modest living painting portraits of Russians living in Batavia, Dutch women who had not been interned, and Malays, Germans and Swiss. The proceeds of a single portrait covered Trechikoff's expenses for a month. Sometimes he was paid in kind – butter, milk, eggs and other commodities that were scarce. One day he met, by chance, a girl who was to become a model for some of Trechikoff's most famous paintings. In his book, *Pigeon's Luck* (Collins 1973), Trechikoff describes this encounter:

> I was gazing into the eyes of the most striking girl I had seen in Java. She was Eurasian, about my height with fine black hair to her shoulders. Her dress was immaculate, a surprise for wartime Java . . . But what riveted me to the spot were her eyes, jet black and with pupils so big they looked like burning coals . . . '

Her name was Leonora Moltema, whom Trechikoff at once nick-named 'Lenka'. Married to a Dutch Air Force pilot who had been evacuated from Java with the rest of the Dutch forces before the Japanese arrived, Lenka lived in a large house with a separate studio, where Trechikoff was able to work undisturbed. Here he painted 'Lady of the Tropics', for which Lenka posed nude with a back-ground of red cannas; 'Madonna of the East'; 'Javanese Half-Caste', also featuring Lenka's Dutch father and Malay mother; 'Lady of the Orchids'; and the most striking of all, 'The Blind Beggar', who became world-renowned.

Trechikoff was picked up one day and taken to headquarters of the Kempeitai, the Japanese Secret Service, in the Dutch College in the centre of Batavia. He was questioned about his contacts both in Java and in Singapore and held in solitary confinement for some weeks. It was evident that they knew of his work for the British Ministry of Information in Singapore and of his relationship with people in Batavia, whom they suspected of being actively anti-Japanese. Somehow he succeeded in satisfying his interrogators that he was innocent of any subversive activities and was released. Lenka too, had been closely interrogated and her house searched on several occasions; but they found nothing incriminating for the good reason that he and Lenka had taken care to hide anything of significance, such as her husband's possessions, articles of clothing and so on.

A few days after the Japanese surrendered on 14 September 1945 (the week after the Americans dropped their atomic bombs on Hiroshima and Nagasaki), the first Allied Intelligence officers (myself included) arrived in Batavia. Trechikoff describes this period in his book:

The Allies arrived and we imagined all would be well. There would be peace and prosperity once again, the Japanese would be sent home and everything would return to normal. Instead, all hell broke out. Suddenly there was guerrilla warfare, street fighting, sniping, machine-gun fire at all hours of the day and night.

Nobody seemed to know what was happening. It was not even clear who was behind the fighting. It was not the Allies, it was not the Japanese. Nor was it the Allies or the Japanese who were the targets. Instead, Malays were fighting the Malays. It seemed to be connected with Indonesian nationalism, rival camps fighting for supremacy. They had got rid of the Dutch, now they had got rid of the Japanese and they wanted their country for themselves. It was only later that I discovered Sukarno was primarily instrumental in all this. The Allies, disturbed by the unexpected violence, made a curious decision. They asked the Japanese to continue administering the Islands. And so, while the rest of the world was at peace with the Axis powers humbled, we in Java remained subject to Japanese rule, and were to remain so for weeks to come.

Although the Japanese were still in control, Allied officers arrived to sort out the mess. In particular the officers of the Allied intelligence corps appeared – and promptly occupied the old Kempetai headquarters I knew so well.

When Lenka heard that her husband was alive and had been a PoW in the Philippines and was coming home, Trechikoff moved out of her house to stay with friends. One day he received a letter from a colleague at the *Straits Times*, Singapore, telling him his wife and daughter were living in Cape Town. I was with them when Lenka persuaded Trechikoff to return to his wife. It was an emotional moment for Trechikoff who was obviously torn between staying with Lenka, of whom he had become very fond, and his duty to his family. Fortunately for me, the latter prevailed.

I was also with Lenka when her husband returned home, but only to collect his belongings before returning to the Philippines to marry a young girl he had met there after his release from captivity. Reunited with his family, Trechikoff struggled to establish himself in a strange new world. Gradually, his fame as an artist began to spread through South Africa, Canada, the United States and Britain. In London, over 200,000 people visited his first exhibition at Harrods. Up to 1973, when *Pigeon's Luck* was published, more than two and a half million people had flocked to forty-three international exhibitions. His name became a by-word and his lithographs, often heavily criticized for being 'chocolate box art', hang in millions of homes throughout the world.

Chapter Eight

Back to Burma

On arrival in Rangoon in mid-March 1946 I had an early meeting with the General Officer Commanding Twelfth Army, who had overall responsibility for the investigation of minor war crimes in his area, and for close liaison with Dominion and Allied War Crimes organizations.

To assist the GOC in this work, a War Crimes Liaison Officer, Colonel Dennis, who also covered French Indo-China, had been attached to his Command. Colonel Dennis decided to divide Burma, over twice the size of Germany, into three parts (like Caesar's Gaul). My Team (No. 2) was assigned to the central and eastern areas, including the Shan States. We were to be based in Maymyo, with No. 17 Team covering the south, based in Rangoon, and No. 16 Team operating in the northern areas, with their HQ in Bhamo, 900 miles up the Irrawaddy River.

With some difficulty, I found suitable accommodation for our HQ in Maymyo, a very pleasant hill station thirty miles or so north-east of Mandalay, the chief city of upper Burma. Maymyo, with its scented pines and relaxed atmosphere, reminded me instantly of Shillong, Assam, the headquarters of my Regiment, 8th Gurkha Rifles.

Soon after my Unit's arrival from Java, we were able, by early April, to get cracking with our investigations. Since the liberation of Burma, a certain amount of groundwork had been carried out by the Field Security Sections, the Burma Intelligence Corps and the civil police. Their efforts, however, did not appear to have been effectively co-ordinated: certain areas had been covered two or three times by different units which led to wasteful duplication of effort. In the absence of any clear directive, the manner in which investigations were carried out had varied considerably. Methods were adopted by units which they considered would suit prevailing circumstances. This inconsistency resulted in generalized and often fragmentary reports being compiled. Lacking sworn statements they were of no legal value. Where affidavits were taken they were not in the correct form and therefore unacceptable in a court of law.

As those who had been there on active service knew only too well, Burma consists of large areas of dense jungle, extended mountain ranges and an intricate maze of rivers and their tributaries. Roads linking the main towns were the only ones usable all the year round, so travel by road transport was very restricted in the outlying regions and impossible during the monsoons. The country had suffered more than any other in South-east Asia from the ravages of war. Economic conditions were poor, the cost of living high: a plain cotton '*lunghi*' (skirt, worn by both sexes) cost thirty-five rupees against the pre-war price of two rupees, and the general standard of living pitiably low. An undercurrent of desire for independence was discernible, and the British Government's attempts to put Burma back on its feet again were, moreover, regarded in some parts with deep suspicion. Notable exceptions were the faithful Kachins, Chins, Shans and the Christian Karens who had bravely helped the British throughout the Burma Campaign, and who remained as loyal as ever. Burma was no exception to the Japanese policy of subjugating the peoples of countries they occupied. Where propaganda failed they resorted to methods of terrorism and barbaric cruelty.

As elsewhere, those who incurred their displeasure, no matter what nationality, class or creed, were dealt with mercilessly. This utter ruthlessness compelled many to collaborate, particularly amongst junior officials and village headmen who had little to lose (in tangible assets) and much to gain by co-operating with the occupying forces, even if this caused as it so often did, untold suffering and barbarous ill-treatment. With the ending of the war these collaborators understandably kept well out of the way to avoid retribution. And those directly concerned with the ill-treatment of their fellow countrymen went out of their way to cover any traces of their misdeeds, enforced or otherwise.

On 4 May 1946, the second edition of *War Crimes Instruction No 1* was issued by Headquarters, War Crimes, ALFSEA (Allied Land Forces, South-east Asia). This was in two parts: Part One laid down the procedure 'whereby perpetrators of war crimes against members of the armed forces of the Allied or liberated countries may be brought to justice'. It defined 'major' and 'minor' war criminals, the main offences constituting war crimes, and crimes against the Laws of Humanity. It went on to outline the duties of the War Crimes organization, the Co-ordinating Section of Registry in Singapore, and the Legal Section; to define the responsibility of Commanders and Staff; and to outline the general policy and procedure regarding the actual investigations. It dealt also with 'press and publicity', the geographical allocation of the seventeen War Crimes Investigation Teams, and such matters as the control of expenditure, the composition of War Crimes Courts, their location and administration. There followed a section on accommodation and the payment of fees and expenses to witnesses; and lastly, in gruesome detail, the procedure for carrying out sentences of death by hanging or by shooting.

Part Two went into considerable detail of the procedure for the preparation and trial of war criminals before British Military Courts.

In my view, based on the recent experiences I had had both in the field and as a senior staff officer, the co-authors of this directive, Brigadier Dowse, who was the DAG (Deputy Adjutant General) and head of the War Crimes organization in South-east Asia, and his counterpart, Brigadier Davis, the DJAG (Deputy Judge Advocate General) went to extreme lengths to ensure that investigations were carried out efficiently, fairly and comprehensively. The rights of the accused were protected, for example, by providing an interpreter and defence counsel – Japanese, if possible – and the opportunity for them to call defence witnesses. Every effort was made to ensure that trials were conducted as fairly as possible, in the interest of justice not only being done, but being seen to be done. Obviously, there were huge problems: the identification of suspects, the corroboration of evidence, establishing the accuracy of the severity of the crimes, the reliability of witnesses, etc. Above all, there was so often the plea of 'I was only carrying out orders . . . ', the standard defence, advanced even by those in direct control of the situation and who could scarcely, therefore, divest themselves totally of responsibility for a crime committed under their very noses.

An Appendix to this document included a 'family tree' of the entire War Crimes organization. This showed Headquarters staff with twenty-four officers, seventeen clerks and sixty civilians; a Legal Section with sixty officers and twelve other ranks; Camp Commandant staff with one officer, forty other ranks and ninety-four civilians. And seventeen investigation teams each with seven officers and seven other ranks/civilians. In addition, there were Liaison Sections in Tokyo and Formosa, Liaison Officers at each of the five Commands and two Liaison Officers attached to Australian Forces. The grand total of 226 officers, 222 other ranks and 157 civilians – 605 in all – constituted a fairly formidable array of personnel with which to fight the war crimes battle over a period of two years.

During May, as we proceeded with our investigations in the field, it became increasingly doubtful that many of the perpetrators would ever be brought to justice. In the early days of liberation (eighteen months previously) many witnesses came forward of their own accord to testify against those they deemed responsible for their sufferings. Since then, a number of these same people had been questioned several times about crimes committed against them, each time by a different person. This led, we soon found, to an avoidance of further cross-examination, which, of course, hampered our investigations considerably.

It has been suggested that in no other country in South-east Asia were so many or such inhuman and brutal atrocities committed as in Burma. This can be explained, to some extent, by the fact that there was almost continuous fighting in some part of the country, and many of the prisoners taken by the Japanese were dealt with by combatant personnel who, in the heat of battle, showed no mercy and either executed them on the spot, tortured them in the presence of locals as a form of admonitory propaganda, or left them to die of starvation. Many cases came to light of Burmese being ordered to carry out the executions of PoW and, occasionally, of their own countrymen. Examples of such cases were unearthed in the Chin Hills by one of my investigators, Captain Jock Crichton, an ex-Shanghai Police Officer, who had joined my team in April. There were widespread reprisals too, whenever the Japanese discovered anti-Japanese underground activities, resulting in the slaughtering of innocent people, such as occurred in Kalagon.

Treatment meted out to Allied PoW in Rangoon and Moulmein Jails was particularly deplorable. Air Force personnel suffered the most, many being kept on a starvation diet in solitary confinement for months on end. Those too ill to work (officers included) were put on half rations as a matter of course, and, with almost no medical facilities, many died. A number of vital witnesses, we discovered, had moved from the scene of the crime and were either out of the area of the Team investigating the case, or in some cases, had even left the country altogether. Attempts to contact these witnesses were made through inter-Team liaison, although the cross-examining of witnesses in cases outside one's area was bound to be less thorough.

A major problem, common to all investigation Teams, was the location and arrest of suspects. In most cases there was no lack of evidence, but this was useless unless those responsible were in custody. It was a well-known fact that, by the time the official War Crimes organizations were on the ground, many of those suspected of war crimes were no longer in the country. Indeed, rumour had it (never, so far as I know, substantiated) that a number of the dreaded *Kempeitai* had donned Red Cross arm bands soon after 26 October 1945 (the day General Kumura, the commander of the Japanese forces in Burma, ceremoniously surrendered to the GOC, Twelfth Army in Rangoon), and were amongst the first to be evacuated to Japan. Also, it must be recorded that the bulk of the Japanese forces had retreated from Burma into Siam, Malaya and French Indo-China towards the close of hostilities.

Identification, too, was extremely difficult. It was rarely possible (or wise) to rely on vague descriptions given by witnesses. Also it was a common practice for the Japanese to adopt a Burmese name by which they were most commonly known. A popular alternative was affixing a Burmese word to the end of their own name, which only added to the confusion. Then there was the phonetic spelling of Japanese names, which was bound to vary considerably, and made the identification of a Japanese from a given list almost impossible. Rarely was even the most educated witness able to provide more than the surname. We, in No. 2 Team, had the added disadvantage of having not one single Japanese suspect in custody within our sphere of operations. We had to rely, therefore, on the Central Registry in Singapore, or on other Teams, to locate suspects from the lists of those 'wanted' and circulated by us to all concerned, and to interrogate them on our behalf.

For these and many other reasons, the number of unresolved war crimes cases in Burma was very great. At the end of May I submitted a lengthy 'Appreciation of the situation' to the War Crimes HQ in Singapore. I recommended that the deadline for the cessation of hostilities should be put forward to October and that efforts should be concentrated on the worst cases to make sure that those responsible did not escape the net, as then seemed more than likely.

A great deal more needed to be done to publicize atrocities to let the Burmese (particularly the surviving victims) know that every effort was being made to bring the perpetrators to justice. In outlying areas, little news of our activities ever reached them, due to the scarcity of radios and the very limited circulation of newspapers. In the Chin Hills, where a large number of war crimes were committed, the successful outcome of Jock Crichton's investigations was to have a far-reaching effect, politically and morally. The tough little Chins, who had resisted the Japanese with conspicuous bravery throughout the occupation, were thirsty for retribution and even demanded the heads of the worst offenders, Colonels Inada and Imamura, to be delivered to them, a request which, though not entirely unreasonable, we were unfortunately unable to fulfil.

Soon after setting up shop, I received a signal from Singapore ordering Major John Walker, who had taken over from Captain Ross Lewis as my Second in Command, to report forthwith to the War Crimes Registry, Singapore, where he would be working in some legal capacity, also acting as Liaison Officer between Burma and Singapore. I objected vociferously to being thus deprived of my right-hand man who, apart from anything else, was doing an excellent job looking after the Team's administration. Moreover, not having been involved in investigation work, John would scarcely be in a position to represent the problems of the three Teams in Burma. As an alternative, therefore, I suggested that Major Lambert, who then happened to be with me on a brief liaison visit, should spend time with each Team before returning to Singapore to fill this vacancy. I wrote to Colonel Dennis, the Liaison Officer in Rangoon, to this effect. In the event, a truly British compromise was reached whereby John was duly assigned to Rangoon to interrogate Japanese suspects on our behalf, and Lambert eventually returned to the War Crimes Registry in Singapore.

Ross Lewis, who had been one of my officers in Java before being attached to a War Crimes Court in Singapore, wrote to say he had been offered a place at Cambridge and would be sailing to England at the end of May. 'Life goes on much the same here, except that I am totally unemployed and bored stiff with the incompetence of this God-forsaken organization . . . and exasperated by life in a town where a narrow-minded military establishment is so under worked that they produce needless regulations in vast quantities to amuse themselves.' He asked me for a testimonial to accompany an application for a scholarship to Gray's Inn (where he would train to be a Barrister), 'signed with all your titles, decorations, etc. . . . to impress aged legal types in a London backwater . . . and omitting references to my signing for your field allowance, pearls, cars, pistols and other nefarious dealings of the past'! I obliged, of course, and my glowing tribute included the comment: 'This officer possesses a remarkably keen personality as well as a somewhat macabre sense of humour'. This latter was further demonstrated when he wrote, soon after arriving in Singapore in early May: 'I got here midday last Sunday, sat in Court the following day, hanged a man on Thursday, went to the pictures last night and am defending a case tomorrow'.

By the end of May, Jock Crichton was working out of Mogok, covering the Northern Shan States, and Jimmy Black had established a base in Taunggyi from which to cover the whole of the southern Shan States. Both of these officers were expected to be in the field for at least five or six weeks. Another officer, Captain Rufus Chater, a red-headed Gunner officer, whom I had known in England before the War, had just arrived from Singapore and had been given the task of dealing with cases in and around Maymyo and Mandalay.

Jock and Jim had travelled together as far as Kalewa, and had then separated, Jim going up the Chindwin River by boat to Homalin, which took him five days, and Jock by jeep to Tiddim. Jock's communications were classic examples of how not to write Army signals: 'driver bloody lucky to get away with it' – referring to a nasty crash in his 15cwt. 'Collected enough evidence against x to send him bye-byes.'

The following extracts from Jock's colourful reports convey some of the difficulties under which my investigators had to work.

28 May – Mogok

. . . after quite an eventful day, reached Khaukme at 1 pm, had a bite to eat, and pushed on again, but alas did not get far before I ran into trouble. Eight miles out got stuck up to the axle in mud and had one hell of a job getting out. Finally got started again at about 3 pm but again no luck, and 30 miles out of Mogok blew a tyre. You might have heard the curses at Maymyo. 7 pm saw us on the road again and the last 20 miles I did in the dark.

Food is plentiful, but very expensive. Had tiffin (lunch) today – cost me 15 chips (rupees) for the two of us. The chow was good but the price hurt, so no more. We'll live on M&V (meat and veg) from now on.

I have contacted several people but all know just a little and appear very reluctant to talk about what happened during the occupation. Even the cases I learned of in Maymyo they deny all knowledge of. The IP (Inspector of Police) is out on tour at the present moment but on my instructions they have sent for him. I have been warned about this laddie and if he doesn't come clean, there is going to be skin and hair flying. I have it on good authority that that is the only way to treat him, if I want to get anywhere. So if anything happens, you will know what it is all about and back me up.

I cannot explain what it is but there appears to be an air of mystery about this place and even the Europeans are not over helpful. They are all very nice but plead ignorance where war crimes are concerned. . . .

I am leaving for Mongmit this afternoon, in order to prepare the ground . . . and where there are quite a number of cases. I met a Searcher Team up here, stuck for want of engine oil. I was obliged to give them enough to see them to Khaukme – one gallon. There is absolutely no petrol or engine oil in the place; in fact if you ask for it they look at you as if you had asked for diamonds . . . '

30 May – Mogok

. . . I have seen the Sawbwa at Mongmit and he asked for a week to collect witnesses, etc.

I returned to Mogok yesterday, still to find the IP missing. In other words it appears he is trying to play a game of hide and seek with me. I have seen the Sub-Inspector but all I can get out of him is that everything is known to Mr Abreu. Fortunately, I have met up with a Burmese Intelligence Officer who was working behind the lines for GSO (I), and being a native of these parts he has turned out a godsend. Already he has given me two cases and there are great possibilities of others including the execution of 16 members of a Wingate operation at a place called Twinnge, over a hundred miles from here and over very difficult country. The village is situated on the Irrawaddy, north of Thadeikkyun. From all accounts it is very hostile country, the natives, I understand, being very anti-British. What do you think? Should I try and make it?

I expect to be in those parts for the best part of a month, and as there is quite a lot of territory to cover, I'm afraid I am running a bit short of gasoline, which will to some extent curb my activities. Hence, if you could send me a 44-gallon drum by civvy truck or any other means at your disposal, I would greatly appreciate it.

I will be stationed in Mogok until Monday, 3 June, or later, as I hear that in certain villages in this area, and stretching as far as the Irrawaddy, there are a number of cases. After completing this area I will be going up to Mongmit, where I expect to be for at least three weeks, so by that time I will be pretty low on supplies. The price of fresh food in this area is scandalous.

I regret to say this but since arriving here I have found out quite a bit of dirty work on the part of members of the FSS (Field Security Section) in this area. So far as I can gather they did very little work and earned for themselves a stinking name, which in no way helped me when I first arrived. However, that has been overcome now and I think things will turn out OK.'

7 June – Mogok

I have returned to Mogok after three days in Longmit, as the cases promised turned out to be a complete flop; 95% of them were claims for damages and looted property. Not one decent case in the lot. After about 36 hours of this I decided it was a waste of time, so I saw the Sawbwa and explained that of all the witnesses interviewed not one was of any use. He explained that most of the witnesses had come from villages within a radius of 40 miles and that if I wanted any more from beyond that area I would have to wait for at least two weeks. Well, that was out of the question so I felt him a specimen statement and asked him to investigate any really important cases. He gladly agreed to this.'

10 June – Mogok

Jock defined the area he had so far covered, pointing out that 'quite a large number of war crimes were brought to light, but unfortunately in most instances they had been committed by retreating troops, hence identifications were impossible, and evidence, in many cases was very poor.'

He enclosed five successful cases against members of the Kempeitai.

Great difficulties have been encountered, particularly in the Mogok area where a very non-cooperative attitude was adopted by the Civil Police authorities, most of whom, it was ascertained, had been in the employment of the Japanese Military Administration, during the occupation of Mogok, and had in many instances collaborated with them to the fullest extent. This attitude, coupled with the fact that many well-known collaborators are still unchallenged in Mogok, (both Burmese and Indians) has had a very detrimental reaction on the local population who are apparently afraid to divulge any information which might incriminate these people.

From many reliable sources it has been ascertained that the services of Mr Abreu, Inspector of Police, Mogok area,

leave much to be desired, and from his non-cooperative attitude . . . it must be assumed that these criticisms are not
unwarranted.'

Shortly afterwards, I received a letter from a Major C. M.
Enriquez, Police Inspector, Mogok, who claimed that it was his
duty to tell me that 'all communities and races in Mogok are getting
extremely uneasy at . . . . the inaction of petty local officers in the
face of rampant sedition and terrorism'. He roundly condemned
Mr Abreu's evasion of Captain Cricghton and his refusal to coop-
erate. 'He was Superintendent of Police here in 1942 and long
before . . . . He was Excise Office under the Japanese. To our great
regret he was reappointed to the Policy on our return. He accused
him of being a collaborator with the lawless and seditious elements
in the town, and as such he and others of his policy are a menace
to security. He talked of 'a bitter hatred roused again the British',
and agreed with Jock Cricghton that 'this remote town, seldom
visited by senior officers, is a centre from which trouble is being
brewed'. He concluded by referring to 'the recent assurances in the
House of Commons that "steps are being taken to counteract the
anti-British feeling in Burma created by seditionists", that grounds
for alarm in Mogok were very well grounded and that the removal
of Abreu was most obviously desirable'.

I replied to the effect that the whole matter had been referred to
the War Crimes Liaison Officer in Rangoon who had undertaken
to bring it to the attention of the proper authorities. I have no
record of the outcome of these complaints.

The *Straits Times* (Singapore) of 10 June reported: 'There are
now only about 4,500 Japanese war crimes suspects remaining in
custody throughout South-east Asia and this figure is being rapidly
reduced. There are still many important cases under investigation
especially in Burma and Malaya. The terrible stores of the Burma-
Siam Railway Labour camps, of the Chinese massacres, of
Kempeitai in Malaya and of the Burma prison camps have yet to
be concluded. Much co-operation is still required . . . In Burma, a
mass of fresh information is now forthcoming . . . It seems likely
that many hundreds more Japanese will be brought to trial and that
trials will continue for many months in 1947 before all of even the
worst criminals have been tried.

'In spite of the rapid demobilisation of legally qualified officers, British War Crimes Military Courts in South-east Asia have dealt with 513 accused persons since the first trial started on January 24, 1946.'

I learned in mid-June that the War Crimes Liaison Officer, Colonel Dennis, had gone home on compassionate leave and that his place was to be taken by Colonel Duggie Clague, who had been my CO in E Group in Calcutta.

On 19 June, the first major war criminal was hanged in Rangoon Central Jail. Captain Uneyo Masakaru was sentenced to death for brutally beating Allied prisoners in Rangoon's Law Courts Jail into 'bloody pulp', as charged by the United States Army prosecuting counsel, resulting in the deaths of two American and one British airman.

The *New Times* of Burma reported on 20 June that the fifth War Crimes trial by the British Military Court at the City Hall, Rangoon, had ended after nine days. Lieutenant Colonel A. M. Sturrock, President of the Court, found all of the accused guilty. Lieutenant Onishi, Medical Officer at the Rangoon Central Jail, was sentenced to death by hanging for ill-treatment resulting in the death of Allied PoWs. Captain Tazumi, CO of the Jail, Sergeant Major Kiyoshi Ueno, the Quartermaster, and Private Koigetsu Ueno, a guard, were sentenced to seven, three and fifteen years' gaol, respectively, for ill-treatment and physical suffering inflicted on Allied PoWs.

The monsoon had broken on 4 June, since when it had rained incessantly. Jock reported that the bridge twenty miles south of Mogok was breaking up. Nothing daunted, he set off again on his travels the following day (11 June) for Monglong, Kyaukme, Nahmsan, Namtu, Lashio and Hsipaw. He asked for supplies of petrol, oil, grease and distilled water to be sent to him at Kyaukme, adding that cigarettes would also be very welcome. Rufus Chater and I drove to Mogok armed with supplies, spending a couple of days with Jock and making a short trip to Mongmit – a most enjoyable and refreshing break.

Jock arrived in Namtu on 30 June after an eventful trip, having unearthed three cases in Nahsam, in each of which the chief offender was a Sergeant Major Yuniyama of the Kempeitai, who was subsequently caught in the jungle by locals and got his 'just deserts'. The Resident Officer in Namtu had provided Jock with a bungalow –'no furniture, of course but I soon fixed that . . . '

In his letter of 6 July from Namtu, Jock reported:

> If there was no crime in Nahmsan they certainly make up for it in Namtu. Ever since I arrived I have been going like crazy, but still they are rolling in. Here, so far, is what it amounts to:
>
> Mass arrest of 800 Indian and Anglo-Indian males, transporting them to Hsipaw State Barracks, and there responsible for the death of some 200 of them. It is very nearly a repetition of the famous Belsen Camp but not on such a large scale. Men were taken out and executed by beheading and bayoneting and I have one witness from the scene of each execution who was left for dead but managed to struggle to safety.

He then listed four accused and, in doing so, revealed some of the problems of identification.

> 1. Lieutenant Colonel Azuma, Intelligence Officer, attached or seconded to the Yaribotai unit (may be CO of this unit)
>
> 2. Major Konda or Kunda or Kundo, 2nd in command of this unit
>
> 3. Captain Sato, Propaganda Officer, attached or seconded to this unit
>
> 4. Eto or Ito, held the position of station master in Namtu, and belonged to the Rikgun Bawdwin Kogyoso, but subsequently was seen in military uniform and left Namtu with the above unit, which was the last to leave.

The third one listed, I suspected, might have been an Army Captain held in Rangoon Jail, named Sato Kitaro (or Kitano).

Jock then asked us to interrogate two vital Indian witnesses, the President and Vice President of the Indian Independence League, both now in Maymyo, who had been interned in Hsipaw but who had been on very friendly terms with the four accused Japanese and 'may be able to supply a complete list of all deaths'. He then identified a further key witness named Balankrishnal, now working with the Supply Department at Taunggyi, who had been Major Konda's interpreter. I immediately signalled the Deputy Superintendent of Police at Taunggyi asking for his help in tracing this man.

Jock's second big investigation involved the mass arrests and torture of Indians, Chinese, Kachins, and Karens by the Namty Kempeitai between 1942 and 1945. This involved dozens of cases. He listed ten accused; four lieutenants, three sergeant majors (one of these was Yuniyama, who had been involved with the three serious cases in Namtu) and three corporals. He urged me to 'get on their tails' as he was 'positive we can sew them up'. He added a footnote: 'The IP (Inspector of Police) here is a gem. What a difference it makes!'

The indomitable Lenka did her best to identify, from all the available lists at her disposal, the Japanese suspects named by Jock. But Sergeant Major Yamamoto could have been: (a) Shochi Yanamoto, Kempeitai, Bangkok; (b) Yoichi Yamamoto, KPT, Rangoon; or, (c) Kenji Yanamoto, KPT, Taiping. Assuming they were still in custody, only intensive interrogation could reveal which one, if any, of these was the culprit.

On 9 July, I issued the first four Suspect Lists, which were distributed to twenty-two jails in South-east Asia and to the Red Fort in Delhi with the request that 'every endeavour is made to locate the suspects named'. Those successfully identified were to be transferred to Rangoon Jail 'with the minimum of delay'. Any available photographs and copies of their war service histories were to be forwarded to my headquarters in Maymyo. In addition, copies of our Suspect Lists went to the War Crimes Registry in Singapore, to HQ Burma Command, HQ North Burma Area, the War Crimes Liaison Officers in Burma and Malaya, and to the other two Investigation Teams in Burma – a total of seventy copies in all. Attached to each was a list of places where the alleged crimes were committed, giving the longitude and latitude of each, plus a list of Japanese Army units involved, to facilitate (hopefully) the location of the units concerned. Altogether, 165 suspects were listed. In each case, the suspect's name, rank and unit were given, a description, for example, 'Age c. 45, height 5' 2"', stout, typical Jap features, husky voice, thick glasses', the date, place and nature of the crime, the jail where he was believed to be held and any other relevant remarks.

Jock proceeded to Hsipaw, reaching it on 11 July after a brief stopover in Lashio 'which, from a crime and pleasure point of view, proved very disappointing . . . '

11 July – Hsipaw
    I shall be here for about one week, as I have just interviewed the Chief Administrator of the State, and he informs me that there are quite a number of cases in this area.

    With regard to the Hsipaw concentration camp, I intend opening the graves wherein I believe some 200 Indians have been buried, and would greatly appreciate the use of a camera. There are only two graves, so it should not be a very long job. If, when you are sending my supplies, you could send your camera, I would take the photographs and send it back right away. Talking of supplies, I am now in desperate need of stationery and would appreciate it if you could despatch some without delay, as it is impossible to get any here.

    In the short space of two weeks I have taken over 60 statements, mostly in connection with the Hsipaw case, and from all accounts I hope to pick up a few more here. I have only sufficient paper to take about six more statements, so it's now SOS stationery.

On 17 July, I wrote to Jock congratulating him on the ground covered and the number of statements he had taken.

The Hsipaw Camp Case appears to be a really big one, in fact it may well develop into being the biggest in Burma, especially as you have got so much firsthand evidence and the names of the accused.

    As you have your hands pretty full, I am sending our new arrival up to join you and give you a hand. I think you knew Corish in Shanghai (in the Police Force). He has been in Java until recently, where his movements were, of necessity, rather restricted, and is therefore dead keen to get out on a job. We checked through the Suspect Lists and picked out all those who might conceivably be the ones you want . . . As soon as

I get your statements I will make out a Preliminary Report to send to the Registry, so they can get cracking and locate the culprits.

I am giving my camera to Corish to take with him. I'm afraid the films aren't very good but they are all I've got at the moment. I advise you to take as many as you can, as it's possible that only one out of three will come out . . .

We are expecting Clague (the WCLO in Rangoon) up here (in Maymyo) any day now and Maddox (OC No. 16 Team) is coming down from Myitkyina for a conference.

I enclose copies of the 4 Suspect lists we prepared before the others went off 'Jap hunting'. Our next big job, which we are busy with, is the consolidating of all our cases into a number of big cases, more or less divided into areas. Corish will tell you the rest of the news. Kyte is supposed to be joining us eventually, and we are also getting Sinclair attached to us, you will be glad to hear.

I am giving Corish Rupees 100/- in case you are getting short of funds; also stationery, petrol (44 galls), cigs and rations. I appreciate all your hard work, Jock, and I can assure you that if I have anything to do with it, it won't be in vain.

Jock was a remarkable person; tough, wild, outspoken, but as solid as a rock and very reliable. He had had an exceptional record of service in the Shanghai Police, having received no fewer than thirty-two awards and commendations for meritorious service, including the Distinguished Conduct Medal. Later (26 October) I recommended him for a Commander-in-Chief's Certificate 'for services rendered under extremely adverse conditions', as well as for promotion to major. I never heard whether he received either of these well-merited recognitions.

I told Jock I had had a successful meeting in Rangoon with Colonel Lambe, the senior staff officer at War Crimes HQ in Singapore, who had been suitably impressed with the Team's work, and had also agreed with my plan for Operation ROUND-UP. I also let him know that Mr Abreu, the elusive Police Inspector in Mogok, had been ordered by the Inspector General of Police, Rangoon, to present himself to me in Maymyo by the end of July, for cross-examination by Jock.

Jock confirmed the safe arrival of Corish and the eagerly-awaited supplies. He spoke of going to interview two very important witnesses, one in Taunggyi and the other in Nahmkan, eighty-five miles north of Lashio. The latter was, in fact, in No. 16 Team's area, but the road from their HQ in Bhamo was reported to be impassable due to heavy rains. He had also picked up some additional evidence in Namtu and planned to return there.

He was anxious to contact an arch-collaborator called Harban Singh, who had worked for the Namtu Kempeitai, and another similar character called Barma, who had been connected with the Hsipaw Kempeitai, both of whom were believed to be in Maymyo. 'If you should be successful in locating these two boys,' Jock said, 'please try to keep them entertained until I get back, as I have a lot of awkward questions to ask them . . . Re your 'grouping of cases' idea, I agree this would be the best solution, as it would save a lot of time and paperwork and appears to be the most logical plan.'

He went on to describe his visit to the mass graves at Hsipaw:

I had a real sickener yesterday . . . It was a sweltering hot day and we had to cut our way into this place. The first grave we opened was alright, but the second (believe it or not) was still 'alive' and the stench was simply hellish. I had a devil of a job getting the coolies to continue, but with the help of a few cigarettes managed to complete the job. Needless to say I lost my lunch, and would have given anything for a real good stiff peg . . .

Two days later he wrote again to say that he was running short of rations and cash and that his Jeep was giving him some trouble, 'No. 4 cylinder piston-ring's gone west and front wheel brake lining finished'.

As local civilians' workshops had no spares, he sent Bombardier Jan back to Maymyo, armed with statements and a plea for help. Jan arrived late that night and early next morning I visited the local Army Workshops. The CO said there were no piston rings to be had in Burma, let alone Maymyo. However, he promised to do his best if Jock were to bring his Jeep in for overhaul and repairs. I got a message to Jock to return to Maymyo forthwith, as in any case Duggie Clague was due to arrive that day (20 July) and it would give Jock a chance to brief him fully on the Hsipaw and Namtu cases in particular and on his operations in the field generally.

Duggie spent nine days as our guest in the Team's HQ in Maymyo, and the change of scenery and cool climate enabled him to recover rapidly from the combined effects of overwork and a generally run-down condition. He had suffered from the intense heat in Bangkok and Rangoon and relished the coolness and quiet of this relaxing hill station. A full colonel, complete with red tabs, at the tender age of twenty-eight, Duggie had had a remarkable war record. After escaping from a PoW camp in Shanghai, he had been posted to E Group, Calcutta, where he masterminded our operations in Burma, Malaya and Siam. He was, in fact, my boss, when I was operating with Jimmie Ferguson on the Arakan coast whence we made sorties behind the Japanese lines, establishing 'rat lines' for aircrew who had been shot down and needed to be rescued.

Duggie had flown into Bangkok clandestinely even before the Japanese had capitulated, and organized a full-scale operation to contact the PoW camps in northern Siam and, in particular, on the notorious Burma–Siam Railway.

Duggie left us on 28 July, a much fitter and happier man and wrote from Rangoon to say he had found everything very congenial, not least the opportunity to pull Lenka's leg which he did mercilessly the whole time he was there. Lenka, it was true, had baffled Duggie at every turn with her facts and figures which (luckily for me) she had at her fingertips. Duggie never caught her out once. He added, 'I fear I have so far not been able to find any mistakes, but even if I have to alter the figures (our war crimes statistics) myself, I will find something in order to redeem my self-respect!' He ended, 'I am sure that in six weeks you and your chaps will have something really good to show as a result of all the hard work put in. Well done, Duggie.' Not normally an easy man to please, his words of praise were a timely shot in the arm for all of us. But, as I wrote home, 'The bulk of the credit must undoubtedly go to those who have worked so hard for me . . . From the dozens of signals that pour into this little office you'd think it was an Army HQ at least! It is a slow business and requires much patience, skill and determination'.

After a couple of days in Maymyo, Jock returned to the field for a further two weeks in the Lashio, Hsipaw, and Taunggyi area. His letter from Lashio of 2 August painted a revealing picture of the conditions under which he had to operate, notably the constant frustration of not being able to tie up vital loose ends.

Fascinatingly, too, he mentioned the questionable activities of Chinese troops who crossed the border into Burma in March 1945 under the eccentric, irascible American General, Joe Stillwell, and were reported to have gone on the rampage in the Hsipaw area. According to Jock's informants, the General commanding the Chinese 50th Division, General Pan Yih Kaung, and his staff were recalled to Chunking and tried for looting, rape 'and God knows what else'.

I had discussed my Operation ROUNDUP with Duggie Clague and Colonel Lambe and both had agreed with my general philosophy. The intention was to speed up the location, interrogation and identification of as many of the 160 suspects on our books as possible. We had prepared four consolidated Suspect Lists in alphabetical order, plus a separate Army Personnel List. These gave sufficient details of the alleged crimes to warrant keeping any suspects picked up in custody. Some of them, of course, would be in Changi Jail, Singapore, but we hoped the majority would be found in Saigon, Bangkok or Rangoon. I planned to send Rufus Chater to Rangoon, Jim Black to Saigon and John Walker to Bangkok. I wrote to Captain Kyte in Singapore asking him to screen the Japanese in Changi Jail but, in the event, he was despatched to Rangoon a few days later.

On 26 May I had sent Jimmy Black, also late of the Shanghai Police, out into the field where he remained for some eight weeks covering the southern Shan States, based on Taunggyi. Like Jock, he encountered almost insurmountable problems in obtaining sufficiently concrete, reliable and corroborated evidence that would stand up in a court of law, as the following extracts from his letter of 6 June conveys.

There have certainly been a lot of war crimes committed by the Japanese in this area . . . most of it from May to July 1945 when the Allied troops arrived and the Shan States were full of retreating Japs from the west and north. The villagers appear to have disappeared into the jungle and witnesses are therefore difficult to find. Interpreters and anyone connected with the Kempeitai, when interrogated, are very evasive and afraid, as there have been two or three tried in the civil courts who get stiff sentences for collaboration. When I opened up here I had a queue for a couple of days, all with their families. I wasn't long in finding the reason . . . they were all after compensation for the deaths of their husbands and sons and didn't seem interested in bringing the Japs to justice, but were more concerned with their neighbours whom they accused of giving the Japs information against their families.

Out of about 15 cases I have been trying to get something concrete. I have only five and they are a bit shaky.

If I have the same experience in the other States I can see me being here for some time, as one has to be patient and go through the cases to see if they can be connected in any way before throwing them up, and it's a long job sometimes.

I have a poisoned heel but it is on the mend. It looked pretty bad, so I saw the MO and have been hobbling around since. It's lovely country up here and I'm very comfortable. I am digging in with the DSP (Deputy Superintendent of Police) in his bungalow, and everyone is very cooperative and pleasant. If you have anyone to spare send them up here. There is plenty of work.

It is clear that Jim was experiencing much the same problem as Jock in persuading the right people to come forward to give statements. In my reply, I suggested:

One possible explanation is that these people realize that there is a strong chance that Burma will be given her independence before very long, and they are afraid of giving any information implicating those of their fellow countrymen who is any way assisted the Japs during the occupation . . . and who may well take the law into their own hands when the time comes.

Jock turned up unexpectedly last night. As you know, there is a very serious shortage of petrol at the moment, so he may be stuck here for a while. Apparently, within a few minutes of Jock arriving in Mogok, there was a general exodus. The place stinks with collaborators, from the DIP downwards! I hope by now your heel has recovered. We thought of putting in the

Progress Report that you had been 'wounded on active service', but decided that the Registry's sense of humour wouldn't appreciate it.

On 12 July, John Walker, whom I had sent to Rangoon on a liaison visit, wrote a long, confidential letter outlining some of the problems he was facing. First, he said Duggie Clague had vetoed his trip to Bangkok and Jim Black's to Saigon. His argument was that all the Kempeitai from Siam were on their way to the Rangoon or Changi Jail, or would be in the near future.

I pointed out that we had already (on 9 July) asked for a number of these KPT to be transferred to Rangoon, but had had no acknowledgement. I was able to give him a copy of the signal, which fortunately I had. He promised to look into the matter. I made all the points I could in favour of going to Bangkok – Lambe's approval, personal knowledge of the cases, the problems of using third parties to do the job, etc.

He then decided that I would go to Bangkok and Saigon, but that Jim was to stay to assist Rufus with the Rangoon cases. As for Saigon, Clague had not very much information about the Jail. Most of the Japanese there were held on French cases, and if I did locate any of them it would depend on the gravity of our case compared to theirs which would settle who tried them.

A message from Rufus said:

We have found a fair number of Japanese down here who will almost certainly prove to be our boys.

17 Team possesses fairly comprehensive lists of the Jails, together with detention reports and war service histories, which we have never seen.

Why on earth all the information should be held in this bottle-neck, I don't know. If we had had the same information at our disposal in Maymyo I feel sure it would have simplified preparation of the Suspect Lists, and also narrowed the field down in the search for possible culprits.

John pointed out that with the promised flow of Japanese suspects into Rangoon Jail at least two if not three officers would be needed to achieve quick results.

He recommended using Corish in Rangoon, rather than in Maymyo, although Duggie thought he could be used going round with photos up-country, adding, 'No doubt you will put the WCLO more in the picture when he arrives in Maymyo.' He continued:

We have started on the Rangoon cases and twelve gents are to be photographed tomorrow . . . These cases should be completed reasonably quickly. Incidentally, due to the difficulties of developing and printing, these photos will be sent to Bangkok, but I understand they should be back in about 8 days. It is difficult to obtain a passage to Bangkok and I doubt if I will get away before the middle of next week.

As a matter of interest, Tony Dumont is probably coming to Rangoon to be the legal advisor to the three Teams. My first contact with Burnett (OC, No 17 Team, Rangoon) was when he was fresh from the wrestling pit, covered in grime and sweat. He thrust a grimy paw in mine and dripped perspiration all over me. He seemed to be full of health and energy, but all I could reply was a request for a few aspirins as I was feeling 'off colour'. He seemed to think me a poor fish. I think he's a ruddy madman! Our work was disturbed this morning to assist him in chasing out two cows from the car park. Our little slumbers are disturbed by gongs at 6.30 a.m. and lots of little men bounding around with medicine balls. Steady snoring is the only reply from No. 2 Team's representatives. Regards from Rufus and Jim and my regards to Lenka, although she is probably reading this over your shoulder . . .

John wrote again two days later (14 July):

We have sorted out a number of case papers which show promise of being completed in a reasonably short time, as it is almost certain that the Japs are in Rangoon. We are handicapped in some cases as we only have the reports. An additional advantage in having the papers here is that Major Airey, the Prosecuting Officer, can 'vet' them prior to our interrogating the Suspects.

Following a brief summary of the cases he was working on, he continued:

I am afraid the above doesn't seem very much but I assure you there is plenty to do. The 'system' down here is in the growing pain stages but we hope things will pep up later. Now that Sinclair is coming to us – in the face of our rival claimants (!) you will probably be able to send another officer here. Burnett does not seem to object to having three or four officers here – we're all War Crimes boys together . . .

I replied to John on 15 July:

The only thing I am not clear about now is the position re Kyte. Corish tells me that Clague is keeping him in Rangoon for a bit, but that he will probably be coming up here in a few days. If he doesn't come with Clague presumably the latter will put me wise as to his fate.

I don't think Clague is being unreasonable (about sending people out on Operation ROUNDUP). He must know best, though it's hard lines on Jim not being allowed to go to Bangkok with you. I am fully confident that you will be able to cope on your own, however. Had we known that the KPT were to be transferred to Rangoon it might have altered our plans in the first place . . . I intend to stick to the plan to send Corish up to join Jock, as Corish is dead keen to go out into 'the field' and Jock desperately needs help . . . They should be back within a fortnight and I shall then certainly send Corish down to Rangoon. Three nights ago we had a burglary and practically all our beautiful China plates were removed from the stores, with the result we are now suffering the gross indignity of having to eat off tin plates. The local police are onto it but were not confident of success until I mentioned a reward of 200 rupees.

I hope this reaches you before you leave for Bangkok. I shall be profoundly relieved when you return, as 'administration' is not my strong point!

Captain Kyte, it transpired, had been officially posted to my Team but was to remain in Rangoon as part of the 'pool' of officers screening Japanese suspects in Rangoon Jail. This suited my books well, as without positive identification the work done on accumulating evidence would have been for nought.

John Walker wrote from Bangkok on 21 July explaining what he had achieved since his arrival there.

> Despite what Clague thinks, I believe it has been worthwhile coming here. Quite a lot of things could not have been done if we had stayed in Rangoon and simply sent out hopeful signals.
>
> I am living in the Colonel's Mess at present and very comfortable it is too. The whole atmosphere reminds me of Java. Even the people, and the countryside I have seen so far, are reminiscent of those halcyon days in Soerabaya. I fear Bangkok is not the town flowing with milk and honey that we expected. Prices are comparable to Burma. Imports of rarities such as rolls of film, cameras, etc., have not yet started and consequently prices are still high. All the Teams here work together in one office, and en masse it looks quite formidable. They are losing about eight officers at the end of the month, however. After seeing the Rangoon fiasco and even here, where it is more organised, I think our sane little set-up in Maymyo has much to be said for it.

Three days later (24 July) John followed up with the results of screening the Japanese on the Bangkwang (Bangkok) Jail list against our suspect lists.

> I have been unable to locate any suspects definitely but it has brought to light a few more possibilities. It is quite likely that some have been sent on to Rangoon by now.
>
> There are no War Histories of the a/m here but Rangoon or Singapore should have them.

He then listed nine 'possibles', e.g, 'List No. 1-A long shot but it might be Sgt ASAHI Shizuo, KPT' and continued,

> I have been to see the Japanese contact office here re Army personnel but I can't expect any definite information until

tomorrow. Incidentally, much of the information we require will probably be available at Jap HQ Moulmein. Perhaps we could arrange for a Jap Staff Officer to come and see us in Rangoon or, alternatively, use No. 17 team's detachment at Moulmein for this.

The next day he sent me three photos of suspects, one of them being of Sergeant ASAHI Shizuo mentioned in his previous letter. His visit to the Japanese Contact Office had proved somewhat fruitless. 'Information is scanty as there are no records. As already intimated, most of the available information is at Moulmein and Rangoon.' He went on to comment on ten of the suspects screened. To illustrate the problem of identification, one of his notes reads:

> This unit must have been part of 31 Division, as 'Litzu' means '31'. This Div. is now in Burma. The Commander was Lt/Gen SATO, Kotoku or Yukinori (alternative renderings). This officer is believed to have gone to Java after being in Burma.

Rufus Chater wrote from Rangoon on 21 July to the effect that the results of a week of hard work had been a little disappointing. His comments reinforced those made by his colleagues, Jock Crichton, John Walker and Jim Black.

> The demoralization which the Japs suffered after their defeat seems to be wearing off and, far from being ready to incriminate their comrades, most of the suspects seem to have got together and agreed to deny even the possibility of any ill-treatment. But there have been exceptions. John and Jim managed to drag some sort of a story out of a suspect early in the week and Jim is in the process of getting another.

He and the other two had decided that they were spending too much time on each interrogation – sometimes two and a half hours to establish one point.

> At that rate I reckon we might have all our cases complete by September next year. I now consider that the best plan is to establish whether the Accused was at the right place at the

right time, put a few questions to any likely people such as his
CO and, if no confession or indictment is forthcoming, send
photos up for identification. Further, Jim and I agree that
going hell-for-leather is hopeless. It is very easy to lose sight
of the fox during the interrogation and then you've just got to
sit back and think for a while. Personally, I don't know if I
want a shave or a haircut.

I have broken my last pair of glasses and the nearest
lens maker is in Calcutta. So now I go around with a
cracked lens seeing a somewhat distorted world through one
corner.

John (Walker) fixed up for a clerk to come to us from
Establishments. He arrived in due course – a chubby, cheery,
slightly stupid Anglo-Indian, who was a Charge-Clerk (whatever that is) and who could *not* type. We bore with him for a
couple of days, retyped all his work and finally he was
replaced by a long, lean Madrassi sub-conductor by the name
of Mr Pedro. This Pedro we still have and he's not too bad,
though a bit on the smart side.

John got away (to Bangkok) alright but before he left the
17 Team Jemadar [Indian Army officer equivalent to a lieu-
tenant] told Burnett [CO No. 17 Team] he felt
uncomfortable in a room with the three of us. So Burnett
decreed that we should move out and double up with
'Shorty' Kyte, with John alone in the Guest Chamber. As
there is no office accommodation for us (No. 2 Team) here,
Jim and I have to do the best we can in the bedroom. It's
rather a shambles sometimes. Lambert said something about
fixing us up with a room in the IORs (Indian Other Ranks)
and dhobi's (laundryman's) house, which would certainly be
an improvement.

The Jeep began to play up somewhat but after it had been
in the hands of one Fitter Mechanic and two Motor
Mechanics for five hours with scant success, Fitter Chater
fixed the thing with one deft flip of a spanner . . . or, at any
rate, he thinks he did. So, you see, everything's fine. But Jim's
main comment is: 'Everything in that bumf about interrogating Japs is bunkum . . .'

I got the impression from Clague that he was very much

toying with the idea of getting all No. 2 Team down here for the Monsoon season. Bloody as it would be for us, it is a reasonable idea . . . from his point of view.

I think he is aiming to doss down with us. He has no proper place to work here and regards Burnett as a sort of circus act.

In my reply to Rufus, I said we had been struggling to get the new Case List out in time for Clague to take away with him after visiting us in Maymyo. As each signal came in from him, Jim or Jock, the List had to be amended.

I then commented on various cases he was working on:

NAMTU Case. This is very encouraging. As you have been able to locate 90% of the accused there is only interrogation to be done. Jock will do this when he finishes up here, which will be in about two weeks' time. I will endeavour to get those now in Japan sent back.

Clague is very favourably impressed with the amount of stuff you and Jim have been sending back. Keep it up! He realizes he is in an even less favourable position to criticize Operation ROUNDUP than when he first arrived. He has seen John's reports from Bangkok and realizes that he hasn't been exactly wasting his time. He is particularly keen on the use made of the four interpreters . . .

Re enclosed Case List: You will see that the 'Basic' cases have been combined to form 'Area' cases, with a view to having each 'Area' case tried in one go. This may not always work, as Legal may not want to hold up the Trial of a 'Basic' case due to non-completion of the 'Area' case (if you see what I mean).

Clague will explain to you that as soon as we have four or five cases completed he wants you to take them down to Singapore. He hopes to be back (from Bangkok) in about six weeks' time. By then we should have at least six or seven cases buttoned up. Re your glasses, I can strongly recommend Lawrence & Mayo Ltd in Calcutta. A cousin of mine, A. W. MacCaw, of 21 Strand Road, Calcutta, would help if you want them quickly. Why not write and ask him?

Clague has enjoyed his stay here. So much so, in fact, that

he intends coming here as often as he can. He has been out riding with the Mountain Regiment several times (including one 18-mile ride) which he enjoyed immensely. When Jock was here we had a binge at the Club, which ended up in Jock's room with Clague lying prostrate on the floor! Jock made up for his month's abstinence with a vengeance.

The officer commanding No. 17 Team in Rangoon (my opposite number) was Lieutenant Colonel J. S. F. A. F. Burnett DSO MC. Most of my dealings with him had been through my officers working in Rangoon. I had, however, crossed swords with him in mid-June over the somewhat belligerent attitude he had adopted to my paper *Appreciation of War Crimes Investigations, Burma* for some unknown reason. On 17 June he wrote describing it as

an admirable document, which I found most interesting. After having been in Burma from the beginning of 1942 to the end of 1945, I find that it is a good survey. So good I realize that my area has been adequately surveyed for me.

Somewhat scathingly he added:

You say that 'the number of incomplete cases is very great'. Are you speaking for Maddox (OC No. 16 Team) and myself? You say 'many of the points raised apply to every War Crimes team'. I wonder.

In the heat of the moment, and no doubt reflecting the stresses and strains of the times, I replied in equally intemperate terms, which, apart from letting off steam, could do little or nothing to improve our relationship. I queried the fact that he had opened a Confidential letter addressed to the Liaison Officer, Rangoon; that no one had troubled to inform me that he was appointed to stand-in for the Liaison Officer; and that, without reference to me, he had arbitrarily appointed Major Lambert to be his second-in-command when, in fact, he had been posted to me as my Legal Major some six weeks previously. Finally, I expressed regret that I had apparently offended him by presuming to survey his area, explaining that:

It was merely intended to give the WCLO an idea of the situation here in Central Burma, as I thought perhaps he might be interested in my views on the subject. As for my reference to the number of incomplete cases in Burma, in view of the fact that the number of Trials concluded in Rangoon amounts to *four*, I still maintain that my contention is correct.

Burnett had had a truly remarkable war record, which, sadly, I only learned of sometime later. Commissioned into the Argyll & Sutherland Highlanders in December 1940, he served with them in Burma and, in November 1942, was transferred to V Force, a clandestine group (similar to my own E Group) operating behind the Japanese lines. He had survived in the jungles of Burma and Malaya for two and a half years and his outstanding bravery had earned him both the Military Cross and the Distinguished Service Order. He became known to the Japanese as 'the officer with the flaming red beard'. He was invalided back to England in November 1945 and spent three months in hospital before being posted back to Burma in command of No. 17 War Crimes Investigation Team. A year later, in December 1946, he was returned to regimental duty as Second-in-Command, 1st Battalion, the Seaforth Highlanders, stationed at Gillman Barracks, Singapore. Unfortunately for him he became involved in an unfortunate incident, which resulted in his court martial. On the night of 3 March, 1947, Burnett was on duty at an anti-looting roadblock outside an ordnance depot in Singapore. A Sikh taxi driver was signalled to stop by Burnett by means of a torch. Instead, the taxi accelerated, Burnett jumped out of the way and then fired a number of shots at the taxi, which crashed. The driver was wounded and later died in hospital. Burnett was arrested and charged with causing the Sikh driver's death: more specifically, ' . . . of doing a rash act not amounting to culpable homicide'. I never learned the outcome of the court martial.

For recreation and exercise, I and my colleagues took advantage of a nine-hole golf course (later extended to twelve holes) although the greens left much to be desired, having been badly mistreated by the Japanese. We played some tennis, too, until the monsoon started when we switched to squash, having successfully procured racquets from the local bazaar and squash balls from the NAAFI. We saw many deer, of the barking variety, and jungle fowl, but otherwise there was little sign of animal life on our frequent walks in the nearby jungle. Rufus Chater, a Mountain Gunner, was able to borrow ponies from the mountain battery stationed in Maymyo, enabling us to enjoy early morning rides round the lake and even on the racecourse. The hills around Maymyo, itself perched on a hill, were thickly wooded, abounding with brightly coloured bougainvillaea and flame-of-the-forest with their brilliant red and yellow flowers.

In the evening we played chess, did the *Manchester Guardian* crossword puzzle, courtesy of John Walker who received this paper regularly, made up our own crossword puzzles and generally managed to keep our minds active and diverted from the gruesome task of reading endless accounts of the Japanese's heinous misdemeanours.

My principal task was to check the witness statements that poured in (112 in a period of one particular week), checking to see that they constituted acceptable evidence before sending them on, via Rangoon, to our HQ in Singapore.

I wrote home:

> You've no idea how exhausting it is to read about the ghastly things that happened, day in, day out, sometimes until the early hours. Also one has to try and remember hundreds of names of suspects, victims and witnesses. Though, in that respect I am very fortunate to have Lenka close at hand. She has the most amazing memory for names and facts. I don't know what I'd do without her.
>
> I could show you statements that would give Dracula nightmares! A favourite torture practised by the Kempeitai was the 'water torture', in which the victim is tied to a bench and a wet cloth placed over his nose, preventing him from breathing. About five or six gallons of water are then poured into his mouth until he is half suffocated. They then proceed to jump on his stomach, before repeating the whole process . . . Charming people!

At the end of July, Duggie Clague submitted a comprehensive 'Resumé and Progress Report' to the HQ in Singapore, covering the month since his appointment as the Liaison Officer, Burma (in addition to being the WCLO, Siam). He had seen the COs of the three Teams and talked to most of the investigators. He explained why so few cases were ready for court, saying that delays were inevitable and that arrangements had been made to ensure greater publicity for War Crimes Trials.

The Government of Burma had been asked to report on coolies used on the Burma–Siam Railway and to collect evidence from the survivors who had returned to their villages. Eighty men from the Japanese 9th Railway Regiment were being interrogated by a detachment from Siam. An RAF War Crimes unit had arrived and was to be allocated to investigate cases on the Arakan coast, which had not as yet been tackled. He went on to outline the structure and duties of the Co-ordinating Section in Rangoon.

(a) This Section is under the direct command of the War Crimes Liaison Officer. It will consist of: WCLO, 1 Legal Major, 1 Staff Captain, and 4 Captains/Lieutenants. WCLO will direct all War Crimes work in conformity with the directives issued by HQ ALFSEA, and co-ordinate the activities of the various agencies employed throughout Burma. He will also liaise with HQ Burma Command on all policy matters. The Legal Major will be available to help all Teams in the completion of their cases. No cases will be forwarded to ALFSEA without his consent;

b) Staff Captain 'A' will co-ordinate all future requests for 'wanted' Japanese. He will liaise with HQ Burma Command on all non-policy matters, and will maintain records of progress of all cases under investigation;

c) The 4 Capts/Lts (all Japanese speakers) will be held in a Pool and will be available to all Teams for the interrogation of Japanese accused in custody in Rangoon. This Pool will maintain complete records of all Japanese in Rangoon Jail and keep Teams informed when wanted men are located.

Duggie's Report then dealt with my own Team's work, general problems and progress.

I visited Maymyo and discussed matters fully with the CO. During my visit I was able to meet all members of the Team not previously contacted. They have 62 'Basic' cases, i.e. crimes for which statements have been taken, the number of accused varying from one to sixteen. All cases were examined and it was found that recommendations made by the AAG as to which should be discarded and which should be amalgamated, had been observed. All cases were divided into geographical groups based on the place where the incident occurred. In the main this coincides with Kempeitai dispositions and as the majority of cases so far involve the Kempeitai, this point is of importance. The result of this division produced 27 Area cases. Very few of the accused have yet been located but when the Kempeitai, who served in Burma but were found in Siam after the War, reach Rangoon a big improvement will occur. Three Area cases can be completed forthwith, the accused having been identified in Rangoon Jail.

A question of policy now arises. Should a completed Basic case be held pending the completion of all 'Basic' cases in the same area, or should it be forwarded to ALFSEA in the normal way? I am of the opinion that where the missing accused required to complete the Area cases are unlikely to be located in the near future, then the Basic case should be forwarded to ALFSEA but that should any evidence come to light that the missing accused are likely to become available, the trial should be postponed pending completion of the Area case.

In my opinion, unless such a step is taken, a bottleneck will result, with Basic cases piling up but few cases ready for trial.

In general, it is fair to say that No. 2 Team have been starved of information due to the lack of Co-ordinating Section in Rangoon and that the locating of accused has lagged far behind investigations with the result that completed cases are nil and, therefore, there is little concrete to show for all the hard work put in by investigators. The majority of two Team's cases involved the Kempeitai and are all of a serious nature, many involving the death of the victims. As in South Burma,

Field Security Sections have done a large amount of investigating and have handed over the resultant cases to No. 2 Team. During the Monsoon it will certainly be impossible to bring any of 2 Team's Chin Hill cases to trial and we will be up against considerable difficulties even when the monsoon is over, due to the fact that it is unlikely that any roads will be motorable.

A decision will have to be taken later when such cases as we have are completed. Considerable assistance has been rendered to No. 2 Team by Field Security Sections and by units of BIC (Burmese Intelligence Corps) in the investigation of cases and the procuring of evidence, whilst North Burma Area has given every possible administrative assistance.

Early in August I received a letter from Rufus (otherwise known as 'Wolfie') Chater in Rangoon enclosing amendments to his previous Suspect Lists. 'The three days I spent on this job were a bloody awful sweat. But I think you will agree that it was worthwhile. Each Team is now allowed to employ six civilian staff: one cook (Indian), one cook (British), one sweeper (cleaner) and three others.' Since there was not a full complement in Maymyo he asked permission to take on a Burmese servant, to which I agreed.

On 22 August I went down to Rangoon, accompanied by Lenka, to see Jock Crichton and Frank Corish who had been there since 17 August. Before leaving Maymyo, I wrote to Bevis Lambe congratulating him on his promotion to full Colonel. I added an apology for having applied (on 29 June) for the job of Officer Commanding the War Crimes Liaison Team in Tokyo, the application, in any case, having been turned down. Lambe replied to say that there was no need to apologize, adding, 'I quite understand but you could not be spared from Burma at this juncture. Also, I had arranged to send Read-Collins before I got your letter.'

Lenka and I left Maymyo in a 25cwt truck. Thirty miles south of Mandalay, en route to Meiktila, we were stopped in a small village and told there had been a hold up by *dacoits* (an armed robber band) six miles further down the road. As we had to catch a train in Meiktila, we decided to take a chance and press on. Fortunately, we got through unharmed, although I felt guilty at having put Lenka at such risk. From Meiktila we travelled in a hospital train. 'Very comfortable', I wrote Home, 'though it turned out that the only two air-conditioned coaches were reserved for some Japanese who boarded the train the following morning. Can you beat it?'

My letter went on to describe our visit to Rangoon:

It rained practically non-stop the whole time we were there – a solid, continuous downpour and the main problem was trying to keep dry. It was also hot, in a sticky, sultry sort of way. Lenka stayed in the WYCA hostel and I was given Duggie Clague's room in the War Crimes HQ, where I also set up a temporary office. Rufus and Jock were very glad to see us. Poor old Rufus had been there for nearly six weeks and was clearly becoming extremely 'browned off'. I soon realized why! The atmosphere in the Mess was anything but congenial and the food so bad we only had three meals there. The four of us retired to the Sun Café where the food was excellent, if expensive.

Nearly every evening we went to the Pegu Club, one of the best I've been to in the East: good food, dance floor and band, and plenty to drink (iced).

I took Lenka to the Jail (nearly causing a riot among the prisoners!), saw our 'friends' awaiting trial in solitary confinement, and listened-in to Jock conducting an interrogation. As we arrived, we heard Jock say: 'Do you realize you've told me enough to hang yourself?'

Major Carter, of the Military Secretary's Branch at HQ Burma Command wrote on 28 August:

Just a line to thank you so much for all the tremendous efforts you and your chaps made to get the dope about Wright (a British civilian who had acted with astonishing bravery throughout the Japanese occupation of Burma). I thought you might be interested to know that the General has forwarded your first recommendation and that it has received the approval of the Governor (of Burma). I am sending it on to ALFSEA and I hope in due course it will receive approval from the Government at Home. You will appreciate that this is for your eyes only; it would be most undesirable for Wright to get an inkling that he has been recommended for an award.

It has taken a long time to get the stuff but your difficulties are fully appreciated and I have explained them to ALFSEA both verbally and in writing.

On 30 August I received the following (somewhat startling) signal from Singapore:

Essential Spooner takes over as AAG (Assistant Adjutant General) War Crimes ALFSEA soonest.

Signal ETA (Expected Time of Arrival). For Clague. Regret necessity owning unforeseen circumstances. Posting Pardoe No. 2 Team on completion investigations Borneo. ETA Burma 20 September.

I signalled Duggie who was then visiting Bangkok: 'Presume no alternative unless you have any objection. Responsibilities entailed rather overwhelming, but could cope if moral support allowed . . . Returning Maymyo 2 September. Anxious hear your views. Will await reply.' Lenka had made it quite clear that she flatly refused to stay in Burma.

Duggie signalled back immediately: 'Report Singapore earliest, handing over to Walker. You will be directly responsible to Colonel 'A' (Lambe) and can rely on all possible assistance and guidance from him.'

He followed this up with a momentous and significant signal: 'Have asked for moral support. Consider it best if Salomonson [Lenka's married surname] proceeds Rangoon with you and awaits instructions.'

On 8 September I wrote Home from Maymyo:

The wheels of Destiny roll on. A year ago today I was enjoying the scenery and fresh air of Kuala Lumpur. Then Bob Stewart turned up to escort us down to Singapore. History is about to repeat itself. Now that the monsoon is over it is as perfect as it could be up here in the hills. But I must pack my bags again and prepare for another long journey . . . to . . . Singapore . . .

I pointed out what a god-sent opportunity this was (career-wise) and that I would be crazy to turn it down, even if I had any option (which I doubted). Judging by what followed, I must have viewed the prospects with some awe:

> The whole shooting match is run almost entirely by Colonel Lambe; the Brigadier only deals with matters of high policy and I will be his right-hand man in complete control of that much-maligned Section known as 'The Registry', with 14 officers, 17 clerks and 60 civilians to supervise and control. It is a wee bit daunting!

The drawback was that this meant postponing my return to England until the job was completed in February or March next year (1947). Little did I realize that it would be a full year before I was finally able to return home. A postscript added succinctly: 'One of our pet war criminals has just been sentenced to death – the first but not the last, by any means.'

The last few days in Burma were frantic. I filled two tin trunks with various possessions not needed in Singapore, had them strongly crated, marked 'c/o Grindlay's Bank, Whitehall, London' and shipped home by sea. A square wooden box and two suitcases were shipped via the MFO (Military Forwarding Office) to Singapore. I did not altogether relish leaving Maymyo, with the monsoon almost over and the weather as near perfect as possible.

I wrote Home:

> It is a place I shall not easily forget – a peaceful refuge in a world of strife and discord . . . and the last in a series of 'homes', which bore little or no resemblance to a military Mess.
>
> Leaving dear old Jimmy Black (a slow, solid dependable and ever-unperturbed Scotsman) to hold the fort, and our newly-joined 'bloodhound', a Liverpudlian, ex-Shanghai policeman, Frank Corish, on the point of starting out on a three-week tour, Lenka (who had firmly packed her bags and insisted on accompanying us), John Walker and I jeeped down the hill, down the road to Mandalay . . . down into the hot, flooded and sticky plains. Then, for Lenka and me, the last nightmarish 24-hour journey in an antiquated, rickety train to the

coast, the two of us sharing a compartment with a stranger.

Rangoon. Incessant rain, in solid, relentless downpours . . . Frantic endeavours to get everything in order for John (Walker) to take over. The annoyance of having to eat out because the atmosphere in the War Crimes Mess could scarcely have been less inviting. The Sun Café for lunch, Pegu Club for dinner, Chinese restaurants (I hate Chinese food!) for variety.

Balancing the books (horrors!), and the relief at finding that I was only 45 chips (rupees) out: visiting HQ Burma Command: going through all the outstanding cases with Colonel Davies, the legal representative from ALFSEA. All this upset my nervous system so thoroughly I was a bundle of nerves. I shudder now to think how bloody minded I was those last few days – with myself, with Lenka, with everyone. But John, Jock and Rufus, bless their kind hearts, were models of patience and understanding. At the height of one of my outbursts they solemnly presented me with a leather writing case, complete with zip fasteners, and a carved ebony cigarette box, which so surprised and overwhelmed me that I nearly broke down altogether!

On Saturday, 14 September, my last evening in Rangoon, there was a farewell party at the Gymkhana Club which lasted until 1 am. Up at 4 am, I was escorted by John, Jock, Rufus and Lenka to the quayside where I boarded a Sunderland flying-boat, which took off at 6 am, just as the sun was rising over the Shwedegaung Pagoda.

I was so utterly exhausted, physically and emotionally, that I slept most of the way, unable fully to enjoy the delectable luxuries of the flying-boat: breakfast and lunch were served by stewards; easy chairs, room to move about the spacious cabin. I managed to glance out of the window, peer down at a group of islands 10,000 feet below, surrounded by emerald-green coral, and memories came flooding back of E Group days when I visited just such islands on clandestine operations to lay dumps of food and water for marooned Allied airmen. But that is another story.

At 2.30 pm we circled the Island of Singapore and touched down lightly on the smooth waters of 'The Roads'.

Chapter Nine

Singapore Slings and Arrows

On 17 September 1946 (my twenty-sixth birthday), two days after my arrival in Singapore, I met Colonel Bevis Lambe for the first time. His wife had just arrived from England so he had moved out of his room at the Goodwood Park Hotel, the headquarters of the War Crimes organization.

Before the First World War the hotel had been the Teutonia Club, the social centre for the German community, where lively Teutonic entertainments were held. The Club had boasted a fine barroom where every kind of German beer and all the best Rhine wines were stocked. Bowling was then a popular sport and the alleys at the Teutonia Club were a popular meeting place, with jolly evenings doubtless ending up with lashings of beer and sausages.

I took over Bevis Lambe's ground-floor room, the best in the hotel, with a spacious bedroom, bathroom complete with shower, and a large, airy veranda. I wrote Home, 'I think I am going to like working for him (Lambe). He is, so I hear, a bit of an old "granny", fussy and absent-minded, but quite easy to get on with.'

I broached the subject of Lenka and he told me to tell her to report to Singapore soonest which, needless to say, I did. I felt lost without her, even after only a few days' separation, which shows how much I had come to depend on her. I felt certain that together we could whip War Crimes HQ into shape in double quick time.

Lenka duly arrived on 22 September. I put her at once in charge of the Central Registry Department, which had the thankless task of maintaining accurate records of the accused in custody and the location of suspects. In recognition of her increased responsibilities she was duly promoted to the rank of staff captain, which pleased her immensely.

Having spent the previous nine months carping about the War

Crimes set-up in Singapore, I now had a chance to discover whether my complaints were justified. On the surface things seemed to be running smoothly: lots of pretty pictures, diagrams and charts on the walls; a bustling, beehive atmosphere, dozens of civilian clerks busy shuffling and typing papers, lots of officers rummaging through endless files. On closer inspection, however, I felt something was not quite right. I sensed troubled waters beneath the seemingly smooth surface. I decided to give myself time to settle in and get accustomed to this strangely different environment before attempting to change the system in any way, if at all. I was acutely conscious of my lack of staff training or experience other than that picked up 'in the field'. The War Crimes HQ was part of the ALFSEA command structure, a huge, many-faceted and somewhat ponderous bureaucratic machine. Its main divisions dealt with Administration (A) which we came under, Operations (O), Supplies (Q) and, of course, Intelligence (I), each subdivided into a multiplicity of specialist units. Staff officers, I soon learned, use a quaint jargon with which I was totally unfamiliar and which I needed to master if I was to make myself understood.

Bevis Lambe was (outwardly at least) patient and understanding and made generous allowances for my shortcomings. As always, I relied on simple common sense, which, in the past, had stood me in good stead. I firmly refused to be overawed by the supposedly sophisticated machinery governing a massive Army headquarters.

I wrote Home on 22 October:

> I've taken on a job and a half this time! What I've done in the past and the responsibilities I have shouldered bear no comparison with the task now confronting me. Running a small unit with four or five officers and the odd clerk isn't quite the same as controlling a dozen or more officers and a staff of almost one hundred. The amount of paper that flows in a steady stream in and out of this place is quite incredible. I don't even have time to draw my pay and have to get someone else to do it for me! Even the long hours are not enough to get through the day's work and more often than not I take papers to my room, working on them sometimes until after midnight. Also, I have never had to work with

constant interruptions, but am slowly getting used to this and to concentrating on more than one thing at a time.

Lambe is a regular Gunner officer, fiftyish, rather distinguished looking and certainly intelligent. Perhaps because of having had to bear such heavy responsibility under an exacting taskmaster, Brigadier Dowse (the Deputy Adjutant General, War Crimes), Bevis can himself be difficult to work for. It is sometimes hard to understand what he says and means. He makes snap decisions and has an unfortunate habit of changing his mind without thinking. I have to listen very carefully to what he says and usually have to ask him to repeat himself. He appears at times to dream and at others to be elsewhere with his thoughts. Worst of all, he takes for granted that even newcomers know all the answers! He would appear unexpectedly in my office, adjacent to his, and fire a rapid question at me. 'Any reply from Tokyo to my letter about Japanese defence lawyers? The Brigadier is on the line and wants to know.' 'I'll find out immediately' is my usual response. For the past three weeks, on top of all this, I have had to deal with all policy matters, normally handled by my second in command, the DAAG (Deputy Assistant Adjutant General) who is responsible for such weighty matters, but he has just got himself married and was away enjoying his honeymoon.

I was able to join the Tanglin Club, situated conveniently nearby, which had just reverted to civilian ownership. This was a very pukka, old-fashioned club where evening dress was de rigueur for dinner. The number of officers permitted membership was quite limited, so I was lucky to become a member. Founded in 1865, it had always been one of Singapore's most exclusive clubs, popular with the 'society' of the day. In the nineteen-thirties it was enlarged and, with the advent of squash, cards, billiards and snooker, lost much of its exclusivity.

The first of the 'big' War Crimes trials in South-east Asia, the notorious 'Double Tenth' case, was reported in the *Singapore Free Press* on 26 July. This concerned the treatment of prisoners held by the Japanese on suspicion of espionage. The evidence was the most damaging indictment yet on the barbarous inquisition which, in Japanese terms, passed for 'investigation and trial'. The aim had been to extract confessions from fifty-seven civilian internees. There was no doubt at all in the minds of the Kenpeitai Tai interrogators of the lengths to which they could go to achieve this aim. 'My orders,' said Lieutenant Colonel Haruzo Sumida, 'were that when a person being interrogated refused to answer, it would be inevitable to use some force – something like hitting him', an understatement of massive proportions. The wretched victims were half-starved men and women, weak with disease, crowded in cells so small that they could not lie down. They were given food scarcely fit for a dog, drank from lavatory pans, were beaten, kicked, clubbed, subjected to water torture, struck in their genitals and given electric shocks. Fifteen of them died. Eight of the twenty-one officers, men and interpreters were sentenced to death, five were acquitted and the rest received prison sentences of eight years to life.

At this point, it might perhaps be useful to review the results of investigations carried out during the previous year in South-east Asia. Up to the middle of September, a total of 414 war crimes suspects had been tried by five British Military Courts – two in Singapore (the first one opened in January 1946), one in Malaya (Penang), one in Burma (Rangoon), and one in Hong Kong. An Australian War Crimes Court was operating in the Chinese Secretariat Building in Singapore and out of thirty-seven accused tried in this court fourteen had been sentenced to death. Of the 377 tried by British Courts, 153 had received the death sentence, 101 had already been executed and sixteen had committed suicide while in custody. A total of 196 had been sentenced to various terms of imprisonment and fifty-one had been acquitted.

In addition to the cases currently being heard, there were a further thirty-seven completed cases pending and, of course, a host of other cases were still under active investigation. On 16 September 1946 there were 28,795 Japanese PoWs in camps in Singapore and Johore Bahru (on the Malayan Peninsula). Some 2,000 Japanese and 650 Koreans or Formosans were being held in Changi Jail as war crimes suspects, of whom thirty Japanese and thirteen Koreans were awaiting the gallows. Notably, there were 1,000 fewer 'inmates' incarcerated in Changi Jail than when the

Japanese controlled it during the occupation. Then overcrowding was utterly appalling, quite apart from the starvation diet suffered by the British and other prisoners. It was estimated at that time that Trials would continue for at least a further twelve months but that investigations would probably cease by the end of the year.

On 16 September, the *Singapore Straits Times* had published a letter from an ex-internee, the Reverend Colin King, concerning sentences passed by the War Crimes Court, Singapore, on five members of the Japanese staff at Changi Jail and at Sime Road Internment camps. These included three death sentences and one life imprisonment. Mr King argued that, whilst the accused deserved trial and punishment, their crimes did not merit the harshness of the sentences imposed; nor were they comparable to those committed by the dreaded Kempeitai.

A few days ago, in the Victoria Hall, I watched the calm, scarcely audible proceedings against five of my former captors. I saw the fairness and courtesy with which the Court heard defence counsel, the freedom from any 'grilling' of the accused. I listened with the most respectful admiration to the evidence given with such moderation by Mr Justice Worley and to his plea for lenience to Myamoto.

I held Camp office under Mr Worley at the time of his detention by these defendants. I remember well the acute and helpless anxiety which we of his committee felt at the time. I remembered the dirty atmosphere with which that contemptible man, Kobayashi, surrounded himself at all times, and particularly at that period. I contrasted it with the atmosphere at Victoria Hall.

I have seen some of the confidential reports of the massacres of our Chinese fellow citizens in Singapore after the Japanese occupation. I assure you, Sir, that I have no sentimental pity for Japanese war criminals. If I am to think of the dead, I have my own poignant memory of the ones drowned or burned, with no attempt to succour, in the hold of the (prison ship)*Tanjong Pinang*.

Yet, Sir, when I heard of the sentences on the Sime Road Japanese I was taken aback with surprise, regret and horror. It is most repugnant to me even to seem to suggest that the

Court committed an act of injustice, or spoke with less mercy than the dictates of humanity require.

I know nothing whatever of military law. But in the depth of my reason I am convinced that, however honourably the Court arrived at its verdict (and not for one moment do I impugn that honour), the strongest possible appeal should be made to the General Officer Commanding to mitigate the severity of these terrible sentences.

Mr King goes on to suggest that his views would be shared by those who 'were themselves the victims of the indifference, callousness, hatred, corruption and brutality of at least four of the men condemned. Nevertheless', he continues,

these men were not Kempeitai. They were not the perpetrators of the massacres of the innocent Singapore Chinese. That they did not care how many internees died through their neglect may well be true. That any of them actively killed or willed the death of any internee is, I believe, not the case. I was but an eye-witness of the cowardly, brutal, drunken, criminal outrage by Kawazue on Mr Baker. It admits of no defence. Like many other incidents, it merits very severe punishment: but not death.

Mr King cited the appalling atrocities

which not even Belsen can have outdone, perpetrated by the fields of the Kempeitai in Penang. I write as an ex-internee who had certain opportunities for learning both what the Japanese did and did not do; and also what the internees thought about them. There was no love lost, little earned; but few internees were, or have remained, so actuated by hatred as to wish for the imposition, let alone the execution of these sentences.

He ended by hoping that the GOC 'may feel able to temper military severity with civil clemency'.

On 25 October, I was delighted to learn that Wing Commander Bill Pitts, who had stayed behind after his release from a PoW camp in Batavia to help me with investigations, had been appointed an Officer of the Most Excellent Order of the British Empire. Bill had been captured in Java and sent to the island of Haroekoe in the Moluccas where, from the beginning of May 1943 until the middle of June 1944, he had been the Senior British Officer in a PoW camp containing 2,070 British and Dutch prisoners. The citation read:

> Working under the most difficult conditions and living in deplorable circumstances, he devoted all his energies to the welfare of his men, and his attitude was such that the Japanese were forced to respect him. A report from the Chief Medical Officer of the camp states that many lives were saved from sickness and malnutrition by the outstanding devotion to duty of Wing Commander Pitts.

A congratulatory telegram, signed by Brigadier Dowse, was sent to him in the Cameron Highlands, a hill station in Malaya, where he was enjoying a well-earned twenty-eight-days' leave.

Lenka and I attended, on Saturday, 26 October, a piano recital given by a fifteen-year-old Chinese prodigy, Lee San San, at the Victoria Memorial Hall, almost exactly a year after the memorable inaugural recital she gave in our HQ bungalow in Batavia. She had a rapturous reception and her programme included Liszt's Hungarian Rhapsody No. 14, which she played with great feeling and maturity. The following evening we went again to the Victoria Memorial Hall to hear a lively concert given by the Singapore Musical Society, which included Hayden's Second Symphony in G Major. So much for our cultural entertainment. Life, on the whole, was pleasant in Singapore, despite the overbearing heat and humidity. The rules about dress too, had been relaxed and military personnel were allowed to wear 'civvies' off duty, which helped to make our lives rather more bearable.

During my first month in office, I learned a great deal about 'War Crimes' that I had never encountered before, particularly on the legal side. As the controlling body, War Crimes HQ issued frequent directives to the Teams in the field on a wide range of subjects, such as the collection and collation of admissible evidence, the search for suspects, rules of identification, interrogation procedures, prison regulations, the welfare of Japanese PoWs, the movement of

Japanese to and from South-east Asia, the movement and staffing of War Crimes Investigation Teams, correspondence with the War Office in London, liaison with our opposite numbers in the Dutch, Australian, French, etc., War Crimes organization.

As for staff work, I wrote Home:

> I realize now what a handicap it is for someone in my position not to be 'p.s.c.' (passed Staff College). Our Section is part of HQ ALFSEA, which comes directly under the War Office and, unless you know the intricate inner workings of the HQ, more often than not you refer to the wrong branch or waste valuable time finding out the right one. Lambe says to me: 'Ask SD3 about so and so.' Until recently I had never *heard* of SD3 and, even now, don't really know what it is!

In the same letter I reiterated the organizational difficulties apparent within our own HQ.

> Things were in a muddle. Lenka and I decided to start a minor 'purge'. Without batting an eyelid, Lenka took on the monumental task of sorting out, rearranging and bringing up-to-date the 6,000 index cards on which the whole system largely depends. She presides over a team of eight clerks, scrutinizing each and every card and insisting on total accuracy. Teams ask for information almost daily and we must be able to give them the right answers.

Later in the same letter I refer again to Lenka's moral support.

> I seem to have talked a lot about myself and my troubles. There are compensations. First, Lenka, who continues to be my main source of inspiration without which I would be completely lost. She is very understanding, particularly on those all too frequent occasions, usually at the end of a hard day, when I let off steam and feel depressed. Often, in the evenings, when I just don't feel like work, she makes me! Our relationship must be a puzzle to others: one could call it platonic, I suppose, but whatever it is, I could never have done what I have without it.

Bevis Lambe went off on a five-day tour at the end of October, leaving me in sole charge. I was becoming more used to his idiosyncrasies and my respect for him increased daily. I got on better with him than most people. His undoubted abilities, I felt, were sadly underestimated. A feature article in the *Free Press* of 5 November described at some length 'How the Japanese Live in Changi Jail' which housed, at that time 2,467 war crimes suspects and those serving sentences. During three and a half years of the Japanese occupation of Singapore over twice that number of British, Australian, American, Dutch and Eurasian men and women had been held captive in Changi under the most appallingly overcrowded conditions, one of them the author of the article, Harry Miller. Soon after the liberation, Changi had held several thousand Japanese generals, admirals, Kempeitai gangsters, ex-camp guards, soldiers and civilians, hastily rounded up for 'screening' as potential war criminals. That screening had been a long process; gathering the men wanted for atrocities committed in Malaya, Burma, French Indo-China, Sumatra, Java, Borneo and the islands of the archipelago, stamping charges on them, and bringing them to trial.

The chase continues and it will be some time yet before the last Japanese war criminal of the most minor degree will stand in the dock for the last trial. The very long arm of War Crimes investigators has stretched out halfway across the world and wanted Japanese have been brought to Singapore by sea and air. The latest arrivals are Lieut. General Kawamura and Major General Meraguchi, who are being interrogated in connection with the massacre of Chinese in Singapore. Japanese officers are stripped of their badges of rank and don prison clothes. They stand in line next to a private, eat in the same dining room as a hundred other men, shave when given the command, bathe when told to do so, and are locked in their three-man cells at four o'clock in the afternoon until 6.15 am the following morning. Each inmate is allowed two pairs of trousers, two shirts, two bathing cloths (or towels), one toothbrush (no paste), one water bottle (no sling – to avoid suicide), two blankets and any books they might have brought. And – prison officials are very proud of this – the cells are bugless. The prison is run as a prison, with specified waking, sleeping and working hours, with discipline reigning for both inmates and guards. A British infantry regiment is now in control, and it has orders that the sole imposer of discipline on the Japanese is the officer commanding the Jail. Their typical daily ration consists of:- potatoes – four ounces fresh and one ounce dry: vegetables – four ounces fresh and one ounce dry: milk – unsweetened, four ounces or sweetened, one and a third ounces: atta flour – six ounces: or biscuits – five ounces: fresh fruit – six ounces, or dry vegetables – half an ounce: fish – one ounce: meat – two and a half ounces: sugar – used to be half an ounce, now seldom on the table: tea – two sevenths of an ounce: cooking oil five sevenths of an ounce. In the interrogation rooms, the suspects are questioned closely on their past. They react to questions like any ordinary criminal who sees either the years stretch ahead of him in jail or his life cut short on the gallows. The health of the Japanese is good, although the British doctor in charge of the jail hospital told me that ninety-five per cent have either syphilis, gonorrhoea, amoebic dysentery, or had been suffering from malnutrition or worm infestation. In an isolated section of the Jail – it was a pretty place during civilian internment days, with the romantic name of 'Hudson's Bay' – are the condemned cells. There were forty-four men in the yard the day of my visit. 'Condemneds' do anything they like; there is no work for them. They play mah-jongg or some other Japanese game, read and talk, or bathe in the yard, which is surrounded by their cells. All of them look astonishingly well fed – and fatalistic about their future.'

My two trunks shipped from Rangoon arrived safely; but Grindlay's Bank reported some trouble in getting my trunks away to the UK, due to the unlicensed gun packed in one of them. However, they kindly offered to 'fix it' with the Commissioner of Police. I had, at this time, to give serious consideration to my future in the Army. I had written to Colonel 'Glaxo' Duncan, who was the Commandant at the Regimental Centre, 8th Gurkha Rifles, in Quetta, asking about the future of the Gurkhas in the light of the impending grant of independence to India. His reply was not

encouraging and it rather looked as if some, if not all of the ten
Gurkha Regiments would sooner or later be 'Indianized' and their
British officers phased out. I decided, therefore to consider other
options, if I was, in fact, to remain in the Army. One of my more
ambitious ideas was outlined in a letter Home:

> My plans for the future are as follows: (a) to go Home direct
> from here and take my overdue leave; (b) attend the Russian
> course (at the School of Slavonic Studies in London; (c) go to
> Russia (that should take me to the end of 1948); (d) study for
> Staff College; (e) attend Staff College in 1950 when I shall be
> 30 (the minimum qualifying age); (f) return to Russia for a
> year or so. I shall then be a qualified Russian Interpreter and
> psc at the age of thirty-one, and so have something pretty solid
> behind me.

Along with others who had served there, I was under no illusion
about the future of India. As I wrote Home on 7 November:

> One doesn't have to be a politician to foresee the mess the
> present trouble (so far very localized) will inevitably lead to.
> How many (Indians) appreciate what the British have done
> for India, even though she may, to a certain extent, have been
> exploited? Would any other Ruler have maintained such
> good order and comparative freedom internally for the
> length of time Britain has? Their apparent ingratitude leaves
> one wondering why we continue to treat them with velvet
> gloves.

Strong words but obviously strongly felt. In the same letter I
mentioned that Lenka and I had been to see 'a very amusing play
called *Worm's Eye View* – a CSE (Combined Services
Entertainment) production with some of the original London cast'.

> We have also seen some good films – *The Invaders* with Leslie
> Howard, *Casablanca* with Ingrid Bergman, and *Jane Eyre*.
> There are some good cinemas here and we usually save a
> dollar by going downstairs – just as good as the three-dollar
> seats in the circle. Tonight we are going to another Sunday

night concert. It's such a joy to be able to hear really good music well played.

Lieutenant Colonel Nick Read-Collins, who had been on my staff in Java, was appointed on 28 September to be OC British Minor War Crimes Liaison Section in Tokyo. He wrote to say he had just visited Hiroshima and Nagasaki and asked me to send him an HMSO pamphlet entitled *Social Implications of Atomic Warfare*, which he said could be obtained from a certain bookshop in Singapore. I duly purchased this booklet and sent it off to him in the hope that the sentiments expressed therein would help to assuage any conscience he might have about the devastation and deaths caused by these horrific bombs. A little later he wrote again, this time to complain about the poor communications between our two offices and that much time was being wasted in attempting to trace special 'wanted' suspects believed (by us) to be in Japan, when it transpired that they were still in South-east Asia.

I can cite examples in my own experience of special wanted suspects being recovered in Changi – I expect you can, too. If we had not sent the signals, we should still be hounding the Japanese and wasting time. Owing to bad weather, thousands of pounds of mail accumulate in Hong Kong and the subsequent clearance often results in lost correspondence. I suggest that because of the lengthy routing of signals, avoidance of abbreviations would help us eliminate corruptions. 'I/PTE' might mean superior private to you but when it arrives 'IPT0' we cannot solve it. I have written about this to try to erase one of the dozen small things which, on top of local troubles, make our day a little heavy. You know the old cry 'Signals should be sent as from a wise man to a fool' – you are the wise men.

Nick was undoubtedly working under considerable difficulties in Tokyo and his frustrations and impatience were thus not unreasonable. Misunderstandings can so easily arise from written communications in any form and particularly the cryptic style adopted in army signals. Happily, a very friendly and informative personal letter from Nick arrived a week or so later, in which he commented on the problems he was having to contend with, as well as on life in general in immediate post-war Japan.

> You can have absolutely no idea how hectic things have been up here since I arrived. I did not realize at first what a terrible state of things. The spate of signals we have been originating represent just a fraction of what has been going on. Everything is just as difficult as it could be. We sit on a knife-edge; collect all the rockets; but when it comes to amenities we are neither SCAP's baby nor Tokyo Sub-Area nor BCOF. Nevertheless we are having a good time – the work is very interesting and Tokyo is probably more cosmopolitan than anywhere else in the world at the moment. Everyone applauds or condemns (according to which side of the democratic fence he sits on) MacArthur's Great Experiment in Japan. While there are a great many things to find fault with, I don't think for a moment that we (the British) could have made a better job of it.
>
> Apart from the fact that America will in due course monopolize Japanese trade, and a good deal of that with China, foreign nations seem to resent most the Supreme Powers of the Supreme Commander. They would, in fact, prefer the mess, argument and muddle (*cf* the Netherlands East Indies) that arises from having a lot of unqualified people on the job. MacArthur has many good advisors and, though he is I think a Christian idealist and therefore dangerous and an appeaser, I believe he is doing well. No one has the faintest idea how long the occupation will last. The pessimists say five years, but several Americans have suggested at least one generation. I don't think 100 years would be too long. The Japanese, though vastly changed, give no indication of regret, or of bona fide attempts to make Japan a really useful member of UNO. As for the towns and cities – a rambling collection of new wooden huts built on the debris of bombed ruins – the amount of damage is astonishing. In Tokyo, 51 per cent was destroyed (and before the war it was the third largest city in the world). The geisha houses are off-limits, but in spite of many precautions, the VD rate soars, fraternization is allowed and everyone behaves in a very European way and very demo-

cratically. I've had no time yet to see the country, other than going to Chiba twice to scan the records held by the former Infantry Training School.

Nick then proceeds to offer some suggestions (in response to my request to do so):

(1) Signals – to avoid corruptions, I suggest our sigs should be as full as possible and avoid abbreviations. Mike Ringer (an officer I had sent him from Singapore) says our sigs to you are not clear. I expect this is due to relays in transmission because I am scrupulously careful in sending out coherent messages.

(2) Please tell everyone to have lots of patience with us. What arrives in Singapore is only the final issue, and only we know all the nonsense that precedes each piece of bumph e.g. to get a single Jap out of Japan we have to go through many channels before we finally get the Chief of Staff's approval. This may take from four days to a fortnight, and so far we have sent back to you forty plus a number of lawyers, etc.

(3) Ships (referring to war crimes committed on transports used to move PoWs and others from one island to another). My plan has been to get from the highest level any documentary evidence suggestive of carelessness, inefficiency or predetermined policy re the transport of PoWs. This has involved a lot of palaver with SCAP and we are raiding the HQ at Hiroshima and the homes of three Lieutenant Generals and two Major Generals and a few minor officers simultaneously to try and produce something on which to base all further investigations. We hope this will reveal all PoW ship movements, draft commanders, ships' captains and the like. We have taken over from the Americans all shipping cases of predominantly British interest because I think it is right that we should prosecute these cases. By the end of this month I hope to have prepared reports on the biggest cases we have here at the moment. I have sent you all the interrogations we have done so far and those of the high level commanders will follow about mid-December. We are certainly leading the

Yanks in this matter and they are, I think, very grateful for such aid as we have been able to give them.

Meanwhile, Lenka was continuing to work wonders in the Registry and getting little recognition (financial or otherwise) for doing so. I wrote Home on 27 November:

She (Lenka) is doing the work of two Staff Captains and getting half the pay of one. She could easily get herself a job for $500/600 a month (£60-£70) instead of $250 (£30) she gets here. I am trying to get her more pay but it is damned hard. She could have been made an honorary Junior commander in the ATS (Auxiliary Transport Service) but they stopped giving any more commissions two months ago.

On 5 December I took the bull by the horns and sent Bevis Lambe a confidential memo about Lenka's pay, mentioning her avowed intention to travel to London or Paris to study art on the termination of her work with War Crimes, pointing out that she could not, on her pay, save enough to cover her fare. Pointedly I added, 'her resignation at this juncture would be a sorry loss to War Crimes.'

A leading article in the *Free Press* of 22 November summarized the history of SEALF (South-east Asia Land Forces), Singapore, which had closed down in November. It expressed the hope that, as a result of the draft agreement between the Dutch and Indonesians, the war in Java and Sumatra, and indeed in the whole of South-east Asia, was finally over.

I got word that General Sir Richard O'Connor, now Adjutant General, War Office (the second highest rank in the Army) was paying an official visit to Singapore in the near future. As described in Chapter 4, I had been involved, with my friend, Jimmie Ferguson, in helping him and another British General (Sir Philip Neame VC) and Air Vice Marshal Boyd to reach the Allied lines after many adventures behind the German lines in Italy. Shortly after Sir Richard O'Connor's arrival in Singapore, I was summoned to the GOC's residence where a reception was being held for a number of senior officers and other important officials to meet the Adjutant General. I was shown into the large room where the reception was being held and asked to wait while someone informed the General of my arrival. I saw him glance over in my direction, turn to apologize to the small group of VIPs he was talking to and immediately come hurriedly over to me, with a broad smile on his face. He took my arm and led me to a sofa in the corner, well away from his guests and for the next half an hour we had an animated conversation, recalling our escapades in Italy. He was keenly interested in what I was doing and said that he had had very favourable reports about the War Crimes investigations in Southeast Asia and the excellent progress we were making. He invited me to visit him and his wife on my return to the UK. I told him about my plans to learn Russian and attend the School of Slavonic Studies in London. He thought this was a good idea and offered to help in any way he could.

Bevis Lambe was out of action for a week with 'flu, leaving me to hold the fort. Poor man, he also suffered badly from lumbago, which did nothing to improve his temper. I was concerned lest his health should make it impossible for him to carry on, and I might conceivably have to take over.

I wrote Home (12 December): 'This is a task which even Lambe, with his long experience of staff work and intimate knowledge of the mysterious ways of the War Office, finds a handful.' The only other person I could turn to for advice would, of course, be the Brigadier (Dowse) who, as the Deputy Adjutant General, SEALF (South-east Asia Land Forces, the new name for ALFSEA) had to bear heavy responsibilities in addition to War Crimes.

> Thank God, so far I haven't committed any serious blunders! My job consists mainly of supervising and controlling the War Crimes Section, including, of course, the Registry, providing Lambe with a constant stream of information, vital statistics, etc., seeing that everything in our HQ runs smoothly and acting as Lambe's deputy on his absence on tour or on leave. I must know precisely what each of the seventeen Teams is doing, how their work is progressing and, at the same time, keep a close eye on the War Crimes Courts to make sure that they have enough cases to keep them going.

One of my least pleasant jobs was being responsible for Changi Jail, reputedly one of the best equipped in the world. Opened in

January 1937, it had been built to accommodate some 650 prisoners. In September 1945, it was taken over by the Allied Command to house war crimes suspects, with Outram Jail being retained as the civil prison. I made periodical inspections to see that everything was running properly from an administrative standpoint and that prisoners were receiving whatever rights they were entitled to. I was determined to release, as quickly as possible, all Japanese prisoners not serving a sentence, awaiting trial or held as suspected war criminals, which would effectively reduce the overall numbers held in Southeast Asia to about 1,500. The numbers in Changi had recently been brought down from 2,500 to about 1,000. For several months, discussions had been held between the Government and the Military authorities on the question of Changi Jail reverting to civilian use, now that the Japanese serving long-term sentences were being transferred to other jails throughout Malaya.

In an article in the *Singapore Times* it was claimed that:

Trial by a War Crimes Court is not quite up to the scrupulously high standard of justice normally associated with British courts of law. The War Crimes Courts are run on lines similar to the Army's Courts Martial, with very important exceptions – the Japanese are not allowed to object to any member of the Court, or to offer any challenge to the jurisdiction of the Court, and the Rules of Evidence are relaxed to admit hearsay and indeed almost any kind of evidence, although it is up to the Court to decide for themselves what weight to give to unorthodox evidence. This rather special kind of trial is reserved for Japanese and Koreans only, as was discovered early in the proceedings when a Chinese was sentenced by a War Crimes Court in Singapore and later transferred to the civil court, where he received a much lighter penalty.

To attempt to transfer considerable numbers of civilian cases to civil courts would have overloaded the already hard-pressed judicial processes in Singapore. Furthermore, a precedent had been set in India, whereby cases against ringleaders of the renegade Indian National Army (formed by the Japanese from regular Indian

Army units, by means of intimidation and coercion) were dropped for political reasons. 'How is it possible,' the article continued, 'for a Government to justify taking stern reprisals against a few local people who were not strong enough to resist the Japanese in Singapore?'

The article ended:

> It will be many months before recrimination over what happened during the Nip occupation of South-east Asia is at an end. The War Crimes organization, depleted by demobilization and always short of trained legal staff, will have their hands full for a long time to come and many more stories of Japanese inhumanity to man will come out before the War Crimes files are closed in Singapore.

On 19 December, the War Office issued a directive that, from 23 December, responsibility for Minor War Crimes Trials would be transferred from the Adjutant General's Branch to the Office of the Judge Advocate General of the Forces. This reflected the view that the bulk of the investigatory work having been completed, it was now a question of concluding the actual trials as expeditiously as possible, otherwise, there would be a tendency for the whole operation to drag on endlessly.

On 15 December, a Japanese Army major escaped from MacArthur Camp, Singapore, where he had been detained for medical treatment, when the Medical Officer's back was turned. Widespread searches conducted by the Military and Civil Police were unsuccessful. Originally arrested in Sumatra, Major Ishijima was wanted by the British for his intelligence activities in South-east Asia, and by the Dutch for an alleged war crime in the Netherlands East Indies. All efforts to trace Ishijima having apparently failed, I called a conference to discuss what further steps could be taken to effect his recapture. It would have been comparatively easy for him to have joined a working party and enter a JSP (Japanese Surrendered Personnel) camp where he could remain under an assumed name. As each of the eight camps held an average of 5,000 JSPs, an identification parade, using a photograph of the fugitive (found, incidentally, under a different name) would have been impractical. The officer commanding 99 Field Security

Service, Captain Tinker, said that Ishijima spoke Chinese, had many Chinese friends and could easily pass as a Chinese. He would provide a list of Ishijima's Chinese contacts to the Defence Security Officer in Singapore, Major Forrest, who would put Chinese detectives, armed with a photograph, on the trail. Other possibilities were that Ishijima had made his way to the mainland (Malaya) across the causeway, or by boat across the Johore Straits; or, that he had boarded a boat and made his way to China, or even to Japan, under the guise of a Chinese. I ordered photographs to be circulated immediately to all JSP camps in Malaya and on Singapore Island, together with a full description of Ishijima. Civil authorities in Hong Kong and Japan would be asked to keep watch on all shipping. Also a photo and description would be published in the leading English, Chinese and Malay newspapers, and a description broadcast over Radio Malaya.

Very concerned that so little had been done to trace the fugitive, I drafted a scheme to deal (hopefully) rather more speedily and effectively with any future escapes, combining all the military and civil resources available to us.

The ten days before Christmas were particularly hectic, so much so that by 2 pm on Christmas Eve (a full working day) I still had not done my Christmas shopping. So I shot off downtown and fought my way through the milling crowds to buy one or two last minute presents, including a new-fangled electric cigarette lighter (operated by a process of suction) for Bevis Lambe, who was forever running out of matches, and a manicure set in a leather case and a powder compact for Lenka, which I was ashamed to find compared poorly with the Reynolds ballpoint pen, grey silk shirt and grey flannel trousers she gave me. On Christmas Eve we danced at the Mountbatten's Officers' Club in Raffles Square. Lenka was looking more than usually glamorous in the slinky evening dress she had designed and made herself.

In December, I received a letter from Captain E.S. Lilley, Commissioner of Prisons, Malayan Union, in which he questioned the need to retain so many Japanese prisoners in the civil jail. I responded on 7 January to the effect that we fully appreciated the problems he faced, but pointing out that since September 1946 over 4,000 Japanese had been released from civil and military jails on the grounds that no charges against them had been or were likely to be preferred. The great majority had originally been arrested and incarcerated as potential war criminals. It had been possible to effect the reduction through a slow process of elimination resulting from a complex screening operation carried out by the seventeen Investigation Teams, each of whom prepared lists of Japanese personnel required to be held in custody as having been either accused or suspected of committing a war crime or as a vital witness. These lists were collated and consolidated at the War Crimes HQ in Singapore and distributed to jails throughout Southeast Asia. Those not on this list would, of course, be eligible for release. However, I went on to point out:

> At the same time this drastic reduction has inevitably resulted in the release of many suspects who would otherwise have been brought to justice had there been sufficient time and machinery to complete the investigation of their respective cases.
>
> Above all, our efforts have been and still are being concentrated on reducing the numbers in the civil jails in the Malayan Union. If, amongst these, a high proportion are 'suspects' rather than 'accused', it is only because the Team concerned has not as yet, for various reasons, been able to complete the case against them. This difficulty will shortly be overcome, however, by the establishment of an additional Team to accelerate investigations in Malaya and another Court to speed up the trial of those cases already completed.

I then told him that JSPs (Japanese Surrendered Personnel, i.e., those not serving sentences as convicted war criminals) in Changi Jail were to receive certain privileges and amenities, e.g., twenty cigarettes a week and the opportunity to write one postcard a month, and asked if he would extend the same or similar privileges to JSPs in the jails under his control. In the event Captain Lilley acceded to our requests and the various proposals were duly implemented.

On 26 February, I visited Captain Lilley in Taiping to discuss the whole question of Japanese held in his jails. He was chiefly concerned with Taiping, this being apparently the only one with workshops in proper working order and which could not be used because of the presence of the Japanese. I reiterated that determined efforts were being made to release all those not still under investigation. He was opposed to accepting convicts from Changi Jail, protesting that this would only exacerbate the situation.

The *Free Press* of 2 December, in a leading editorial, had applauded the policy decision to proceed only with the most serious charges against Japanese war criminals.

> Singapore has long been the headquarters of the War Crimes organization in SE Asia. This comprises a Co-ordination Section and Registry and a Legal Department, and employs as many as seventeen teams of investigators, interrogators and interpreters, who have toured all over South-east Asia obtaining evidence from local people of Japanese cruelties. They have not only provided masses of evidence against Japanese but they have also investigated – and reported – cases in which local persons other than Japanese have been accused of being responsible for the deaths and suffering of people during the occupation. More than 9,000 Japanese have been detained, nearly 600 brought to trial and hundreds more will follow them into the dock.

Next day, while Lenka and I were opening our presents, Bevis came to my room and thanked me profusely for the wonderful present I had given his wife! I suspected that either he had misread the label (in his typical, absent-minded-professor's way) or couldn't be bothered with the sucking business. We then adjourned to the Mess, where a rollicking party was being given for the non-commissioned officers and other ranks, with turkey and plum pudding, together with all the seasonal trappings, washed down with gallons of good old British beer. Bevis, somewhat inebriated, swayed visibly when he rose to say a few appropriate, if somewhat incomprehensible words of good cheer. On Boxing Day morning, I gallantly if a little unwisely, took part in the traditional 'officers vs other ranks' football match, full of alcoholic remorse and fervently wishing I was elsewhere.

Lenka and I celebrated New Year's Eve at the Mountbatten Club which was so overcrowded that dancing was almost impossible.

Some Naval types livened up the proceedings by throwing Chinese firecrackers on the jam-packed dance floor until they were forcibly ejected.

I sent a rather pompous note to Lieutenant Colonel Wright, President of the Mess Committee, on the 'marked improvements in the standard of catering, the provision of an ante-room with papers and periodicals, and the efficient management of the Mess in general [which] have created a far more favourable atmosphere than was evident in the past'. On behalf of the officers of the War Crimes Section [the Mess was shared with the Legal Department], I expressed our gratitude, too, for their efforts to make the Christmas celebrations such an outstanding success.

Early in January, the London correspondent of the *Free Press* reported on a letter from a Mr John Sharp, a former PoW, which had been printed in the *New Statesman and Nation*, London, expressing surprise at the sentence of twenty-five years passed on Lieutenant Colonel Yamada Ida of the No. 2 Railway Construction Group, Siam, better known as 'the Little Colonel' by British PoWs working on the infamous Burma-Siam Railway. 'The PoWs believe the Japanese Colonel did his best to secure better conditions for them, "though he fought a losing battle against the apathy of the PoW Administration and against the ruthless dictation from the far more powerful railway engineers".' Mr Sharp hoped that there would be no miscarriage of justice. His viewpoint was shared by a former officer PoW who agreed that the Japanese Colonel personally was decent enough and committed no crimes. On the same day, 4 January, the *London Times* carried a criticism by an 'ex-prisoner of war in Siam' of trials of Japanese war criminals, which had been 'proceeding in Tokyo, Singapore and throughout South-east Asia during the last few months'.

Declaring that those concerned with the building of the railway were mostly being tried on evidence obtained from sworn 'atrocity forms' signed by returning ex-prisoners of war, the writer said that very little publicity was being given to these trials in the Home press, and claimed that considerable uneasiness was felt by many ex-PoWs concerning some of the verdicts that had been published so far.

'It seems to us that the humbler the rank of the Japanese the more severe is his punishment,' the letter continued, and we seem to be dealing out the severest punishment to the most primitive and therefore the most expectedly brutal of the Japanese guards. For instance, Sergeant Shoji, the notorious basher and bully, has been sentenced to be hanged for brutality that did not include murder. Lieut Colonel Yanagita, whom thousands of ex-PoWs will remember as a comparatively humane Japanese commander of 'Two Group', was sentenced to twenty years in prison because four escapers were shot outside his camp, the order coming from the highest officer. Colonel Sugasawa, supreme boss of all forces in Siam, and as callous and insolent a Japanese as we ever saw when he very occasionally made a lightning tour of our camps and told us we were very well off, got twelve years. He was Yanagita's immediate superior. Lastly, Lieutenant General Ishida, Commander-in-Chief of the whole Railway in 1943, and the man responsible at the highest political and military level, got just ten years.

'What we would like to ask is this,' he ends. 'On what principal are these Japanese being tried?'

I took the Indian Government representative, Mr Chetthur, to the Victoria Memorial Hall on 6 January to attend the opening of a big war crimes trial in which the victims were men of the 5/2nd Punjab Regiment who were slaughtered wholesale by the Japanese in the Solomon Islands. Unfortunately, the evidence was mostly hearsay and not very strong. Mr Chetthur was himself a barrister so he understood very well the procedures of the Court, which was just as well, this being my first attendance at a war crimes trial (see photo of Mr Chetthur and myself in court).

Shortly afterwards, I was invited to meet General Sir Ouvry Roberts, the Vice Adjutant General of the British Army, when he visited Singapore with the Vice Chief of the General Staff and the Quartermaster General. I wrote Home, 'General Roberts recognized me immediately and even remembered my name, which was flattering considering it is sixteen months since I had tea with him and his wife in Bombay before leaving for Malaya'. I asked after General Sir Richard O'Connor, the Adjutant General and now his boss. General Roberts said, 'Oh yes, I remember now. You helped to extricate him from behind the enemy lines in Italy, didn't you?

I will certainly give him your regards'. He also asked if I still planned to go to Russia (fancy remembering!) and I told him my plans hadn't changed. He noticed my promotion to lieutenant colonel and was very interested in the work I had been doing. 'Yes,' he said, 'War Crimes have done exceptionally well in South-east Asia. In fact,' he added, 'the War Office's opinion is that the War Crimes people here have done a better job than their opposite numbers in Germany,' a nice compliment and a well-deserved tribute to Bevis Lambe's splendid achievements.

An article appeared in the *Sunday Tribune* on 5 January, gruesomely headed 'Japs Now in Changi Await Death', saying that thirty-seven Japanese war criminals were in the condemned cells awaiting execution. I had a slight altercation with the Major commanding the Jail for having agreed to be interviewed by the press without my permission. I fully expected angry letters to this newspaper demanding to know why these men had not been hanged. The fact was that it took, on average, two months from the time a death sentence was passed for it to be carried out, allowing time for petitions and confirmation of sentence by the GOC. Also, it was more practical for executions to be carried out in batches of twelve or more, rather than in ones and twos. Up to that time seventy Japanese had been executed.

I had learned that in order to function with reasonable efficiency, one really needed to master the many acronyms used to identify military organizations and units. To give a few random examples, SCAP stood for 'Supreme Command Allied Powers (Japan)'; JCOSA – 'Joint Chiefs of Staff (Australia)'; BIEJCOSA – 'British and Indian element of JCOSA'; BCOF – 'British Commonwealth Sub-Area Tokyo'; UKLIM – 'United Kingdom Liaison and Intelligence Mission'; and, very importantly (to us), BMWC – 'British Minor War Crimes', our very own Liaison Section in Tokyo.

Lieutenant Colonel Cameron, my opposite number in A (Administration) Branch, GHQ, visited Japan later in January and found that our BMWC unit, consisting of ten officers and three other ranks, had become submerged in red tape and bureaucracy; moreover, that few people seemed to be aware of their existence. They gave every impression, in fact, of being 'nobody's baby'. They lived, somewhat under sufferance it seemed, in Headquarters

BRICOSAT's Officers' Mess and were regarded as rather a low-powered outfit compared to other odd bodies in Tokyo, so tended to be overlooked, if not forgotten.

They had no means of maintaining their three vehicles, nor was it possible for them to employ civilians because (a) they would be a security risk (the leakage of names of suspects would result in many of them 'going underground' or even committing suicide), and (b) there was no way of paying them.

Locating suspects in Japan and having them sent back to Southeast Asia had proved to be extremely difficult, although this was hardly surprising under the circumstances. Cameron found that Headquarters BCOF, who controlled shipping from Kure, would have no shipping available for the next three to six months.

There had even been an unfortunate instance when a Royal Naval commander had refused to take Japanese suspects on board his ship but this was an isolated case. In an attempt to overcome the problem, I arranged with Q (Movements) GHQ for the initial transporting by sea to Singapore of 150 suspects, and thereafter 100 per month.

BMWC had requested a legally qualified officer to deal with minor legal matters that arose from time to time as they were the only unit in Tokyo without one. None being available in Japan, I had asked the War Office to send us three civilian lawyers, one of whom would be sent on to Japan.

One of the problems of tracking down suspects in Japan was that, once traced, there was then a long and complicated procedure for getting them out of the country, as has already been mentioned. It took at least eleven weeks from the time BMWC received a request from us for an arrest to the time the suspect (assuming he was found) was in custody and waiting for despatch to South-east Asia. Highly unsatisfactory though this was, Cameron and I had no alternative but to accept the situation. At the time of Cameron's visit, there were no fewer than seventy-five suspects awaiting shipment, and 463 were still being searched for by Read-Collins and his staff.

Bevis Lambe and his wife left on 14 January for a ten-day visit to Borneo, leaving me to hold the fort and to be responsible for the entire War Crimes organization, which apart from the Legal side, comprised 189 officers, ninety-eight British other ranks and 205 Indian other ranks and civilians – quite a formidable family.

My opposite number, Lieutenant Colonel John Davies, the Assistant Judge Advocate General, who was in charge of the Legal Section of War Crimes in Singapore, flew to England on 27 January. Before leaving, I had briefed him fully for his meetings at the War Office. Brigadier Dowse, who was also in London then, sent us a memo confirming the take-over of all war crimes investigations by the JAG's department, except for administration, and that investigations would cease on 31 May, and War Crimes generally, including Trials on 31 December 1947. The London Bar Association had been approached for legally qualified personnel to help in the War Crimes Courts. Only one candidate had responded!

On 30 January, Lenka and I went off on ten days' leave to the Cameron Highlands, a delightful hill station to the north of Kuala Lumpur, to enjoy a welcome respite from the heat and hassle of Singapore. I took advantage of the opportunity to pay an official visit to the Team in Penang at the end of my leave.

Nick Read-Collins wrote from Tokyo on 5 March regarding the official notification to the Japanese Government of all war crimes sentences imposed in South-east Asia. He expressed some concern that, not infrequently, relatives read in the Japanese press of the execution of their husband, son, brother or other male relative.

> Both Legal Section SCAP and ourselves are often contacted by worried Japanese Government officials whose job it is to dispose of the assets of convicted criminals. Since there is so much similarity in Japanese names, exact details of the criminal's Unit and last whereabouts are required to establish their identity. It would be much more satisfactory to us and to SCAP if all information in this connection could be passed directly to the Japanese Contact Bureau, Singapore for their direct transmission to the Japanese Government. This would, I think, cover the Press release aspect.

'The next point,' he continued, 'is in connection with No. 4 Team's Suspect Lists.'

While I was in Sumatra we produced a total of five lists consisting of approximately 650 names. I know that many of these suspects have returned to Japan but we have no record of them being requested by SEALF. It seems likely that Suspect Lists Nos. 3, 4 and 5 have in some way been mislaid. I mention this to avoid requests for a tremendous number of Dutch suspects at a future date.

In reply I offered to send him the results of all trials as soon as they were known, pointing out, however, that the next-of-kin could not be officially informed until the sentence had been confirmed or promulgated. The Public Relations department of GHQ, Singapore, transmitted Trial results to their opposite numbers in Tokyo where they 'may or may not be published'.

On the question of the missing Suspect Lists, I told him that Lists 2, 3 and 4 had been found amongst No. 4 Team's records but there appeared to be no trace of Lists Numbers 1 and 5. Seventeen of the suspects concerned with crimes in Sumatra were being questioned in Changi Jail but none of the others were wanted by us.

Lenka, meanwhile, had applied to the Government Immigration Office, Singapore, for entry into the United Kingdom 'to study commercial art'. Bevis Lambe willingly agreed to support her application and gave her a glowing testimonial based on her excellent record of service and her devoted loyalty to the War Crimes organization. 'Mrs Salomonson has proved herself to be conscientious, hard working and efficient at all times' and he strongly recommended that favourable consideration should be given to her application. This was duly awarded, much to Lenka's undisguised delight.

I received a letter from Lieutenant Colonel Dickie Kerr, who had taken over from Duggie Clague as our Liaison Office in Burma.

I am having a good time up here and am settling down to Rangoon life. There is not very much to do and therefore the best thing is to be busy. I am, too! I find my time fully occupied with many peculiar problems but they are all interesting. I think things are going well and with more bods here we could do so much more.

In my reply of 25 March I told him that I had had precisely four months at Home in the past seven and a half years and hoped to be going on Longer Leave in May or June.

I don't envy you your task. Your reports make very interesting reading. Burma has always been desperately short of personnel but I think the situation now has improved a good deal. I am sure the atmosphere amongst the War Crimes units in Burma is much better now. When I was in Rangoon there seemed to be a complete lack of enthusiasm or Team spirit: and the Mess, as no doubt you will have heard, was anything but convivial. I shall be very sorry to leave War Crimes. It has been a most interesting and enjoyable phase in my life; we are planning a get-together with Duggie Clague who soon returns to England.

By 10 April 1947, of the 653 Japanese who had appeared in 201 trials in South-east Asia, 186 had been sentenced to death, 379 to imprisonment and eighty-eight had been acquitted. By then, War Crimes Courts were sitting almost continuously in Borneo, Rangoon, Hong Kong, Malaya, Singapore and Java, Indonesia. Trials had been conducted too, in fairly remote places, which had necessitated the setting up of travelling courts, complete with judges, and prosecution and defence counsel. On one occasion, I recall having to provide rope for possible use in Borneo, in the event of a death sentence being passed. It was the declared policy for the accused to be tried in or as near as possible to the place where they had committed the crime. This also made it easier for witnesses to attend, when they would otherwise have to be brought, with some difficulty and at considerable expense, to one of the main centres.

On 16 April, I wrote to Nick Read-Collins in Tokyo, giving him the latest news. On the subject of recent and fairly dramatic changes, I said:

Now that the JAG (Judge Advocate General) have taken over from AG Branch, the set-up here has consequently changed, with Legal Section under Lieutenant Colonel Stewart (soon to be a full Colonel), late President of a Hong Kong Court, taking over direction of investigations from Lambe. This means that very soon the War Crimes Section will also come directly under Legal and Dowse will cease to have any say in War Crimes at all. Lambe's position has become increasingly difficult in that his hands are tied and he cannot make any decisions without prior reference to Legal. He has, therefore, decided to leave as soon as the change-over has been finally completed, which will probably be at the beginning of June.

I have also decided to leave in the early part of June and a Major Howard (a regular) is taking over from me. That briefly, is the position here. Confidentially, I think Legal are regretting their insistence on taking over the reins and are beginning to realize that they have bitten off more than they can chew. In actual fact, however, it will merely mean that the Assistant Adjutant General (myself) will continue to run the Registry and deal with certain policy matters, and the rest will be in the hands of Stewart under Brigadier Davis. Basically, that appears to be the only change.

On 29 April I was the guest of honour at a small luncheon party given by Major General Sir Reginald Kerr, Head of the Adjutant General's Department at SEAC, and Lady Kerr.

Plans went ahead for my departure for the UK early in June. However, a major problem arose over the appointment of my successor. The first choice, Major Howard, a regular officer, was turned down. Then a Major George Lewis, who had been commanding an Investigation Team, was designated to succeed me and started to understudy me at the beginning of May. However, soon after he arrived, it transpired that under a new War Office dictum, no officer under thirty-five could be promoted to a Grade One appointment, and George was twenty-nine. Unknown to us, moreover, the Military Secretary's Department at SEAC, who selected Grade One appointments, had, in fact already chosen my relief and referred their choice to the War Office for final approval.

I wrote Home on 25 May:

The gradual process of changing over commands has been going on for over a month now. When Stewart, Lambe's opposite number in Legal Section, heard that George Lewis could not take over from me, and in order to avoid having to get a complete outsider in from outside, he decided to have Ben Massey, my Deputy Assistant Adjutant General (Policy), promoted. Rather foolishly, he told Ben before checking up with MS Branch, with the inevitable result. 'No, we've already got someone,' MS retorted! It is an awful mess up and could so easily have been avoided. As it is, it looks as if I shall now have to wait for the War Office to get their OK, which leaves me somewhat in the lurch.

I could not have chosen a worse time to leave, with all these changes taking place. Brigadier Davis, the Deputy Judge Advocate General, left for the UK on 24 May, his place being taken by Colonel New. Stewart, who had succeeded Kerrin as Colonel, Legal Staff, had been President of a War Crimes Court in Hong Kong and so was comparatively new to the job. Lambe himself had by this time already started in his new appointment. My DAAG (Admin), Major Laurie Pike, was due to leave for the UK on 1 June, to be replaced by a young RAC officer, John Walkerdine, which left me as almost the only person who really understood the workings of the Registry, apart, of course, from Lenka.

Luckily for me, the RAF officer running the Air Booking Centre in Singapore had, until recently, been commanding a WCIT in Burma and had promised to get me on a plane whenever I wanted. On the other hand, I had absolutely no intention of allowing my plans to be totally disrupted. I had already been mucked about quite enough! Come what may, I would leave Singapore in June. On 26 May (Whit Monday), I was invited to a cocktail party at Flagstaff House by General Sir Neil Ritchie, Commander-in-Chief, ALFSEA. At 9 am the following morning, I had a formal meeting with him when he thanked me for all I had done and wished me luck in the future.

In my last letter Home (16 June), I voiced my resentment at the delay in my departure, and the frustrations I was experiencing through having to cope with the heavy workload resulting from Bevis Lambe's transfer.

It is a really hard struggle to keep our Courts going these days, what with chaps going on leave, release and repatriation, illnesses and staff courses. Stewart is much easier to work for than Lambe. He knows what he wants and leaves me to work out the details, which is the way I prefer it. Not that the changeover has gone smoothly. Many complications have arisen as is only natural when two opposing factions (a slight exaggeration!) are united. Previously Legal occupied separate offices in one of the Hotel buildings. I strongly advocated that they should move into the Main Building where we are and this was agreed. So now we are all together and this should make things much easier. Remote control never works satisfactorily.

The promotion of one of my Staff Captains has been turned down on the grounds of his youthfulness, which means that a stranger from outside War Crimes will have to take over the important job of DAAF (Admin).

My successor, Major Percy Hardman, is expecting his relief to arrive by the next boat from the UK (due in tomorrow). He hopes to be able to hand over to his relief within a week, so all being well he should be available to start work here by 23 June. Strictly speaking, it should take him at least a month to get to know even the basic principles and current problems of War Crimes but if he is reasonably quick on the uptake I think 7–10 days will suffice. In any case it will be at least another two weeks before things are running smoothly again.

I hate this delay and am tempted to blame Lambe for having messed things up so completely by not thinking ahead. In many ways it is a pity this reorganization didn't take place long ago. Still, you find that in all walks of life and particularly in His Majesty's Army!

The heat doesn't improve matters either and I am longing to get away from it. It saps one's vitality and leaves one a wet rag at the end of the day. You will be glad to hear I have been dosing myself with vitamin pills called VIKELP – 18 a day – and they are doing me a lot of good. I don't exactly bounce out of bed in the morning but at least I don't get the backaches I used to. I'm just as lazy as I always was about getting up in the mornings. Work starts at 8 am. and I am often still in bed at 7.40, though I am never more than a few minutes late in the office, even if I have to miss my breakfast (porridge and tea). I have an excellent Chinese 'boy'. Until recently he used to creep into my room with my early morning tea and leave me snoring my head off!

I worked all Saturday and Sunday the last two weekends and every night except two until 11 o'clock. The days just have not been long enough. I have never been nearer to earning my pay than during the past hectic month.

I've learned a good deal, too, since taking over from Colonel Lambe.

My successor, Percy Hardman, came in last week to say he would be ready to start work on Monday (tomorrow). We both agreed that it would take three to four weeks for him to settle in.

My final contribution to War Crimes was to draw up a detailed plan for the move to new office and living accommodation. On 31 August, Goodwood Park Hotel was to be handed back to the proprietors who had plans to restore it to its former glory as a private residential hotel. I worked out a phased timetable so that the entire War Crimes organization would move into their new quarters over a four day period, the whole operation being completed by 5 pm on 29 August.

On Friday, 1 August, I held a farewell party in the Officers' Mess at the Goodwood Park Hotel, which was attended by some sixty members of my staff, plus officers from GHQ and other units in Singapore. A fairly formidable guest list included two brigadiers, two full colonels, seven lieutenant colonels, twenty majors, one wing commander, two squadron leaders and ten captains! It was, for me at least, quite a moving occasion and immensely gratifying that so many turned up to say 'Goodbye' and wish me well.

I had a charming letter from Bevis Lambe after I arrived Home.

The very best of luck to you and very many thanks for your most able and loyal assistance during a time which must have been most frustrating and irritating. I admired your quiet firmness and constant commonsense. It will be a lesson to both of us never to go to law.

P S I was glad to hear that the Deputy Adjutant General (Brigadier Dowse) turned up to your farewell party. He always speaks very highly of you.

Brigadier Dowse was kind enough to write the following, which I received early in December, a most welcome Christmas present!

Naval Military Club
94 Piccadilly, W1
30 November 1947

My dear Spooner,
I enclose a Testimonial. Let me know if I can do anything more. Good luck to you and I hope you get the job you are after.
Yours ever
M. B. Dowse

Testimonial in respect of
Lieutenant Colonel A. P. Spooner MBE

This officer worked on my staff since December 1945 and only left me in August this year. In December 1945 he was specifically selected to take over command of a War Crimes Investigation Team and was promoted to Lieut. Colonel.

His unit operated for a period of five months in various parts of Java when disturbances were at their worst.

In May 1946 he, with his unit, were ordered to Burma to carry out similar investigation work, namely running to earth and collecting evidence against Japanese war criminals, no easy task in an area the size of Germany.

In September 1946 I applied for Lieutenant Colonel Spooner for special War Crimes work in Singapore at the GHQ of the Army in South-east Asia. At that time, as now, I was Deputy Adjutant General. While at Singapore he worked directly under my control and was responsible for the co-ordination and control of our War Crimes Registry where a complete record of the current activities of all War Crimes Teams was carefully indexed and recorded.

The experience Lieutenant Colonel Spooner gained in routine office work, including the drafting of reports and high policy letters, and the supervision of a number of officers,

British other ranks, and Indian and Chinese civil employees, should stand him in excellent stead in any work of a similar nature which he may have in the future.

Lieut Colonel Spooner has plenty of self-confidence and initiative, will readily accept responsibility, and gets on very well with his seniors and juniors alike.

I was extremely sorry to lose him as he proved himself a very valuable officer.

M. B. Dowse
Brigadier
Deputy Adjutant General
Far East Land Forces
Singapore.

Chapter Ten

Wind Up

The title of this chapter is misleading if pronounced to rhyme with 'sinned'. It could thus be interpreted as a reference to the physical fear induced by exposure to danger. Indeed, I experienced this on several occasions during the war, as did many others. They say that fear of fear is worse than fear itself, more so in the case of an officer in the company of his men in battle. Any respect would vanish at the first sign of cowardice, as would his power of leadership.

Courage *per se* is indefinable. No one knows how they will behave in the heat of battle. Inextricably linked to instinctive self-preservation, and regardless of their training, each individual will react differently. Acts of extreme valour (winners of the Victoria Cross, for example) have been carried out by the gentlest of men, the most unlikely of heroes.

I make no claim to be any more 'gutsy' than the average soldier. Most assuredly I had the 'wind up' when I was captured in the Western Desert and lay trembling in a sand pit while fierce fighting raged around me. I was scared during the hair-raising drive from the Monastery to a safe house on the Italian coast by the odds-on chance of encountering a German roadblock and the Italian driver's vow to keep going regardless of the inevitable hail of bullets. I was no less fearful when Jimmie and I paddled shorewards to land agents on the Burmese coast during our clandestine operations at the end of the war with Japan.

'Wind up' has, however, no gaseous connotations in my book. It is, in fact, an attempt to summarize the contents, like a judge's summing up before passing sentence.

Little did I know, when I entered the historic portals of the Royal Military College, Sandhurst, that the next eight years of my life would be so amazingly eventful, fluctuating between fluid campaigns in the arid deserts of Iraq and Libya to lurking in the dense jungles of Burma. I was privileged to witness first-hand the surrender of both Italy and Japan, the former a reluctant ally of Nazi Germany, the latter a bitter enemy of the West bent on conquering the Indian sub-continent and much more beside.

I experienced many conflicting emotions; of fear (as mentioned above); of elation, as when the fishing boat that took us down the Adriatic on the final lap of our escape landed in the safe harbour of Termoli; of frustration and disappointment, as when bouts of malaria prevented me from accompanying Jimmie on his Burma–Siam railway mission (which I probably would not have survived).

Other than the year spent languishing in an Italian PoW camp I could claim to have had what was euphemistically called a 'good war'. The immediate aftermath, too, was an incredible experience for a young officer. Coping with the unfamiliar and stressful responsibilities of a senior staff job was daunting enough. Dealing with the horrors perpetrated by Japanese and Korean soldiery in the Far East was far more unpleasant than anything I had ever been exposed to during the war years. The flip side was that it brought home to me, in no uncertain terms, how fortunate we are to live in a country that enjoys the blessings of a free and democratic society.

Chapter Eleven

Potted Pot-pourri

The Scorpion and the Moustache

In 1941 with 2/8th Gurkha Rifles in Iraq the author's orderly was Pahalman Gurung.

To make him laugh Pahalman had a habit of twitching his long, spiky moustache. He did this memorably one day at our temporary rest camp in Baghdad.

I was not too happy with the way he made up my camp bed and insisted on showing him how I wanted it done. I placed my hand on the bedclothes to pull them back and what felt like a red-hot needle pierced the third finger of my right hand. Flinging back the sheet exposed the culprit – a vicious-looking scorpion.

Pahalman stood at the foot of the bed – and twitched his moustache; whereupon we both roared with laughter. I then ran to our Medical Officer's tent for treatment. He asked me whether the scorpion was black or white, one being far more poisonous than the other. I could not enlighten him and he did not waste time on finding out. He assumed the worst and gave me an injection, whereupon I passed out.

By the time I got back to my tent Pahalman had disposed of the evidence. So I was left forever ignorant as to whether my abortive bed making demonstration might have led to fatal consequences.

Dangerous Engagement

In March 1944, during his post-escape leave in the UK, the author was invited to talk to a boys' school near London about the Gurkhas.

India Office, Whitehall
  8th March 1944

My dear Spooner

I shall be very grateful if you can do something for me. It is this. A School in Middlesex has adopted the Gurkhas to assist them to reach their 'target' in the Salute the Soldier campaign. They asked for Lalbahadur Thapa [who earned the Victoria Cross in Tunisia in April 1943 whilst serving with Eighth Army] to go down and talk to them but, of course, he is not in the country and as far as I know there are no Gurkhas here.

I should like you to go down to the school and give them a talk on the Gurkhas. It will not be a difficult job, for the children just want to hear blood and thunder about the Gurkhas. I gather you escaped from Italy, and if so you could tell your story as well. The whole thing should last not more than half an hour, be simple, exciting, and of course talk about the Gurkhas. If you can take a kukri down with you and show how it is used, I am sure that would raise the greatest enthusiasm. I am sending them a batch of photographs for them to show.

The engagement would be somewhere about March 25th. If you will take the job on, I will give you as good a warning as possible, and I will also recover for you the cost of the train, bus, etc. The schoolmaster is an old Gurkha Officer.

Yours sincerely
Walter Hingston Lt-Col

India Office, Whitehall
  13.3.44

Dear Spooner

I am so glad you can go down to Isleworth and lecture on the Gurkhas. I attach a copy of a letter to the Headmaster and you will no doubt hear from him. Let me know what your expenses are.

Yours sincerely
Walter Hingston, Lt-Col

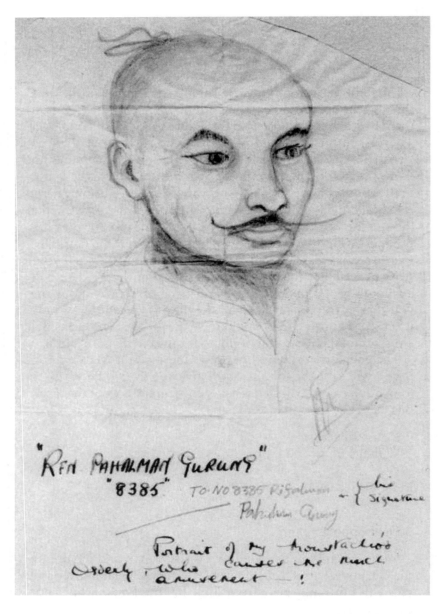

Sketches of Gurkhas, drawn by the author during active service with 2/8th
Gurkha Rifles in the Iraq Campaign, 1941

"8947 Rfn. Narsam Gurung."
. 6/6/41.

India Office, Whitehall
13.3.44

G. D. E. Douglas, Esq., Spring Grove Central School, Thornbury Road, Isleworth, Middlesex

Dear Sir

I have obtained a lecturer for you on the subject of the Gurkhas. He is Captain A. P. Spooner of the 8th Gurkha Rifles. He has seen service in North Africa and was captured in 1942. He recently escaped to Italy and is now in England. He would be very pleased to come and talk about the Gurkhas at the School.

Would you get in touch with him and arrange dates and so on. His address is . . .

I am so glad you have got a kukri for Spooner has not got his here. No doubt you will be able to let him demonstrate with yours.

I do hope you have a successful week. I am sure Spooner will be very interesting and exciting.

Yours sincerely G H

Spring Grove Central School, Thornbury Road, Isleworth, Middlesex
20 March 1944

Dear Sir,

I have received a letter from Lt Col Hingston of the India Office telling me that you have kindly agreed to come to my school and give a talk to the children on the Gurkhas during our local Salute the Soldier week, commencing on Monday 27th inst.

I will leave you to fix the day and time most convenient to yourself, although I should prefer early in the week and in the afternoon if possible, but if you cannot manage this, please do not worry as I can easily adjust my timetable accordingly.

I have stated that your talk is to be about the Gurkhas,

simply because I am an ex-Gurkha Officer of the last war but I am sure you will be kind enough to throw in some of your exciting personal experience.

Yours faithfully
G. D. E. Douglas, Secretary of School Savings Group

Spring Grove Central School, Thornbury Road, Isleworth, Middlesex
28 March 1944

Dear Captain Spooner

I wish again to thank you on behalf of the Staff and Pupils of the above for so kindly coming and giving us such a splendid and interesting talk.

The pupils are still full of it and in their modern way of expressing their best appreciation of anything, your talk was referred to as 'smashing'.

I personally feel honoured that you should have gone to so much trouble in the preparation of your talk and you also should feel very satisfied keeping nearly 400 children interested for an hour as I know from experience.

Wishing you and the 8th Gurkhas the best of luck and every success from the staff and pupils of Spring Grove Central School.

Yours sincerely G. D. E. Douglas

Gurkha PoW 1944

No 9269 Havildar Indrajang Rana
PoW Repatriation Camp
Italy 14/10/44

Sir

You will be surprised to get this letter from Havildar 'JANG' since such a long time. As a matter of fact I was a prisoner of war in Germany. I escaped from PoW Camp and entered in Switzerland where I met Lieut McDowell 2/4th G R who gave me your address. Lt McDowell died in the Hospital in Switzerland after 24 days illness.

Major Wall is still in the PoW camp in Germany. We are 81 Gurkhas here. Out of these 22 are from our Bn. i.e., 2nd Battalion 8th Gurkha Rifles.

I stayed for 4 months in Switzerland. I liked Switzerland like anything. We spend a good time in this pretty little place. Gurkhas won two football tournaments and one basketball tournament. Unfortunately we lost one Naik (2/7 GR) in the final match who died in Hospital after 9 hours. I am sending you my Photograph taken in Switzerland and one copy of Gurkhas Group photo taken in Switzerland.

Nothing to write more, reply me in India 8th Gurkha Centre Quetta Baluchistan.

Salaam from the Gurkhas

Your obedient Indrajang Rana. Havildar. 2nd Battalion 8th Gurkha Rifles

The Final Burma Reunion

AUTHOR'S REPORT

Four thousand five hundred members of the Burma Star Association, their families and friends, assembled in the Royal Albert Hall on Saturday, 22 April 1995 for their forty-ninth and, sadly, final reunion.

My wife and I had the privilege and pleasure of attending this splendid occasion. It began with a representative from each unit entering the arena carrying a furled standard. There followed a brief but moving Service of Remembrance conducted by Bishop Mann. This included two hymns, sung loudly and lustily by the assembled gathering and accompanied by the Central Band of the Royal Air Force, an Act of Dedication, the Last Post, The Epitaph and Reveille.

Brief speeches were made by the Chairman of the Association, the Vice Patron, Countess Mountbatten of Burma, the President, Viscount Slim, who stressed that this was not the end of the Burma Star Association, merely the last Reunion 'for sound and sensible reasons,' and by the Patron, HRH the Duke of Edinburgh.

Prince Philip referred to the Burma campaign as a war that was 'forgotten' by many people in this country, but will never be forgotten by history, 'and that is where it really matters'. 'Generations from now,' he continues 'will read about the exploits, the failures, the successes and the sacrifices of those we knew who tried to defend, and then triumphantly restored freedom and hope to millions of people in South East Asia and the Pacific . . . they will also become aware of the raw courage, dogged endurance and sheer determination of that gallant brotherhood of friends and relatives.'

And it has been grand working with and for so many excellent people.

Then came the fun part – a lively programme of bands, the South Wales Burma Star Choir, Scottish girl dancers (performing Irish jigs), tumbling girl gymnasts and, for good measure, a Barbershop Harmony Club. Howell James led the roof-raising community singing of *Fall in and Follow me*, *When You're Smiling* and (inevitably) *On the Road to Mandalay* (where those mysterious flying fishes play).

The Band of the Brigade of Gurkhas, the penultimate item on the programme, performed brilliantly, as always. And then, finally, came our old friend, Vera Lynn, at seventy-eight still in excellent voice, singing a selection of war-time favourites (*The White Cliffs of Dover*, *The Lights of London*, *Roll out the Barrel*, and of course, *I'll be Seeing You*), with *Land of Hope and Glory* as a fitting end to an evening of unashamed nostalgia and comradeship.

Surely it is quite remarkable that, fifty years on, so many still sprightly veterans of the Burma campaign were able to gather together for this final, most moving and memorable reunion.

The Admiral's Baby by Laurens van der Post

REVIEW BY THE AUTHOR

This is the story of the twenty-two months Laurens van der Post spent in Java after his release from three and a half years as a prisoner of war under the Japanese. He tells the fascinating tale of how, although weakened by his years of incarceration, Mountbatten asked him to stay on in Java and use his knowledge of the Japanese, Javanese, Dutch and British to bring about a peaceful transition and prepare the way for the return of the Dutch colonial rulers.

For over a year after the Japanese formally surrendered, troops from the old Indian Army occupied Java. Their tasks were: to maintain order, to round up the Japanese armed forces, and – a priority – to locate, feed, safeguard and repatriate the thousands of ex-PoWs and civilian detainees of many nationalities, all in poor or desperate states of health. The PoWs were in camps scattered through the islands of Java and Sumatra, many of which were under threat of massacre by fanatical Indonesian insurgents.

For a further task soon developed: the thankless one of trying to reconcile the returning Dutch administrators and the Indonesian nationalists who had proclaimed independence when the Japanese surrendered.

Two of our battalions, the 1st and the 4th, were among the 92,000 soldiers rushed to Java and Sumatra. Many of them had endured years of arduous campaigning in the jungles of Assam and Burma.

Van der Post's task was a well-nigh impossible one. Because of his close ties with the Nationalists he was disliked and mistrusted by the Dutch, many of whom saw his role as part of a sinister British plot to undermine the Dutch Empire for commercial reasons. Nor was he much liked by some of the British officials and diplomats who regarded him as 'a bit of a phoney', 'too one-sided in his views'.

The book contains a surfeit of rather portentous 'philosophising' which tends to rankle. As one who commanded a war crimes investigation unit in Java during the period in question, I am bound to disagree with van der Post's views on war crimes trials, and his tendency to 'turn the other cheek' in his lenient attitude towards his former captors, the evidence of whose brutality was overwhelming and absolute.

Nevertheless, one has to admire this Afrikaner's tenacity of purpose and sheer physical courage, and pay tribute to his instinctive recognition of Dr Sukarno's extraordinary qualities of rhetoric and power over massed populous, and as the future leader of a fully independent Indonesia. He was proved right. Within a year of his departure from Java in June 1947 there would be rebellion and, in the end, Indonesian independence.

Whatever one's views of him as a person, there is no doubting his devotion to duty and his dedication to what he saw as more of a spiritual crusade than a military or diplomatic campaign. It was, moreover, quite remarkable that anyone should so readily assume such huge responsibilities after three years of pure purgatory as a prisoner of war.

EPILOGUE

Understandably, readers may wonder what happened to Lenka, who had supported me so faithfully and loyally in our efforts to bring Japanese war criminals to justice. All who knew and worked with her sang her praises, notably my boss, Brigadier Dowse.

Lenka had always wanted to visit England, so I arranged a free passage from Singapore to Southampton. Through a family contact with the Chairman, Lady Reading, I got her a job at the WRVS HQ in London. After six months Lenka decided to move to the Netherlands to visit her Dutch family and friends. Some time later I learned that she had met and married a wealthy Dutch industrialist. Trechikoff's famous painting of her, *The Green Lady*, became the highest-selling print in history (likened to the *Mona Lisa*).

Following Indian Independence my regiment, 8th Gurkha Rifles, was assigned to the Indian Army which had no need of British officers. I accepted the offer of a transfer to the British Army, landing up in the Royal Army Ordnance Corps. After several miserable winter months at their HQ in Didcot, the Commandant and I came to the mutual conclusion that I was totally unsuited to this branch of our military establishment. Consequently, I resigned my commission and joined the unemployed in civvy street.

A stroke of luck found me employed at the Head Office of the Hudson's Bay Company in London, albeit as a lowly trainee, sorting Persian lamb skins in their warehouse. Subsequently I was promoted to be the Publicity Manager of the Fur Department.

In 1951 I married Frances Dunlop and we had two children, Christopher, now married and living in New York, and Caroline, born in New York and now living with her parents in Guildford, Surrey.

We moved in 1956 to Chicago where I spent five years

promoting tourism to Britain as Midwest Manager of the British Travel Association. In 1960 I was headhunted to be General Manager of the British-American Chamber of Commerce in New York, helping British firms to find a market for their products in the USA.

Returning to England in 1970 I qualified as a professional director of fundraising, masterminding international campaigns raising millions of pounds for St Paul's and Canterbury Cathedrals and for the Royal Opera House. I organized campaigns overseas with members of the Royal family, including Prince Charles, Princess Margaret and the Princess Royal, an eventful and glamorous period of my diversified and colourful career from which I finally retired in 1990.

Pat Spooner
Guildford
October 2011

Bibliography

Churchill, Winston, *The Second World War*, Vol. 3 *The Grand Alliance* (Cassell, London 1950)
The Second Word War, Vol. 4, *The Hinge of Fate* (Cassell, London 1951)
Johnston, M. & Yearsley K., *Four-Fifty Miles to Freedom* (Blackwood, London 1919)
Moynihan, M., *God on Our Side* (Leo Cooper, London 1983)
Newby E., *Love and War in the Apennines* (Hodder & Stoughton 1971)
Tretchikoff, Vladimir, *Pigeon's Luck* (Collins, London 1973)

Index